T0314742

The World Bank and Global Managerialism

In recent years, a great deal of scholarly and popular ink has been spilled on the subject of globalisation. Relatively few scholars have addressed the political sociology of globalisation and, specifically, the emergence of global class formations and a nascent global governance framework. This book is a contribution towards redressing this imbalance.

The book traces the emergence of the World Bank as a key driver of globalisation, and as a central source of an evolving form of elite-driven transnational governance which the author describes as "global managerialism". The book argues that the Bank has expanded its sphere of activity far beyond provision of low-cost capital for development projects, and plays a central role in pursuing global economic and social policy homogenisation. *The World Bank and Global Managerialism* features a new theoretical approach to globalisation, developed through an analytical exposition of the key stages in the institution's growth since its creation at the Bretton Woods conference of 1944. The author details the contemporary Bank's central policy framework, which includes the intertwining of public and private initiatives and the extension of global governance into ever-wider policy and geographic spheres. He also argues that contemporary globalisation marks the emergence of a transnational elite, straddling the corporate, government and civil society sectors. The book provides two detailed case studies that demonstrate the practical analytical utility of the theory of global managerialism.

The theoretical approach provides a robust but flexible framework for understanding contemporary global development. It is essential reading for courses in areas such as International Organisations, Global Political Economy, and Globalisation and its Discontents, and is also relevant to students of development policy and international economic architecture, among others.

Jonathan Murphy is Lecturer in International Management at Cardiff Business School, Wales.

Routledge studies in international business and the world economy

The World Bank and Global Managerialism

Jonathan Murphy

Routledge
Taylor & Francis Group

LONDON AND NEW YORK

First published 2008
by Routledge
2 Park Square, Milton Park, Abingdon, Oxon OX14 4RN

Simultaneously published in the USA and Canada
by Routledge
270 Madison Ave, New York, NY 10016

Routledge is an imprint of the Taylor & Francis Group, an informa business

© 2008 Jonathan Murphy

Typeset in Times by Wearset Ltd, Boldon, Tyne and Wear

British Library Cataloguing in Publication Data
A catalogue record for this book is available from the British Library

Library of Congress Cataloging in Publication Data
A catalog record for this book has been requested

ISBN10: 0-415-41269-2 (hbk)
ISBN10: 0-203-93619-1 (ebk)

ISBN13: 978-0-415-41269-8 (hbk)
ISBN13: 978-0-203-93619-1 (ebk)

Contents

Illustrations

Figures

Table

Foreword

This book began life in Ulan Bator in Mongolia, in the mid-1990s. I was visiting the country to write some articles for Canadian newspapers about gold mining. The usual mix-and-match expat dinners in the faded Soviet splendour of the Ulan Bator Hotel's dining room were enlivened by the company of various global business pioneers whose loquaciousness was, I suspected, in inverse proportion to their real prospects of landing that big deal. One of the less plausible of these fellows was a frayed old man from Peckham in south London, whose most convincing story was that his wife encouraged him to travel as far, and as often, as possible. But what was most striking about Peter was his companion, a tall, lissom Mongolian beauty, who spoke English in the grammatically perfect but over-formal style that is the hallmark of those who learned the language behind the Iron Curtain under the tutelage of a teacher whose pedagogical materials reflected, even into the 1990s, an England of bowler hats and afternoon tea. Valentina was the lead dancer of the Mongolian National Ballet. The Ballet had once been a symbol of the fraternal friendship of the Soviet bloc, and Valentina had studied dance in Moscow and Sofia, where she had adopted her Russian name. After graduating, she had toured across the world, or at least the bits of it to which she was allowed to travel, danced at the Bolshoi, returning home to garlands and adoring press clippings. Now she performed classics and national adaptations in the crumbling concrete theatre on the edge of town, in front of ever diminishing crowds, with her increasingly disconsolate troupe. When Valentina stepped away from the table, Peter whispered loudly in my ear:

> Isn't she beautiful? Every Monday evening, when she doesn't have a performance, I give her a good meal here at the restaurant, and we go upstairs and have sex. I give her a twenty dollar tip. It feeds her and her son for the week.

Globalisation is a good thing. How could it not be? We are all members of the same species, and have much to learn from each other, from our diversity and our commonalities. The idea that walls can be built to constrain us from meeting our fellow humans always struck me as a barbarity that fatally discredited Communism. But contemporary globalisation, the globalisation of high-flying consultants, of the World Bank and International Monetary Fund, of corporate restructurings, even of the Millennium Development Goals, has not freed the ordinary person. According to statute, Valentina might now be permitted to travel to visit the Lincoln Center, to practise with the National Ballet in London. But actually, she has to sleep with seedy Peter to earn enough money to buy bread, and the furthest she journeys these days is five kilometres in the lopsided trolleybus to her one-bedroom flat overlooking the Russian-built power station, which no longer pollutes the pristine mountain desert air because the government can't afford the coal to fire it. It struck me then, that for Valentina and other ordinary people around the world, liberation from authoritarian bondage has been replaced by another more subtle powerlessness, the faceless and inexorably grinding exploitation of a global managerial order. I decided to make it my mission to understand, from as many perspectives as possible, how and why the New World Order has not delivered on its promises of prosperity and democracy.

I have travelled many thousands of miles in the past twenty years, lived and worked on four continents, genuflected before presidents and written lies for prime ministers. I have slept in mansions and castles, consulting for the World Bank, and bedded down with hobos on a urine-drenched railway waiting-room floor in Siberia. I am sure that there are people who know the diverse corners of this world better, but perhaps not too many. Personal experience does not ensure insight, but it does provide a foundation upon which to build understanding. The unifying feature of the different societies I have observed is the ubiquity of inequality and domination. These features transcend political and economic systems. The composition of dominant elites is different in different societies and at different times, and diverse means are used to assert and safeguard their power. But the elites are always there.

Since the end of the Second World War, the nature of elite domination has substantially changed. The defeat of National Socialism was constructed on a fundamental logic of human equality. This logic also led to the collapse of colonialism, the universalisation of the principle of democratic governance, and ultimately to economic and political globalisation. These developments did not end elite rule, but rendered its assertion and maintenance infinitely more complex and sophisticated. Brute force and absolutist ideologies have been replaced by managerialism, whose authority is based on the efficient and value-free resolution of the problems of human organisation. This book traces the rise of the global managerial elite through an exploration of the World Bank, a central organisational driver of the international institutionalisation of managerialism.

I set myself an ambitious objective of capturing, or at least sketching, the broad outlines of the emerging structure and dynamics of a global order. It is an objective that inevitably will fail to be fully realised, not only because of my own limitations as a writer and researcher, but more fundamentally because of the infinite complexity and ambiguity of social organisation. Nevertheless, it is an objective worth attempting. The alternative, far too commonly accepted in this "post-ideological age", is to abandon the general right to a global normative vision. In shying away from such a vision, we cede the authority to define social objectives to a managerialism that relentlessly disassembles any comprehensive and motivating imaginary into a series of technical issues whose resolution requires managers' "expertise". In the process, the overall interconnecting structure of inequality is effaced, and managers' elite status legitimised.

There is no "right" way of seeing. Each of us interprets the world from an explicit or implicit standpoint. Anyone claiming any special significance for their viewpoint, which is surely inherent in all non-fiction writing for public consumption, has an obligation to explain that viewpoint. This allows readers to make their own interpretation of the information they are being provided. I have always identified with the left, or progressivism, or a critical approach – terms that possibly have different meanings through time, but that seem to me to overlap consistently and broadly enough to be interchangeable. In recent years the left has spent much of its time soul-searching about what it means to be progressive. Whatever the reasons for this, and some answers to that question are implicit in this book, the definition of a left-wing or progressive perspective is much simpler than we have often made it out to be. It means asserting the spiritual equality of all people (Domhoff, 2003).

Of the countless books that have been written about globalisation, and the smaller but nonetheless impressive catalogue of monographs about the World Bank, this is the first that approaches these subjects from a critical management viewpoint. Critical management is an analytical approach that has developed quite rapidly in recent years, mainly in European business schools. It aims to deconstruct the dominant instrumentalist approaches of mainstream management science. I find critical management studies useful because it focuses attention on the role of organisations and organisational life in shaping broader social dynamics, and because the new transnational order that is being constructed is one that is managed, or at least is one in which power is exercised by those who claim to manage.

The book is comprised of several elements that connect together to present an overall argument from different methodological viewpoints. The first chapter defines the analytical standpoint through a discussion of alternative critical perspectives on development and globalisation. The second and third chapters explore the historical rise of the World Bank as a key globalising and managerialist institution. The fourth chapter focuses on the discourse of managerialism as embodied in the World Bank. The fifth and sixth chapters include case studies of the Bank in action. The case study in Chapter 5 illustrates the extension of global managerialism into transnational social policy and the importance of international civil society elites to this new, comprehensive managerialism. The sixth chapter examines the central role of the World Bank in forging global economic restructuring.

Readers approach books with a variety of different objectives and interests. Many who are unfamiliar with or unengaged in the theoretical issues of the contemporary left may find some of the discussion in Chapter 1 arcane. These readers might want to read the introductory pages in Chapter 1 and then skip to

Chapter 2. They can always return to the first chapter if the historical account and case studies in the rest of the book whet their curiosity about the overall theoretical approach that guides the analyses presented in the more empirical chapters. The reader who is only really interested in the "punchline" of what I have to say, could just read the Conclusion.

The book is not intended to be gratuitously provocative, but it is based on the critical deconstructive principle that what is taken for granted often reflects the hegemony of particular interests rather than any objective truth. Although the World Bank is a favourite target of many leftists, often with good reason, the Bank is only one instance of a global managerialist approach that links together international economic, political and social leaders in common purpose. Doubtless some readers will find it offensive that I argue that international civil society leaders are complicit in institutionalising a comprehensive managerial order, or that I describe the Millennium Development Goals as a managerialist exercise. I am not impugning the good faith of international NGO leaders, or suggesting that the MDGs are not in themselves laudable objectives. However, it is precisely when interests and strategies are deemed beyond debate and reproach that a critical eye is most keenly warranted.

Many people have directly and indirectly helped me to write this book. I would particularly like to thank Hugh Willmott, who has been a wonderful intellectual inspiration, Chris Grey and Bill Cooke, who encourage me by urging that I have something useful to say, Timur Tulushuev was an invaluable research assistant in Kazakhstan. Nira Ramachandran helped edit the book and convinced me of the value of charts. Above all, I thank my wife Joan Howe for her unfailing support, and my children Michelle and David, for their inspiring joie de vivre.

A version of parts of Chapters 1 and 6 is in press at the time of writing in *Critical Perspectives on Accounting*, in my article "International financial institutions and the new global managerial order", reproduced here with kind permission of the copyright holder, Elsevier.

An early version of part of Chapter 5 was published in my article "The World Bank, INGOs, and civil society: converging agendas? The case of universal basic education in Niger", *Voluntas*, 2005, volume 16, pages 353–374, with kind permission of Springer Science and Business Media.

Jonathan Murphy

Abbreviations

ADB	Asian Development Bank
CDF	Comprehensive Development Framework
CMS	critical management studies
CSO	civil society organisation
DAC	Development Assistance Committee
DFID	Department for International Development
DPEP	District Primary Education Programme
EBRD	European Bank for Reconstruction and Development
EFA	Education for All
EI	Education International
FTI	Fast Tract Initiative
HIPC	heavily indebted poor countries
IBRD	International Bank for Reconstruction and Development
IDA	International Development Association
IFC	International Finance Corporation
IFI	international financial institution
IMF	International Monetary Fund
IUCN	International Union for Conservation of Nature and Natural Resources
MDG	Millennium Development Goal
MNC	multinational corporation
MPS	Mont Pèlerin Society
NGO	non-governmental organisation
NPM	New Public Management
OECD	Organisation for Economic Cooperation and Development
OSCE	Organisation for Security and Cooperation in Europe
PRSP	Poverty Reduction Strategy Paper
RBM	results-based management
SAP	structural adjustment programme
SPA	Strategy for Poverty Alleviation
TCC	transnational capitalist class
UNCTAD	United Nations Conference on Trade and Development
UNDP	United Nations Development Programme

UNESCO	United Nations Educational, Scientific and Cultural Organisation
USAID	United States Agency for International Development
WHO	World Health Organisation
WTO	World Trade Organisation

1 Towards a theory of global managerialism

Introduction

Global managerialism describes an ambitious elite project – both orchestrated and spontaneous – to construct a durable human management system on a global scale. The theory of global managerialism that I present here argues that managerialism is the driving force underpinning the colonisation of ever greater swathes of the ideal and physical worlds. Global managerialism is both more and less than an economic or political system; it is a modus operandi, an infinitely reconfigurable worldview, justifying continuing elite domination and inegalitarian resource distribution.

Global managerialism revolves around three core propositions:

- A globally organised managerial elite dominates contemporary society.
- The elite straddles economic and geographical boundaries.
- The elite is institutionalised through global institutions such as the World Bank, that play a key role in promoting and enforcing the new global order.

This book explores the theory of global managerialism from within a critical management studies (CMS) perspective. This represents something of a departure from the typical application of CMS approaches. CMS is best known for exploring the micro-processes of power within organisations. It has identified the burgeoning of managerial practices that seek to colonise organisations through an increasingly comprehensive set of practices extending far beyond twentieth-century Taylorist industrial management techniques. The new practices, propagated formally (e.g. business school education) and informally (e.g. popular management manuals), disavow mechanical management methods such as production lines, quotas and time-clocks, preferring to secure consent through enlisting the worker as a willing and enthusiastic partner in corporate success (Willmott, 1993). This approach has been generalised beyond the corporate environment and become managerial*ism*, an all-purpose organisational solution (Parker, 2002). Despite the common CMS claim that managerialism represents a widespread and generally undesirable feature of contemporary society, little attention has been paid to the sociological meaning of this development. Does managerialism represent the emergence of managers as a distinct social grouping?

Critical management theorists are divided about the appropriateness of tying the concept of managerialism to a class of managers. For Grey (1999), managerialism is totemic of contemporary life, and thus managers cannot be neatly distinguished from managed. However, it is argued here that management is still an activity that belongs predominantly to certain social roles: within the organisation, to managers over workers, and in broader society to politicians, senior bureaucrats, opinion-leaders and corporate lobbies. Governing has become a matter of managing systems and people. Increasingly, management's focus extends beyond national boundaries, through the activities of transnational corporations, the emergence of transnational systems of economic and social regulation, and the management of popular consent to this transnationalisation of social norms.

Global managerialism theory's most celebrated ancestor is James Burnham's (1941) managerial revolution hypothesis. Burnham argued that a managerial class had come to dominate political and economic life in New Deal America, Communist Russia and Fascist Germany, which he claimed were about to eclipse the old empires. Despite apparent ideological differences, Burnham believed that the Soviet, German and Russian elites shared a corporatist, scientific and totalising perspective to which traditional democracies had no answer. In retrospect, it is evident that Burnham greatly exaggerated the potential of statist planning while underestimating the resilience – and managerial tendencies – of liberal democracy. New Dealism in America had only superficial similarities with the authoritarian European movements, neither of which could escape from their own ideological and organisational rigidities. Burnham mistook Fascist and Communist states' aggressiveness for durable strength and fatally minimised the importance of consent in the managerial project. Burnham's inaccurate predictions somewhat discredited his theory and, more generally, managerial class theories. Managerialism was not dead, however, and in recent years has assumed a more flexible guise, adapting to ideological fashions while continuing to extend the domain of the manageable.

Today's globalised order is a seamless web of public and private networks extending over the human terrain. While the networks are not strictly hierarchical in the manner of the authoritarian movements of the first half of the twentieth century, power is distributed unequally within the networks, and institutionalised nodal points exist from where the discourse and practice of globalisation are developed and propagated; Czarniawska (2004: 780) uses the term "action net" to describe such an institutional order.

The World Bank is one of these crucial nodal points, and the following chapters will trace its development into a pre-eminent globalising institution. It is not argued that the World Bank is the *only*, or even necessarily *the* pre-eminent, institution in this process. In particular, it is affirmed that private multinational corporations play a crucial role in pursuing elite-led globalisation, and that their executives are also part of the global managerial elite (Sklair, 2001). However, most previous critical research on globalisation has focused much too narrowly on its private capitalist content and insufficiently on the process of institutionalisation of globalisation. This book aims to help redress that imbalance.

The theoretical framework

The New World Order is one in which the fundamental cleavages of interest cut across national lines, as well as traditional economic categories. It is an order structured around the construction of governmentality, even while it lacks the nation state's explicit authority superstructure. This order is the product of three dynamics: the seepage of managerial approaches into all facets of life; the gradual, worldwide homogenisation of human organisation; and the emergence of a global managerial elite straddling the public and private sectors.

Elite theory and existing critical theories

I begin by comparing the underlying assumptions of the global managerial elite theory with those of other critical perspectives of globalisation. While there are a variety of iterations of critical globalisation theories, which are discussed in some detail below, these fall essentially into two families: those that explain globalisation in terms of the unfolding of objectively existent economic factors; and those that are based on organic, culturalist explanations. By and large, the economistic critical accounts have roots in Marxism, while the culturalist accounts are based on a poststructuralist approach. Neither approach is satisfactory. Purely economic accounts can only offer a partial explanation because economic power is only one manifestation of power, while poststructuralist approaches are oblivious to the unequal distribution and reproduction of power. I will take some pains to underline the importance of a more nuanced analytical approach than either of these theoretical starting points can provide.

The ramifications of economistic approaches to understanding social dynamics are wide ranging and restrictive. These accounts grossly oversimplify the operation of power, tending to create a morality play in which agency is attributed only to holders of economic capital and the proletariat, their historically blessed "gravediggers". Those who hold critical economistic views are unable to account for power in the state and civil society sectors except as derivative of one or other of the two power groups, leading to a repeatedly tragic "tourism of the revolution" in which demagogic populist movements are held up as harbingers of universal freedom.

The popularity of poststructuralism is in large measure a reaction to this authoritarian problem in economism (Derrida, 1994: 13–15). However, the poststructuralist approach eviscerates the potential for authentic critique in asserting that "real" structure does not exist outside discourse. This argument tends to be constructed in the process of a logical leap: economic determinism cannot be sustained, thus power is not structured (Laclau and Mouffe, 1985). Whatever the political position arrived at by poststructuralists, it cannot by definition be derived from an analysis of existent social structure and reproduction, and thus tends to be random, declamatory and irrelevant in exposing the reproduction of deep social inequalities such as exist between the managers and the managed in an emerging global order.

Elite theorists Mosca and Pareto (see Bobbio, 1972) provide a more inclusive starting point for understanding social stratification than Marxism can provide. Marx began by assuming that a hidden explanatory engine must lie underneath social manifestations; his task was to uncover this essence and then refit presenting social phenomena into the defining dynamic. Because Marx selected the economic transaction as the fundamental social moment from which all other human phenomena are derived, social power must thus be traced back to the economic power holder. Mosca and Pareto's method moves in the opposite direction; they base their theory of elite domination on the prima facie observation that dominant elites appear to exist in all different types of society. They assume that this is preordained, and focus their attention on the various mechanisms whereby elite domination is assured, threatened and renewed. In the democratic age, the assertion that elites dominate all societies is an impolitic one, but borne out by all presenting evidence. Ironically, in comparison to the putatively progressive theories of Marxism and poststructuralism that seek respectively to exclude the possibility of some, or all, forms of social domination, the "reactionary" elite theory acknowledges this reality without shame. From a critical perspective, acknowledging structured inequalities in human organisation does not assume that this is either a desirable or immutable feature of life: "the ubiquity of domination does not exclude the possibility of relative democratisation" (Wacquant, 1992: 52).[1] From an analytical perspective, the elite approach draws attention to this unequal structuring of power while leaving open the forms in which this structuring takes place. Elite theory provides a basic starting point of the global managerial elite theory presented in this book.

Elite theory was further developed into an authentically critical approach by the post-war radical American sociologist C. Wright Mills. Mills sketched a contemporary picture of who, specifically, was running things, and how their domination was operationalised. He described a power elite of real people: people who went to school together, married each other, and helped each other out. From his angle, it wasn't evident that the ones who ran companies were necessarily more important than the ones who ran countries or the ones who planned nuclear war. Beyond petty squabbles between different elite segments, they tended to see things the same way, and they often changed hats. In the half century since C. Wright Mills wrote *The Power Elite* (1957), the lifestyle details and the personal ambitions of elites have changed, but the basic characteristics of elite reproduction and control have not:

> If social origin and formal education in common tend to make the members of the power elite more readily understood and trusted by one another, their continued association further cements what they feel they have in common. Members of several higher circles know one another as personal friends and

even as neighbours; they mingle with one another on the golf course, in the gentlemen's clubs, at resorts, on transcontinental airplanes, and on ocean liners. They meet at the estates of mutual friends, face each other in front of the TV cameras, or serve on the same philanthrophic committee; and many are sure to cross one another's path in the columns of newspapers, if not in the exact cafes from which many of these columns originate.

(Wright Mills, 1957: 281)

Wright Mills's definition of the power elite carefully avoided exclusive membership criteria; he envisaged elite membership as gradated or tiered, in the manner we see today in frequent flyer programmes that have both basic and various "elite" tiers. For Wright Mills, elite membership, although correlated with wealth, was more directly related to location in an intertwined social order. Thus the senior government official is as legitimately an elite member as the corporate executive. There were three main circles of institutional power: business, government and military, although he emphasised their overlapping and the tendency of elite members to move between the circles.

The French social anthropologist Pierre Bourdieu (1994) provides a dynamic structural explanation that grounds Wright Mills's sketch of a cross-sectoral elite. Bourdieu expands the notion of capital to include social and human as well as economic capital, like Wright Mills, justifying the extension of the ruling class to incorporate those who possess abundant non-economic but little economic capital. For Bourdieu, the various capitals cannot be simply translated into each other, but they can in principle be combined together in varying quantities to create what he calls "symbolic capital", an aggregate capital that approximates an overall class position and social power. Bourdieu's multiple capital theory is complemented by John Higley's notion of elite "settlements", which asserts that a stable hegemonic order is based upon the concurrence of major elite groups in a particular formula for the exercise of elite power (Higley and Burton, 2006). I will argue in this book that such an elite settlement, or compact, now exists on a global level.

Bourdieu's other key contribution to post-determinist class analysis is the concept of "habitus". Habitus, simply put, is the translucent web of social signals such as definitions of "taste" that semi-consciously structures social allegiances and permits coherent class positions to emerge in the absence of overt concertation. Bourdieu's approach allows navigation of the waters between determinism and atomism, and is of fundamental importance in this book's conceptualisation of the process of emergence of the global managerial elite.

Global managerial theory compared with other critical theories of globalisation

In this part of the chapter, I examine more closely some key alternative critical perspectives on the emergent global order. This discussion will permit an enriching of the bare bones of the theory of global managerialism described above, as well as clarification of the distinctions between this theory and other alternatives. By and large, the discussion will move chronologically, beginning with early theories of imperialism and leading to contemporary analyses of global class formation. Although some of the earlier perspectives outlined in the discussion might seem outdated, they continue to influence, both explicitly and implicitly, critical thinking on the global order, as I will discuss briefly at the end of the chapter. It is important, then, to understand the strengths and weaknesses of these positions.

Before venturing into a discussion of transnational theorising, it should be mentioned that there are some relatively well-known theorists who question the extent and the inevitability of globalisation. When globalisation discourse first became popular in the late 1980s, critical social science responses were often cautious and even disbelieving. Callinicos (1989) argued that the "postindustrial economy", often represented as underpinning globalisation, is mythical, and that the shift between industrial and service employment is actually bi-directional. Hirst and Thompson (1996) reject the claim that the nation state can no longer regulate national economies, and are sceptical of the prospects for global economic and political integration. Although both works are important in checking over-exuberant globalising rhetoric, their themes have not been replicated in recent major scholarship. While the desirability and inevitability of current globalisation patterns is highly disputed, most scholars accept that we are witnessing a rapid expansion of transnational social, political and economic activity.

Imperialism and globalisation

Although Marx predicted the global spread of capitalism, and wrote about problems of economic development in "underdeveloped" countries such as India, China, Ireland and Russia, he never systematically analysed colonialism and imperialism, whose golden age arrived after his death (Carty, 1993). Marx acknowledged the human cost of colonialism, but associated the worldwide expansion of capitalism with progress and the eventual victory of socialism. Few subsequent writers in the Marxist tradition attempted to apply this logic, apart from Warren (1980) who argued controversially that capitalism plays a fundamentally progressive role in developing countries.

By the First World War, it was clear that imperialism was making social structure more, rather than less, complex, undermining the central law of motion of Marx's system. Capitalism faced not a relentless concentration of conflict in the crucible of industrial class warfare, but a series of guerrilla conflagrations on the periphery of the world economy. Lenin's *Imperialism* (1964 [1916]) is the best-known attempt to restate Marxism for the imperial age, and continues in various guises to illuminate critical discourse on globalisation and development.

Written just before the Bolshevik revolution, it is based on the work of Hobson (1961 [1902]) and Hilferding (Winslow, 1931) (neither of whom, significantly, was a Marxist). For Hobson, monopoly characterised the modern era, with demand suppressed through excessive savings in the hands of the monopolists, resulting in a crisis of underconsumption. Chronic demand weakness leads finance capital to attempt to export capital, resulting in pressure on the state to engage in imperial adventures. Hilferding believed imperialism was motivated by the desire of monopoly capital to extend protective tariff zones beyond the nation state (Hozumi, 1996). Given that domination over the world market was not feasible, this could only be achieved through colonial expansion. Capital concentration in the hands of the financial sector provided socialists the opportunity to seize state power (Foster, 2002). However, if socialists did not grasp this opportunity, the capitalist order would dissolve into a series of imperialist wars. Lenin adds an explanation of how imperialism divides social classes. A labour aristocracy in developed countries is "bribed" into supporting the imperialist state through high monopolist profits reaped at the expense of colonial workers. The bourgeoisie in developing countries becomes divided between a "national-progressive" component that chafes under imperialist domination and thus allies itself with the workers' movement in an anti-imperialist nationalist struggle, and a "comprador" element that is satisfied with a subordinate position, administering the local affairs of imperialist capitalism. Lenin's imperialism theory remains an often uncited but nonetheless decisive component of mainstream critical thinking about globalisation, as will be shown later in this section.

Dependency theory

Samir Amin's *Accumulation on a World Scale* (1974) extended Leninist imperialism theory into a global theory of capitalist development in which peripheral countries were made to serve the needs of the developing mercantile capitalist class in Western Europe. America originally served as a periphery, with Africa the "periphery of the periphery". African slaves were forced to work on American plantations whose production was sold in Europe. This simultaneously demolished the European feudal production system and permitted European mercantile capitalists to accumulate sufficient capital to launch industrial capitalism (Amin, 1972: 511). The lopsided relationship continued after the end of slavery through cheap colonial labour set to work in plantations and extracting natural resources for European industry. African infrastructure was developed only to the extent that it served the interests of the colonial powers; this meant the coastal regions received far more investment in capital infrastructure and human resource development than did the hinterlands. This "dependent development" established a framework for a continuing unfavourable relationship between Africa and Europe. Amin, and Emmanuel (1972) developed the term "unequal exchange" to characterise the First World's exploitation of the Third in a cycle of low wages and low prices for Third World labour and goods, exacerbated by constraints on the free flow of labour and the flow of capital towards high-wage and thus high-demand First World countries. Autarky, or "delinking", was the only means to achieve Third World development.[2]

Amin's model can be criticised on two main grounds: weak empirical evidence that imperial plundering was fundamental to capitalist development, and the incompatibility of unequal exchange with the Marxist mode of production analysis. If correct, the theory is not an addition to Marxism but its refutation (Laclau, 1971). The theory also lacks a change dynamic, and appears to condemn underdeveloped regions to perpetual subjugation; its nub is that engagement with the capitalist core economy is what keeps poor areas of the world poor. Recent history seems to demonstrate the opposite; there is an undeniable positive correlation between engagement under certain conditions and development. In 1962, the Republic of Korea and Sudan had similar per capita income levels (Jenkins, 1994: 83). By 2001, Korea had a per capita income of $15,090 compared with Sudan's $1,970 (UNDP, 2004: 237, 239).

Amin called for developing countries to isolate themselves from the capitalist world and practise autarkic development; this proved disastrous. Autarkic economic policies deprived undercapitalised economies of needed production technologies, while not guaranteeing that what development did occur would equitably benefit all citizens. Through defining conflict between developing regions (as homogenous entities) and the developed world as fundamental, dependency theory obscures conflicts of interest between developing country elites and the masses. In dependency theory, the wholesale abandonment of autarky in the 1980s could only be explained as an outcome of imperialist pressure, although the benefits many developing country elites enjoy through enrichment and incorporation into global networks seem evident.

World-system theory

Immanuel Wallerstein's (1976, 1979) world-system theory extends dependency theory, analysing in greater detail the historic processes through which the core came to control the periphery; world-system theory has largely replaced dependency theory as the dominant (post)Marxist[3] approach. The theory's descriptors are misleading. World-system denotes not that the system operates globally, but simply that it transcends national political boundaries; Wallerstein says this world-system has been in existence for several hundred years. Similarly, Wallerstein's "division of labour" describes not workplace-based structuration, but a "new international division of labour" between the core countries where skilled workers use advanced technology to produce high value-added goods and services, and the peripheral countries where a largely untrained workforce conducts extraction and basic processing. Wallerstein's theory of class structure "proper" is loosely derived from Marx and Weber, and he also incorporates in his model the Weberian concept of "status groups", typically "ethnonational" identifications. Given the multiple-celled identification matrix, individuals have a number of possible subject positions. World-system theorists combine core–periphery and traditional class positions in order to determine overall status:

> The differences in absolute wealth between core and periphery, say between the United States and China, affects the comparative status and power of the classes within each society. To be upper middle-class in the core United

States involves more wealth and power than being upper-middle class in semi-peripheral China".[4]

Skocpol (1977: 1088) questions Wallerstein's methodology, which she finds based on teleological assertions that create circular arguments: "Repeatedly he argues that things at a certain time and place had to be a certain way in order to accord (or seem to accord) with what his system model of the world capitalist economy requires or predicts". She also disputes his historical analysis as fatalist and instrumentalist; the role of class conflict and political leadership in shaping patterns of development is disregarded in favour of "market-technological" determinism, a perspective that does not square with the historical record.

It is doubtful whether either trade between the core and periphery or investment by the core in the periphery have ever been sufficient for the relationship to be central to global capitalism: "Core investment in peripheral areas was a very small percentage of the total of all core investments, and overall the new colonies never provided markets or investment opportunities of sufficient size or profitability to justify the cost of acquiring and administering them" (Shannon, 1996: 170). Between 1950 and 1995, Africa's share of world exports and imports declined from 5.3 per cent to 1.5 per cent (Hoogvelt, 2001: 73). From a purely economic perspective, Africa is irrelevant to the success of the world capitalist system. Munck paraphrases the Cambridge economist Joan Robinson: "[i]f there is one thing worse than being exploited, it is not being exploited at all" (1999a: 65).

The merits of dependency and world-system theories, like all theories founded on the Marxist-imperialist paradigm, include their attention to the core–periphery problem, which is marginal to the concerns of many critical thinkers, particularly in the critical management tradition. While this problem is not necessarily central to the formal functioning of the global economic system, it is central to the world's human system, where "advanced" countries can, for example, blithely negotiate with a North African dictator to build prison camps in his country to house undesired economic migrants to Europe.[5] The increasing tendency of the excluded within and outside the core states to resort to internationally organised acts of rage suggests that relationships of exclusion are the sharp end of class stratification in the global managerial era. It is not insignificant, however, that groups involved in terrorist attacks are often comprised of individuals from both "developed" and "developing" countries, whose common cause reflects a cultural opposition to the global order rather than a reaction to spatial exclusion,[6] as the world-system approach would suggest.

One important extension of world-system theory is global commodity chain analysis, which studies the processes of value creation through the production and distribution process (Gereffi, 1996; Gereffi and Korzeniewicz, 1994). Close cousin to value chain theory in mainstream business strategy, it argues that in a globalised economy, commodities are often produced in a process chain beginning in a peripheral country and ending in a core country. The value added at each process stage of the chain depends on market competitiveness, although some commodity chain theorists emphasise the importance of power relation-ships in securing value at different stages of the process. Increasingly, the great-est share of value is being added in the branding and product differentiation process, a factor reflected in the decision of a number of large corporations, notoriously Nike (Klein, 2000), to contract out all physical production and focus entirely on design and marketing. Commodity chain analysis permits a decon-struction of the power relations involved in the world system, demonstrating that the "free operations of the market" are underpinned by a hegemonic discourse of differential human worth. This process is facilitated by the global financial order administered by the international financial institutions (IFIs). The commodity chain approach is particularly salient in unmasking exploitation relationships lurking behind the relentlessly upbeat discourse of branded transnational capital-ism. While global commodity chain analysis has grown out of world-system theory, its application is not restricted to analyses working within this model. It is a promising vehicle for exploring the changing distribution of value realisa-tions between social groups at different stages of the production process, and between different fractions of the transnational elite over time.

Post-developmentalism

Post-developmentalism is in the poststructuralist tradition and it likewise rejects the possibility of a meta-theory of society. In his seminal post-developmentalist study, Ferguson (1990) showed how the World Bank and other development agencies had constructed a discourse of "underdevelopment" in Lesotho that validated their presence while simultaneously dislocating the country's inhabit-ants. The Bank's Lesotho projects failed to meet their stated objectives, but criti-cism was futile as they did meet their subtextual function of justifying Bank involvement.

Arturo Escobar extends Ferguson's perspective to articulate a general post-structuralist and explicitly non-Marxist development theory, grounded in his research on development practice in Colombia. Escobar asserts that the economy is "above all a cultural production, a way of producing human subjects and social orders of a certain kind" (1995: 59). He traces the origins of the development dis-course to the immediate post-war period and the decline of colonialism. During the colonial period, natives were believed incapable of acquiring western know-ledge and attaining "developed" status. As former colonial states achieved at least nominal independence, such a perspective was no longer sustainable. American President Harry S. Truman announced the new development era: "we should make available to peace-loving peoples the benefits of our store of technical knowledge in order to help them realise their aspirations for a better life". Poverty was "a handicap for them and for more prosperous areas" (cited in Escobar, 1995: 3).

For development discourse to take root, the Third World had to be constructed as underdeveloped: overpopulated, backward, illiterate, malnourished and abnor-mal. Armed with unshakeable faith in scientific method, research teams went into the field to collect data on a "seemingly endless specification of problems". The organising principle of development discourse was that modernisation had the task of sweeping away the "archaic superstitions and relations" of the underdeveloped world. The end result was "a discursive practice that systematically produced interrelated objects, concepts, theories, strategies, and the like" (Escobar, 1995: 42). Using the power and authority of international institutions such as the United Nations and the newly created Bretton Woods institutions, a discursive edifice was constructed and enforced around the diagnosis and treatment of the "disorders" of the Third World. Economic issues were accorded primacy, because it was assumed that, "only through material advancement could social, cultural, and political progress be achieved" (Escobar, 1995: 39–40).

The biggest problem to be constructed was poverty: "Almost by fiat, two thirds of the world's peoples were transformed into poor subjects in 1948 when the World Bank defined as poor those countries with a per capita income below $100". It was ironic, according to Escobar, that the First World should show such concern with poverty, given that it was only with the onset of capitalism that "systematic pauperisation became inevitable" because it "deprived millions of people from access to land, water, and other resources" (1995: 24, 22). While poverty existed before capitalism, "vernacular societies had developed ways of defining and treating poverty that accommodated visions of community, frugality, and sufficiency".

Poverty was broken down into discursive subsets, each imparting a label of abnormality on the recipient, whether illiteracy, excessive fecundity, or poor hygiene. No aspect of poverty was more laden with signification of First World power than that of hunger. Indigenous societies understood periods of hunger in terms of their relationship with the land: "There is a relationship of give and take between humans and the earth, modeled in terms of reciprocity and ultimately validated by Providence (God). The land may produce abundance or scarcity" (1995: 96). In contrast, development's representation of hunger is epitomised by:

> the body of the malnourished – the starving "African" portrayed on so many covers of Western magazines ... A whole economy of discourse and unequal power relations is encoded in that body ... there is a violence of representation here. This violence, moreover, is extreme; scientific representations of hunger and "overpopulation" (they often go together) are most dehumanising and objectifying.
>
> (1995: 103)

Development's failure – he claims the people of the Third World are worse off now than they were fifty years ago – reveals its true meaning, a discourse designed to perpetuate "the Third World as different and inferior" (1995: 54). Escobar's themes have been extended by other scholars to form the "post-development" or "critical development" school (Rahnema and Bawtree, 1997).

Munck (1999a, 1999b) shares Escobar's perspective that the modernist development paradigm is exhausted, in both its mainstream modernisation and neo-Marxist dependency versions. However, Munck warns that "the problems of underdevelopment (however defined) … cannot simply be wished away" and criticises post-developmentalism for the "breathtaking simplicity" of many of the alternatives it proposes (Munck, 1999a: 202–203).

With the exception of Munck's measured use of poststructuralist themes, post-developmentalist analyses of globalisation have many weaknesses as ana-lytically operational theories. Escobar combines a devastating critique and destabilisation of materialist essentialism – in this case developmentalism – with absolutist assertions that questions such as economic underdevelopment and poverty are purely discursive in nature. While it might be arguable in the West that social and even economic questions are largely discursive construc-tions, this is implausible in the developing world, where material reality is reflected in disease and mortality statistics. Faced with this rude challenge, Escobar responds with a methodologically unsound and politically conservative charitable policy approach. His assertion that the West invented development and imposed it on the Third World is at best only partially true; it is noted in Chapter 2 below that Third World country delegates at the Bretton Woods con-ference talked of little else but their desire for development, and in Chapter 3 below it is shown that their pressure led to the expansion of the World Bank's mandate into social development through the establishment of the Bank's Inter-national Development Association arm.

Undoubtedly, the discourse creation machine usually operates as post-developmentalism proposes; bright ideas are developed in the World Bank's comfortable offices in Washington and foisted upon the citizenry of developing countries. However, as will be seen in Chapter 2, whether these ideas are imple-mented, and under what terms, is intimately linked to the material conditions of the client state and the predilections of local elites.

Nevertheless, post-developmentalism's deconstructive insights can greatly expand understanding of the Bank's hegemonic development practices. As will be seen in Chapter 3, the Bank goes to great lengths to hegemonise development discourse, thus establishing a taken-for-grantedness about the "need" for its intervention into ever wider spheres of global life. The interpretation of this process that is reflected in this book relies heavily on post-developmentalist concepts.

Post-developmentalism often relies on a narrow caricature of globalisation, with the relationship between First and Third Worlds viewed as simple exploita-tion. In contrast, the theory of global managerialism argues that relations of inequality and exploitation are fluid and subvertible. While unequal relationships are continually created and recreated through the interplay of material and discur-sive representations of power, the nature of these relationships and the victims of oppression change over time. Further, the construction of First and Third World needs to acknowledge internal differentiation within First and Third World soci-eties, and the increasing tendency for elite interests to coincide across the world. As an example, the global business process outsourcing industry is largely con-trolled by developing country elites. Chapter 6 of this book offers another example of a changing, globalised elite dynamic. It describes the rise of Mittal Steel, a corporation originating in the Third World, and owned and managed by postcolonial elites, building a global steel empire under World Bank tutelage on the foundation of often non-transparent relationships with developing and transitional country state elites. No spatially dyadic system, whether of the Marxist-imperialist or the post-developmentalist type, can adequately account for the emergence of global elites.

Gramscian international theory

A number of thinkers within the field of international political economy reject the dualism of determinism and poststructuralism, seeking a framework that acknowledges both material and cultural factors in the construction of a global order. Gramsci's method (1992) provides a base for such an inclusive framework. Material power, institutions and ideas interact to create a "historical bloc" that underpins a stable ruling order. Understanding social dynamics requires analysis of the elements of the bloc and the dynamics of their dialectical interrelationship.

Robert Cox (1981, 1983, 1987, 2002) has pioneered the use of Gramscian methodology in international relations. Cox emphasises the distinction between Gramsci's definition of "hegemony" and the common modern usage that is coterminous with domination. In Gramsci's hegemony, the social order is generally accepted as legitimate by the population; rule is by consent. Translating this to the world system in which states are the "population", Cox argues that hegemony rests on states' acceptance of the particular social and ideological order. If states were homogenous and discrete units, insoluble conflicts would frequently arise, and hegemonic articulation would be inherently unstable. However, states are themselves comprised of complex social structures dominated by elite formations more or less successfully articulating a hegemonic order. The global system's stability rests not on the formal architecture of inter-state collaboration, but on the articulation of an international hegemony through the interweaving of multiple national hegemonies to serve the needs of social classes across state boundaries, for example in underpinning an international mode of production (Cox, 1983: 171).

Cox's international hegemonic overlay is centred upon the transformatory economic and political ideology of the dominant class in one state. In the nineteenth century, British classical liberalism supplied the foundation for the hegemonic ideology while in the current era the United States dominates through corporate power and ideology underpinned by an international neo-liberal architecture. Dominant classes within other core states tie into this system as subordinate supporters.

The strength of Cox's model in comparison with traditional historical materialism includes its ability to explain apparent historical anomalies, such as the persistence of hegemonic systems even after they no longer reflect material conditions. Elements of British hegemony such as the City's coordinating role in global financial markets continued long after the locus of economic power had shifted away from Britain, because the ideology and institutions of British-led hegemony remained attractive to a world nostalgic for the golden era of the nineteenth-century world economy (Cox, 1981: 140). Similarly, hegemonic power in the process of becoming, such as the United States in the early years of the twentieth century, may not immediately view itself as representing a New World Order. However, for Gramscian theory, ideology is in the last analysis rooted in economics. For example, British hegemony in the nineteenth century, while articulated through the global ideological and social leadership of its ruling class, was predicated upon the British manufacturing industry's dominance in the international economy.

The state, for Cox, is neither all-powerful, as it tends to be seen in mainstream international relations theory, nor largely irrelevant, as suggested by many globalisation theorists (Sklair, 1995, 2001). States "play an intermediate though autonomous role between the global structure of social forces and local configurations of social forces within particular countries" (Cox, 1981: 141). The role of the core hegemonic state within the global system is essential. In its absence, the system is fundamentally unstable, and multinational institutions function poorly, as did the League of Nations in the interwar period. Present-day international organisations can be characterised as "weak" (United Nations) or "strong", like the International Monetary Fund and the World Bank, depending on the extent to which they are under the control of the hegemonic state. Multilateral institutions that cease to represent the interests of the hegemonic state are re-categorised from strong to weak (World Trade Organisation (WTO)) and are circumvented by bilateral arrangements.[7]

By the 1980s, Cox acknowledged the growing internationalisation of the world system and its more extensive institutionalisation than during the nineteenth-century period of British hegemony. A "machinery of surveillance" (1981: 145) had developed, rooted in the growing supervisory role of the new Bretton Woods institutions, while international policy harmonisation developed from the Marshall Aid fund criteria and NATO annual reviews, which created a habit of mutual consultation on national economic policy. The internationalisation of economic policy restructured national governments, favouring ministries of finance and executive policy offices such as prime ministers' offices over central planning agencies and ministries of industry that had occupied a central role in the period of national corporatism between the New Deal and the triumph of neo-liberalism in the 1970s. Thus, internationalisation of the economic system resulted in its further politicisation.

Internationalisation of the state takes place at three levels. At the top level, the advanced capitalist countries collaborate in achieving consensus through their central agencies in formal structures like the OECD, IMF and World Bank, as well as less formally through *ad hoc* fora and bilateral discussions. There is increasing involvement of private business in these fora and discussions. The second tier of internationalisation involves the relationships between the state socialist countries and the world economy; this level is obviously now defunct.

The third level is the hierarchical relationship between the advanced countries and the Third World, typically organised around the financing of debt and aid. Cox notes that:

> Third World elites do not participate with the same effective status as top-level elites in the consensus. The consensus does, however, gain ideological recruits and places ideologically conditioned agents in key positions within Third World countries. ... These people are often graduates of major advanced-capitalist country universities and have often passed through the IMF Institute and similar bodies that bring Third World technical financial personnel into personal contact with the milieu of international finance.
>
> (1987: 260)

In an extension of this process, and presaging Sklair's theory of the transnational capitalist class, Cox detects a tendency to the internationalisation of social classes, "alongside or superimposed upon national class structures" (1981: 147). The nascent "transnational managerial class" includes the officials of international institutions, executives of multinational corporations and national enterprises focused on global markets, and senior officials in internationally oriented government ministries.

The Gramscian-based model permits the introduction of a variety of different factors into the explanatory model, while its emphasis on the centrality of hegemony to human organisation prevents it succumbing to directionless empiricism or decentred poststructuralism. But Cox's transposition of Gramsci's class hegemony model to inter-state relations is problematic. Gramsci wrote about *class systems. States are not social classes. States do not represent common interests but are themselves made up of hierarchical class orders.* In defining dominant states as homogenous bearers of a certain mode of production, as Marx did in describing dominant classes such as the feudal aristocracy and the bourgeoisie, Cox renders the emergence of an authentically transnational (rather than imperialist) social and economic order logically impossible, notwithstanding actual social and economic developments. His recent attention to globalisation and his tentative discussions of the emergence of a transnational managerial class are juxtaposed uncomfortably with his continuing insistence on a rigid, US-dominated international hierarchy. Thus the role of his "transnational" managerial class is to negotiate the terms of interplay between nation states rather than being authentically transnational, in other words reflecting an emergent supranational order.

Cox has been legitimately criticised for not adequately accounting for the fundamental changes in the international order unleashed by the collapse of the Soviet bloc (Schechter, 2002: 9). It can be argued, employing his categorisation of ideological modes of production anchored in one country, that the era of American ideological and institutional hegemony is over (reflected, for example, in the inability of the United States to generate substantial support for its 2003 attack on Iraq), and that the world is entering either an interregnum before the likely dominance of China and other Asian countries (the direction in which Cox's state-based thinking would logically lead) or, as is argued here, the global mode of production.

Cox makes clear in his writings that his personal preference is for a state-based international order. The problem, however, is not the desirability of a world of independent but interconnected nation states, but rather its plausibility. As many "hyperglobalist" thinkers have emphasised, recent technological trans-formations have increased the speed and reduced the cost of the multiplicity of transnational communications, creating a global capital, labour and consumption market. Thus, "[e]conomic geography and political geography both are desta-bilised in such a way that the boundaries among the various zones are them-selves fluid and mobile". This in turn calls for

> a new mechanism of the general control of the global process and thus a mechanism that can coordinate politically the new dynamism of the global domain of capital and the subjective dimensions of the actors; it has to be able to articulate the imperial dimension of command and the transversal mobility of the subjects.
>
> (Hardt and Negri, 2000: 254)

If, instead of building the "transnational managerial class" from state-bound roots, it is conceived of as a putatively global phenomenon, Cox's application of a Gramscian framework is useful, especially when elite membership can be understood in Bourdieu-style terms as deriving from the broader concept of symbolic capital. The elite can be viewed as a historical bloc composed of a number of different elements that are constituted partly in political geographic terms (because the global elite is unevenly distributed between different parts of the world), but also in economic classification (most obviously finance and pro-ductive capital), appurtenance to the public and private sectors, and through popular legitimating structures, such as international civil society organisations (whose emerging role will be discussed in Chapter 5 below). The relative power of these different groupings, and even their adherence to the global managerial elite, depends upon an effective "war of position" involving the manufacture of consent for the global order through material and ideological persuasion taking a number of forms.

The transnational capitalist class

Laurie Sklair (1995, 2001) has sketched out a globalisation paradigm called "global system theory", a sociology of the global system, and, most extensively, the theory of the transnational capitalist class, a "central inner circle that makes system-wide decisions" (2001: 21). Sklair argues that transnational corporations (TNCs) dominate the world: "The building blocks of the theory are the TNCs" (2001: 4). In contrast to Cox, he downplays the role of international state struc-tures such as the IMF and World Bank in the globalisation process because, as

creatures of nation states, they are not truly transnational. He also rejects Wallerstein's world-system theory because it, too, is founded upon distinctions
between states. TNCs are run by a transnational capitalist class (TCC).

A definable TCC substantially controls the "processes of globalisation". It
is "beginning to act as a transnational dominant class in some spheres", it
reproduces itself through the ideology of consumerism, and it is trying to
address the problems global capitalism is creating, such as poverty and
inequality, as well as ecological problems (2001: 5–6). Sklair claims that his
concept of a transnational ruling class is both new and controversial. Its key
characteristics are:

- The "economic interests of its members are increasingly globally linked
  rather than exclusively local and national in origin". TCCs look in terms of
  markets and not a nation state (2000: 18).
- The TCC exerts political as well as economic power. The TCC successfully
  dominates the political system through its control of the "TNC-generated
  culture-ideology of consumerism". However, this system also results in a race
  to the bottom for market share in poor and rich countries alike (2001: 20).
- TCC leaders have outward and global rather than inward local perspectives
  on economic, political and culture-ideology issues. The multinational
  representation of students at business schools is an indication of this openness to different cultures.
- TCC members portray themselves as citizens of the world rather than of one
  country: corporate barons such as Rupert Murdoch have even gone so far as
  to give up their "native" citizenship in order to pursue global business
  opportunities.

Sklair tests his theoretical framework through a survey of Fortune Global 500
companies. About three-fifths of the Global 500 corporations have headquarters
in Japan or the United States. Most companies responding to his survey (fewer
than 20 per cent) considered themselves either already global or in the process
of globalising, or were planning to globalise, though a significant number
expressed no global ambitions. He explores the involvement of transnational
corporations in several key moments of the globalisation process, including the
campaign to establish liberal foreign investment regimes (2001: 93), the assertion of corporate citizenship, best practice regimes as a globalising tool, and the
incorporation of environmentalism (2001: 206).

While he enumerates globalising international bureaucrats and state officials
as part of the transnational capitalist class (2001: 17), Sklair addresses their role
in the global system only in passing, preferring to focus almost exclusively on
the corporations that are central to his system. Although Sklair's approach is
hardly economistic (he rarely mentions production dynamics), almost exclusive
power in his model rests with transnational corporations, and state and transnational governance institutions are either irrelevant or under their control
(Sklair, 2002: 160). Sklair's hypothesis of a transnational ruling class is shared

by global managerialism, and his analysis of transnational corporation elites can help round out the theory presented here, which focuses mainly on the role of the World Bank and other international institutions in fostering a global system of elite domination. However, his theoretical premise – that transnationalisation is a *fait accompli* rather than under construction – sets the evidential bar very high, leading him to make questionable interpretations of the results of his empirical research. While most – but by no means all – of the corporations he surveyed either operate internationally or plan to do so, and many seem keen to describe themselves as global companies rather than imperialist operations centred in the United States or another developed capitalist country, Sklair's evidence does not justify describing many MNCs as truly transnational.

For example, Mitsubishi, despite being almost entirely dependent for its survival upon global acceptance of its product, acknowledges that it is a national company with units abroad rather than an MNC, although it says that it wants to change that situation (2002: 51). Only one-third of Mitsubishi's employees are outside Japan. Similarly, the comment of Matsushita's president that, "We've grown into a global enterprise, but we still carry Japanese passports, so to speak" (2002: 98), seems to sum up a globalising economy where corporations continue to have homes.

Sklair's corporate-focused view of globalisation also leads him to claim that existing multilateral institutions such as the World Bank and the IMF are not transnational, because they are representative of states and, therefore, apparently not worth examining. However, if an authentically global system exists, there must logically be a homologous global regulatory framework that permits it to operate. If, on the other hand, as I argue in this book, the world is undergoing a (lengthy) process of transition from a nationally based economic system to a global system, one would expect both transnational corporations and the economic regulatory framework to contain national and transnational elements – which seems to be the case.

Sklair's work on transnational class formation has been continued by the American sociologist William Robinson (2004, 2005), who also writes of a new transnational capitalist class. Robinson focuses to a greater extent than Sklair on the theoretical conditions for the emergence of the global spatiality of the new order, and emphasises the rise of transnational elites from within the Third World (although Sklair and Robbins (2002) had already documented this phenomenon). However Robinson's model is primarily distinguished from that of Sklair by his assertion that global ruling class membership can by definition only be secured through actual ownership of the means of production. Where Sklair's privileging of the transnational corporations' driving of globalisation is asserted primarily through his selection of corporate executives as his source of empirical data, Robinson takes pains to establish the theoretical necessity that corporate owners are the main drivers of globalisation. He evades the familiar logistical difficulties with this position (ownership positions in major corporations are typically widely held, and senior managers usually only own an insignificant proportion of the companies: see Berle and Means (1932)) by sticking to a purely theoretical description of the transnational class, without descending into uncomfortable empirical details.

Sklair's and Robinson's work on the transnational capitalist class is a break-through in attempting for the first time a clear schematisation of transnational class formation, but it is hampered by an outdated determinist view of class formation that views state and global quasi-state institutions primarily as con-veyor belts for private capitalist power. Their work is an example of the limits to understanding of the new global order imposed by a rigid corporate-driven understanding of transnational class formation. This book provides some strong empirical evidence that transnational institutions and their leaders play a key role in structuring the new global system, and that along with corporate and civil society leaders, they are essential contributors to an emergent global elite system in which power is expressed through the exercise of human and social, as well as economic, capitals. As will be seen in Chapters 2 and 3 below, the World Bank, in particular, has been proactive both in forcing global governance and in promoting a particular economic agenda. If anything, it is globalising quasi-state institutions that are leading the push towards the global order, rather than private corporations.

Management scholarship and globalisation

At first glance, it might appear that management studies has little to offer in terms of a theoretical approach to the new global order. Mainstream manage-ment research tends to take globalisation for granted, focusing mainly on means to adapt to or take advantage of it. As mentioned in the introduction to this chapter, CMS theorists have only cautiously moved beyond explorations of organisational dynamics to hypothesise the possible wider social ramifications of managerialist control technologies. Remarkably few critical management scholars have directly paid attention to international developments; until the journal *Critical Perspectives on International Business* started publishing in 2004, only a handful of CMS-inspired articles had been published on globalisa-tion themes.

This section begins with an examination of some of the limited CMS liter-ature that deals with globalisation themes. This is followed with an examination of how insights from CMS and institutional theory can contribute to the devel-opment of a theory of global managerialism.

CMS scholarship on globalisation – unrealised potential?

One of the first CMS treatments of globalisation was Bobby Banerjee and Stephen Linstead's 2001 journal article, "Globalisation, multiculturalism and other fic-tions". Banerjee and Linstead adopt a catholic analytical approach combining globalisation-sceptic, Marxist and post-developmentalist viewpoints along with some specifically CMS insights. Applying what they call a "critically discursive approach", they argue that globalisation is the result of contestable and contested political decisions, rather than an inevitable development of the market economy. Following Hirst and Thompson (1996), they question whether the world economy is truly global, pointing out that some aspects of the economy were more internationalised in the period before the First World War. They view the globalisation discourse as a manifestation of postcolonialism, in which poorer countries are subjected to "resource expropriation and economic control by the industrialised countries". Banerjee and Linstead emphasise the political aspects of globalisation rather than the economic development logic that is inscribed in both traditional and Marxian accounts of human development. They adopt Arturo Escobar's (1995) post-development discourse which rejects the "post-enlightenment discourse of Progress" and claims that poverty in the Third World is a discursive construction.

They identify various mechanisms through which globalisation is spreading. On one hand, they draw on the imperialist paradigm to argue that the pressure for globalisation has come about through concerted efforts by powerful western interests, implemented through coercion, surveillance, legitimacy-granting and authority. This involves direct pressure from western powers, particularly the United States, as well as regulation through multilateral organisations such as the WTO, IMF and World Bank. On the other hand, they draw on culturalist paradigms in asserting that globalisation is inculcated in the world's citizenry through a "culture-ideology" of consumption integrated within the meaning of democracy which has reconceptualised the citizen as a consumer. They reject the "old world, new world, third world and fourth world" (the underclass of the developed countries) schematic, proposing instead a division between those who live in time ("a first-world financial district full of high and frequent flyers") and those living in space; perhaps only a mile away from the high-flyers, people are confined to their locale, have difficulty crossing borders, and are frequently placed into a demi-monde of illegality when they do travel, "prey to traffickers and debt-bonders". Peasants make up a large proportion of the excluded, living in space rather than time.

Banerjee and Linstead offer some useful insights for a critical management research agenda on globalisation. In contrast to most dependency and world-system theorists they acknowledge that globalisation, for poorer countries at least, is "not the result of free and self-regulating market economies but the result of co-ordinated economic and political management" (2001: 689) by the World Bank and IMF. Globalisation is "grounded not only on capitalist economic systems but also on culture and the polity". This perspective on globalisation as a process, a managed phenomenon as much as it is natural and inevitable, is central to the argument here. At the same time, their insistence that globalisation is merely western imperialism flies in the face of actual developments. Is China's rise as an industrial powerhouse and putative superpower part of a western scheme? Does the shopping spree of Indian corporations purchasing key western assets (Elliot, 2007) reflect some hidden imperialist strategy? While Banerjee and Linstead legitimately point out the many losers in globalisation, their attempt to shoehorn this phenomenon into ill-fitting and worn descriptors such as colonialism robs their analysis of credibility. If British Corus workers in Port Talbot, Wales, are laid off by new Indian owners Tata Steel, is this an example of western imperialism operating through sleight of hand? Banerjee and Linstead's article is a classic example of the problematic application of existing critical theory, no longer fit for purpose as an analytical framework for understanding human organisation in the global era.

The critical accounting subspecialisation has generated more discussion of globalisation than other areas of CMS. Critical accountants have a long tradition of moving beyond traditional accounting frameworks in order to analyse broader regulation issues. The emergent system of supranational regulation, in which the World Bank and other transnational institutions play a key role, is a natural area of interest, and has generated lively discussion in recent years.

Annisette discusses the role of the World Bank through a perspective grounded mainly in Wallerstein's world-system theory and its argument that there is "a single ongoing international division of labour" (Annisette, 2004: 304). She argues that the World Bank's role is to maintain this international division of labour. Thus, its failure to effectively address poverty, even though this is its principal mandate, is not the result of organisational incompetence but is hard-wired into the imperialist raison d'être of the institution. The Bank's activities in developing countries are geared towards extracting profits for the benefit of the rich shareholder nations. Despite being exploited, developing countries have little choice but to borrow from the Bank because it is easily the largest source of development capital. Through the system of unequal exchange, injustice in the world economy has deepened and solidified.

Annisette captures many of the key features, to be discussed later in this book, which make the World Bank a leading vehicle for elite-driven globalisation. Her description of the institution's ability to coordinate the globalisation drive is particularly effective. However, as with Banerjee and Linstead, and several other writers in the critical accounting tradition (Arnold and Sikka, 2001), her analysis is weakened by an attempt to fit it into the constricting and outdated framework of post-Leninist theories of imperialism.

Her assertion that the World Bank was founded as a "conspicuously capitalist institution" (2004: 310) is at odds with the historical record; the Bank was explicitly designed to accommodate socialist as well as capitalist economic systems. Second, her characterisation of financial extraction from the Third World as the Bank's primary institutional driver is inaccurate. From the early 1980s, the institution's focus has been on making loans in return for policy reform. These carry a negligible interest rate; their purpose is not to extract profits but rather to impose the Bank's political economy on debtor nations. Thus, governmentality rather than profits lies at the heart of the Bank's mission. Third, Annisette's assertion that the Bank is not serious about poverty reduction is incompatible with the Bank's insistence that recipient countries recast all of their domestic policies to fit the comprehensive framework of its poverty reduction strategy, an issue that will be discussed at length in later chapters of this book. While the content of poverty reduction programming is problematic, there is little doubt that the Bank is serious about enforcing it (Cammack, 2002). Fourth, Annisette's claim that the Bank does not engage adequately in "participatory methods" is naïve. The Bank has extensive participatory programmes; the salient critique is that these form part of a managerialist "tyranny" through which potential critics of the Bank's activities are neutralised (Cooke and Kothari, 2001), as will also be discussed in a later chapter. Finally, Annisette's argument is built around the belief that the Bank is at the centre of a system that serves to "freeze [developing countries'] economies, preventing them from transcending patterns of production set during the colonial era" (2004: 315), a statement that is impossible to square with the rapid growth and transformation of China, India, and several other developing country economies.[8]

Dean Neu and his various collaborators have approached globalisation from a more nuanced perspective, also within the critical accounting tradition. They focus on the World Bank as a key coordinating institution of globalisation, introducing Foucault's concept of governmentality, Bourdieu's (1994) theories of fields, habitus and multiple forms of capital, as well as Dimaggio and Powell's (1983) theory of institutional isomorphism into their analytical framework.

In contrast to Annisette's stock critique of the World Bank as a muscular financial agent of imperialism, Neu and colleagues concentrate on the institution's use of human and social capital (perceived expertise and networking centrality) as well as economic power to place itself at the centre of a globalisation "consensus" that enables "supranational organizations to structure the cross-border flows of much more than capital" (Graham and Neu, 2003: 452). They emphasise the crucial role of information in the Bank's strategy, creating the opportunity to "name" the new global system and thus legitimise the extension of a hierarchical system across ever broader fields of human activity (Neu *et al.*, 2002: 275–276).

Another significant difference between Neu's and Annisette's analyses is his assertion that globalisation is more than simply the rearticulation of the interests of the hegemonic nation states on a supranational basis; the supranational, embodied by the World Bank, develops a persona of its own, "outside of the direct control of even the largest and most powerful individual states" (Graham and Neu, 2003: 451). Neu and collaborators do not, however, follow the wide-ranging implications of their insights to their logical conclusions. If supranational institutions like the Bank are beginning to operate independently of nation states, this must imply development of a transnational social structure and the emergence of a nascent global elite, as argued in this book.

Neu aside, CMS accounts of globalisation have been weakened by their reliance on standard critical explanatory frameworks, which I have been at pains to show are no longer very relevant in a post-imperialist and post-postcolonial era. In the remainder of this chapter I will argue that, in fact, the critical management studies discipline can bring key insights into an explanation of the functioning of a global managerial system. CMS's understanding of how managerial domination is constructed at the level of the firm through corporate culturism and concertive control can be extended into the broader social field to characterise core modalities of global managerialism. In order for these insights to be used, they must, however, be translated from the micro-organisational level.

The relevance of CMS to understanding global managerialism

Management, in its broadest sense, has been around for as long as human organisation. However, interest in management as a specific function in organisation is most often traced back to Weber's analysis of bureaucracy (Parker, 2002: 18). Weber identified two predominant ideal types of rationality in modern society, instrumental rationality and value-rational action. A person operating through instrumental rationality will take the dominant value system as given, and derive their wants from this given value system. Value-rational action, on the other hand, is founded on critical self-reflection. The individual's autonomy is formed through the conscious choice of ethical standpoints and their realisation in everyday action (Willmott, 1993: 532).

Although value-rational action is a subjectively superior foundation for human self-realisation, it lacks the concerting potential of instrumental rationality. The dangers of relying for control on the operation of one or other of these methodologies became evident in the mass strikes in the United States during the 1930s (Preis, 1994); if the economic system gathered thousands of people in the same location to produce through scientific industrial organisation principles, the assembled masses could generate value-rational action antithetical to the existing industrial system. They would also possess the instrumental-rational organisational framework necessary for collective action: from the manager's point of view, the worst of all worlds. This conundrum underpins Marx's theory of revolutionary transformation (Marx and Engels, 1999: 73–77).

However, continued elite domination would be more certain if an order could be constructed in which instrumental-rational and value-rational systems of social action complemented each other in order to further the pre-existing hegemony. The new project would have to find a way to deliver the self-realisation of value-rational motivation, while safeguarding the instrumental goals of the organisation. It is this project that has seized the post-war managerialist imagination and lies at the core of global managerialism.

Tompkins and Cheney (1985) contribute useful conceptual tools for understanding managerialism, from within management communication theory. They sketch four separate but interconnected managerial control strategies within the corporation. The first three could be labelled "traditional": direct control, control through machine production discipline, and bureaucratic control. Tompkins and Cheney's addition to the theory of organisational power is the fourth strategy, that of concertive control, where employees come to share the organisation's worldview. Concertive control derives from "post-bureaucratic" organisational life built on teamwork, "flexibility and innovation", "flat hierarchy", "blurring of line and staff distinctions", "intense face-to-face interaction" and "relative value consensus". Ultimately, concertive control's success depends on employees' internalisation of the organisational mission, so that bureaucratic controls can be "replaced by common understanding of values, objectives, and means of achievement" (Tompkins and Cheney, 1985: 184). The concertive approach is epitomised in popular management manuals, from which Tompkins and Cheney select an early example, Peters and Waterman's *In Search of Excellence* (1982).

Other CMS writers have analysed contemporary corporate control techniques and noted the centrality of self-motivation to successful management. Kunda (1992), in a rich empirical study, noted the extent to which management of a high-tech firm consciously sought to re-engineer the identity of its employees to conform with the needs of the corporation. Willmott (1993) explores a related theme in his discussion of "corporate culturism", drawing a dark parallel between concertive managerialism and George Orwell's *Nineteen Eighty-Four*, in which the Party uses similar techniques to maintain control and marginalise opposition.

The theories of concertive control and corporate culturism resonate with the internal working and development practice of international institutions such as the World Bank. Internally, great effort is made to flatten hierarchy through inter-locking teams and networks, compensate for geographical distance through videoconferencing technology, 360° evaluation, collectively designed mission and value statements, etc.[9] These technologies are discussed in detail in Chapter 3 below.

While concertive control is mainly viewed within CMS as an internal organi-sational control mechanism, this insight is extended in global managerial theory to explain the emergence of managerial strategies underpinning wider social control technologies. In this book I will focus particularly on the export of con-certive control strategies to the international development domain by the World Bank. World Bank concertive managerialist keywords include "country owner-ship", "partnership", "participation", "empowerment", "coordination" and "inclu-sivity". Concertive managerialism reflects an organising principle underpinning contemporary organisations ranging from Third Way political movements to the nascent institutions of global governance.

Institutions and global managerialism

Institutional theory, an overwhelmingly popular analytical framework within mainstream organisation studies, is typically rejected as a useful approach by critical management theorists (Lok and Willmott, 2006). However, the roots of institutional theory are not as quietist as either CMS scholars or conservative American business school academics might appreciate. Institutional theory was developed by the former Trotskyist Philip Selznick in his quest to understand why Bolshevism had been transformed from a movement for liberation into a repressive government. Selznick employed Weber's concepts to explore the process through which an organisation acquires value meaning beyond its strictly technical and instrumental raison d'être, including through the embodi-ment of the ideals of the individuals who are its members (Selznick, 1948,

1949). As individuals collectively infuse the organisation with value, they too find meaning through participating in the organisation's activities. Organisational identification becomes more than loyalty to an external entity, it is also the realisation of self in the institutionalised entity (Scott, 1987: 493–495).

Particularly in its broader "old" manifestations[10] institutional theory can strengthen a critical explanation of the development and institutionalisation of global organisations such as the World Bank. The Bank's instrumental tasks, as defined by the Bretton Woods agreement that launched the organisation, undoubtedly remain relevant to the organisations' missions, as will be discussed in the next chapter. Path dependency alone, however, cannot account for the organisation's trajectory, and particularly its ideological oscillations and continual growth (Peters, 2000: 3). The Bank pursues a global civilising mission beyond its mandate that has become institutionally embedded through an iterative process of value infusion into the originally relatively modest, but nevertheless global, ambitions of the organisation. This analysis might help explain why the Bank's flirtation with market fundamentalism during the 1980s, far from expressing the "true essence" of the organisation, was abandoned as soon as the force of the neo-liberal tsunami had abated. Nevertheless, the Bank adapted to the ideologically hostile external environment by expanding its organisational responsibilities to include the supervision and correction of underdeveloped and deviant national economies, an adaptation consistent with the survival instincts of an institutionalised organisation. The Bank's venture into political economy conflicted with the organisation's founding vision (because of its intrusiveness into states' internal economic organisation), but was the outcome of an interplay of that vision with the Bank staff's value-rational vision of a competent organisation able to deliver its instrumental goal of a "world free from poverty".

Concepts of path dependency have been employed relatively widely within mainstream organisation studies. Hannan and Freeman's population ecology theory (1977), for example, strongly emphasises path dependent factors in organisational survival. Organisational inertia is reflective not of lacking vision but of the likelihood that organisational resources cannot be adapted to changing external environments. Berger and Luckmann's symbolic interactionism (1972), which provides methodological grounding for much contemporary institutional theory, places a strong emphasis on the importance of routinisation in patterning human behaviour. These accounts have tended to reinforce a quietist orientation in institutional theory which is not consistent with critical approaches (Cooper *et al.*, 2007). An alternative, more change-oriented approach to path dependency is provided by historical institutionalism, a rapidly growing school in political science that has received little take-up within organisation science despite its obvious relevance (Skocpol, 1995). The discussion of the World Bank's history in Chapter 2 below is built around a historical institutionalist approach; the method is examined at greater length in the introduction to that chapter.

Another small theoretical school has emerged in recent years within the institutionalist tradition, applying institutional approaches to understand the emergence of transnational organisational structures (Brunsson and Jacobsson, 2002).

Their research, which is largely descriptive rather than analytical, centres on regulated standardisation as a vehicle for supranational governance. Marie-Laure Djelic (2001), writing in this tradition, does offer one meta-explanation for the globalisation trend and its institutionalisation in its particular market-oriented form: the expansive drive towards global Americanisation. While this has resonance for the immediate post-war period when America acted as the driving force in replacing the imperial systems, it is less convincing when extended to the contemporary era. As will be discussed in the next chapter, the period of unconditional US support for transnationalisation was actually very short, essentially ending with the death of Roosevelt and the onset of the Cold War. Since then, American actions have tended to be instrumentalist.

Brunsson and Jacobsson and some of their collaborators do cautiously broach critical questions about the expert-driven nature of the transnational society that is being built. However, there is considerable room to deepen and sharpen the questions they ask about the legitimacy of the semi-formal expert networks that set rules, norms and standards in ever wider areas of human activity. The implications of expert-driven standardisation are considered in the discussion of global networks in Chapter 5 below.

While the Bank's own organisational trajectory can be partially understood through institutional theory, an economic version of the same theory shapes the organisation's own definition of its rational-instrumental development mandate, as reflected in the post-Washington Consensus and the Bank's consequent emphasis on the institutionalisation by developing countries of "good practices" in economic and political governance. This aspect of the Bank's project, which post-developmental theory might categorise as postcolonialism and dependency theory as neoimperialism, is an important extension of managerialism and, in combination with the Bank's adoption of a development supervision role as argued above, places the Bank at the heart of the ambitions of global managerialism.

Conclusion

In this chapter I have outlined the foundations of the theory of global managerialism. I have emphasised the importance of grounding critical analysis on a defensible social theory. The disintegration of the socialist project in the latter years of the twentieth century was both caused by, and produced, contradictions in the ways critical thinkers viewed the world. Central in these contradictions was the inability of Marxist class theory to explain how the elimination of the capitalist "motor" in the Soviet Union had resulted not in emancipation but in the entrenchment of an elite and the relentless physical and moral exploitation of the ordinary citizen. Critical theorists who continue to depend on economic explanations of contemporary social developments, including globalisation, are increasingly unable to construct plausible accounts. The many critical theorists who have understandably abandoned economism have tended to spiral into poststructuralist analyses that by definition cannot assist an understanding of structured inequality.

As an alternative to both (post)Marxism and poststructuralism, I have proposed the use of elite theory, enriched with Wright Mills's and Bourdieu's insights, as the basis for a post-economistic account of global social stratification. Several critical theories of globalisation have been reviewed from within this framework, and their relevance to a theory of global managerialism assessed. None adequately describes the processes through which a global elite is being built, although the model proposed here draws on aspects of several of these theories.

The various (post)Marxist globalisation theories (actually better described as Leninist) abandon central features of Marx's model: capitalism's conquest of anterior modes of production and the intensification and simplification of class conflict. Instead, the imperial stage of capitalist development complicates class relationships, creating contradictory class positions. More recent iterations such as dependency and world-system theories extend Lenin's postulations into hierarchical global systems in which an international division of labour is superimposed upon national class structures. But, as poststructuralists have pointed out (Laclau and Mouffe, 1985: 57–65), once the essentialist dynamic of the Marxist system is removed, it is no longer possible to "objectively" assess class dynamics and "scientifically" predict the ultimate outcome of the class struggle. Particularly problematic is the tendency of the (post)Marxist theories to belittle developing country elites as mere "comprador" agents of imperialist capitalism although much of the world economy's recent growth and dynamism originates in the developing world.

Refinement of a (post)Marxist theory of social stratification dynamics required further breaches in the Marxist economist edifice. In the Leninist theory of evolutionary strategy, the working class can split developing country elites between "nationalist progressive" and comprador elements and ally itself with the former to accomplish the "democratic" phase of the revolution; this political task has necessarily indeterminate outcomes. Gramsci extended Lenin's unacknowledged deviation from Marxism to explore the processes whereby hegemonic social alliances are constructed. Robert Cox has applied Gramsci's method to the international relations field, and his approach assists in understanding international elite dynamics. Nevertheless, Cox's scholarly focus on relations between nation states means that international class formations are little more than extensions of national classes, and his global hegemonic model in turn rests upon an assumption of a dominant national power: at present, the United States. However, as shall be seen later in this book, the US administration is at odds with the globalising initiatives of transnationalising institutions including the World Bank. These institutions are not mere appendages of the United States; the nuanced relationship between the Bank and the United States is discussed in Chapters 2 and 3 below.

Post-developmentalism and postcolonialism are invaluable in deconstructing taken-for-granted explanations of human organisation. However, these poststructuralist-inspired theories have difficulty moving beyond deconstruction to social explanation. A particular problem in applying them to the constitution of transnational hierarchical social relations is the inherent lack of a "change logic".

The strength of poststructuralism's critique of developmentalism as the imposition of a disempowering hegemonic discourse on the poor of the Third World is acknowledged. However, post-developmentalism and, particularly, postcolonialism are susceptible to deconstruction as articulations of the elite aspirations of postcolonial intellectuals (Žižek, 1997; Hardt and Negri, 2000: 146, 155–156). One common version of this manoeuvre entails exposure of the discursive and material processes of oppression of developing country subalterns by the forces of imperialism/colonialism, elision of the distinction between the oppressed subaltern and the postcolonial intellectual, and consequent assertion of the postcolonial intellectual's claim to morally privileged status. Examples of this process are found in Spivak (1999) and in Chakrabarty (2000). The taken-for-granted equivalence of postcolonial subaltern and postcolonial elite obscures the key social hierarchical relationship argued in global managerial elite theory, which is of a transnational power elite extending to developing countries, with internally congruent interests and fundamentally conflictual relationships with transnational subaltern classes. This phenomenon is denounced in dramatic terms by the prominent Indian novelist and social activist Arundhati Roy:

> What we're witnessing is the most successful secessionist struggle ever waged in independent India – the secession of the middle and upper classes from the rest of the country. It's a vertical secession, not a lateral one. They're fighting for the right to merge with the world's elite somewhere up there in the stratosphere.
>
> (Roy, 2007)

Despite these cautions about some of the uses to which poststructuralist theorising on globalisation has been put, one of the breakthroughs of poststructuralist-inspired CMS is an emphasis on reflexivity and an enhanced sensitivity towards underlying social agendas and power dynamics masked by overt truth claims. The deconstructive approach to understanding organisational dynamics has been particularly useful in exposing the manipulative core underpinning participatory management techniques. While CMS writing directly addressing globalisation has been of mixed quality and particularly prone to the (uncritical) use of stock critical explanations such as postcolonialism and post-imperialism, a critical literature is emerging that uses CMS approaches to understand globalisation discourse. From within more mainstream management theory, institutional theory can contribute by documenting the important role played by supranational institutions such as the World Bank in rooting discourse within an elite-driven transnational governance practice. In the following chapters I seek to extend the approach outlined in this chapter, through explorations of case studies on "moments" in the World Bank's rise as a global managerialist powerhouse.

2 The genetic code of global managerialism

Introduction

The first chapter discussed various critical approaches to globalisation, including the Gramscian international political economy of Robert Cox. Cox argues that the world system is effectively controlled through the hegemony of an economic system based on a "mode of production" associated with a dominant state; at the present time, this is the United States. This perspective is ultimately a sophisticated variant of the "imperialism" theory that was also discussed in the first chapter, although the economic driver is extensively mediated through cultural and political hegemonisation processes so that no direct or immediate correlation can be drawn between the dominant economic power and the systems of institutional and cultural hegemony. If the argument is correct, the global elite would be largely tributary of the dominant class of the hegemonic power. Further, the role of the transnational institutional framework of the global system would primarily be to support the hegemonic mode of production. In other words, institutions like the World Bank, if not directly controlled by the dominant power, would be dominated by the United States and its hegemonic order. In fact, this point of view is routinely expressed by many radical critics of the World Bank and the other global governance institutions (Monbiot, 2005). It contradicts the global managerial hypothesis, which asserts the emergent transnationalisation of elite identity, structured through a global institutional framework.

Consequently, this chapter will address the key issue of whether the international system is subordinate to the United States, as Cox and Monbiot argue. This question will be answered through an exploration of key historical junctures in the development of the World Bank, and specifically of the relationship between the Bank and the United States in the course of those defining moments. It will be argued that the World Bank, since its inception, has been motivated by a vision that transcends the interests of the United States, and that the institution carries the genetic code of global managerialism.

The presentation of the history of the Bank's formation and subsequent development and relationship with the United States is guided by the historical institutionalist approach. As noted in Chapter 1 above, historical institutionalism is an analytical method mostly used in political science, best known for its emphasis on the importance of path dependency in institutional development: "dynamics triggered by an event or process at one point in time reproduce themselves, even in the absence of the recurrence of the original event or process" (Pierson and Skocpol, 2002: 666). Historical institutionalism views institutional organisation as a key factor in structuring behaviour and producing differential social outcomes, in contrast to behaviouralist models in which outcomes were perceived to derive from aggregated psychological traits of individuals, or Marxist-inspired models in which institutions are derivative of the primal relationship to the means of production. In particular, historical institutionalists view the state as crucially important in structuring outcomes. "The state" is logically extended in this book to the emergent structures of global governance that are embodied in the Bretton Woods institutions and their derivatives.

Ma (2007: 63) identifies six core features of contemporary historical institutional theory: focus on historical movement as opposed to tendency to equilibrium; inclusion of informal as well as formal institutions; a blend of utility maximisation and cultural factors as individual motivators; an emphasis on power asymmetry; the contextualisation of institutional developments within the broader social and cultural environment; and an interest in explaining macrorather than micro-phenomena. A refinement of the concept of path dependence within historical institutionalism is the notion of "positive returns", an idea drawn from heterodox economics. Positive returns is essentially the opposite argument from classical economics' faith in the tendency to equilibrium: "the probability of further steps down the path increases with each move down that path" (Pierson, 2000: 252). The positive returns argument responds to a common criticism of institutional theory as poorly explaining change. Positive returns suggest that change begets change.

Although the positive returns insight was developed in the economic field, it is likely to be a more predominant phenomenon in the political and organisational fields, for several reasons. The logic of collective action is much stronger; individual success depends on institutional success, and individual exit is rendered difficult. Power asymmetries tend to be exacerbated as typically only one institutional orientation or policy option can be pursued, and particular (elite) interests become institutionally entrenched. Finally, among extra-market institutions such as the World Bank, there are no "market signals" of success. Success is largely self-defined. In this vein, Chapter 4 below documents the extraordinary efforts the World Bank makes in order to preserve its capacity to define the parameters of success in the development field.

The implication of positive returns for social science researchers is that close attention should be paid to the historical path that has led to specific social outcomes. Further, because outcomes tend increasingly to be locked in, critical junctures tend to arise early in institutional development, and are most likely to occur in a context of broader social flux. Such circumstances were undoubtedly present in the later years of the Second World War, when existing institutional arrangements had irretrievably broken down and the edifice of the post-war international order was being conceptualised and built from a virtually blank page. It was in such circumstances that the ideas of a radical economist, Harry White, could act as the germ for a new, global system of human organisation.

In the following sections of this chapter, I highlight three critical junctures in the World Bank's development. The first of these junctures is the period including the conception and realisation of the project for the creation of the Bretton Woods institutions. An exploration of the motivations underlying the foundation and early development of the World Bank allows an assessment of whether the Bank was from the outset intended to be a genuinely global institution or whether, as Cox and Monbiot suggest, it was primarily an extension of American hegemony. The second juncture is the later Cold War period, and specifically the aggressive expansion of the Bank's activities and vision from the late 1950s. Finally, this chapter examines the dramatic rise of neo-liberalism and the Bank's adoption of "structural adjustment" as its version of this phenomenon (see Table 2.1).

The formation and early years of the World Bank

The best means to understand the nature of the World Bank at its moment of creation is through an appreciation of Harry White, the American economist who conceived the Bretton Woods system.[1] White rose like a meteor from a modest immigrant family to become the architect of the Rooseveltian internationalist project for a post-imperial world economic order. White's even more precipitous fall with the onset of the Cold War, a fate shared by most of his colleagues, also provides an understanding of the longstanding divisions within the American elite on globalisation, the roots of American unilateralism and the construction of internationalism as treason. However, as the next section of this chapter indicates, White's legacy was the institutionalisation of a global managerial momentum within the Bretton Woods architecture.

Harry White and the origins of global managerialism

In the aftermath of Pearl Harbor and the entry of the United States into the war, US policy experts turned their hands to post-war problems, a task important for war propagandist as well as long-term policy reasons. Harry White, one of the US Treasury's leading economists, began work on a post-war economic reconstruction plan. He envisaged global institutions geared to increasing social justice and overall prosperity, and reducing or eliminating cyclical crises. His proposals argued that the world would face three outstanding economic issues at the conclusion of war: re-creation of a functioning international monetary system, restoration of foreign trade; and the reconstruction of national economies (White, 1942). These problems could not be addressed by countries individually; they would require new multilateral institutions that should be established before the end of the war so that the world would not spiral into another post-war economic crisis. According to White, two new institutions were needed: an international

Table 2.1 Four stages in the development of global managerialism

Period	Ideological orientation	Institutional developments	Emblematic policy orientations	Geographic orientation
1942–1946	Rooseveltian internationalism	Foundation of Bretton Woods institutions	Reconstruction and stable monetary system	Wartime allies; failed attempt to include USSR
1958–1975	Cold War liberalism	Creation of International Development Association	Capital projects and low-cost loans	American dominance; inclusion of least developed countries
1979–1993	Disciplinary neo-liberalism	Shift from project to policy-based orientation	Imposition of structural adjustment: privatisation, export-driven development	Western triumphalism
1995–	Third Way managerialism	Integration of Bank and IMF activities; convening of other international stakeholders	Comprehensive development frameworks; poverty reduction strategies	Absorption of the former socialist countries; tentative rebalancing of institutional power towards emerging powers

Fund to stabilise the foreign exchange system, and an international Bank to supply capital for reconstruction. The Bank would provide capital for reconstruction and short-term capital to support international trade, and help create economic stability by redistributing gold, thus stabilising prices, raising living standards worldwide, and reducing or eliminating financial crises and economic depressions. The Fund would establish international parameters for monetary and trade policy, with an emphasis on convertible currencies with managed exchange rates, reduction of trade barriers, elimination of export subsidies, and consultation with the Fund on economic policy and, especially, exchange rate changes. Both the Bank and the Fund would be financed by subscriptions loosely based on comparative national incomes; countries would take short-term loans from the Fund up to the value of their subscription in order to support their currency or deal with balance of payments imbalances, while the Bank would underwrite longer-term loans to help countries rebuild after the war.

White was aware that his proposals would encounter opposition, particularly from American isolationists:

> There is an urgent need for instruments which will pave the way and make easy a high level of cooperation and collaboration among the United Nations[2] in economic fields hitherto held too sacrosanct for international action or multilateral sovereignty. A breach must be made and widened in the outmoded and disastrous economic policy of each-country-for-itself-and-the-devil-take-the-weakest. Just as the failure to develop an effective League of Nations has made possible two devastating wars within one generation, so the absence of a high degree of economic collaboration among the leading nations will, during the coming decade, inevitably result in economic warfare that will be but the prelude and instigator of military warfare on an even vaster scale.
>
> The Fund and the Bank ... can facilitate that high degree of economic collaboration. It will be at once apparent that the resources, powers and requirements for membership, accorded both agencies, go far beyond the usual attributes of monetary stabilization and banking. They must if they are to be the stepping stone from short-sighted disastrous economic nationalism to intelligent international collaboration. Timidity will not serve.
>
> (White, 1942: 9)

White's economic ideology had its roots in his background. Born in 1892 in a modest Boston neighbourhood, the youngest child of recent Russian Jewish immigrants, Harry White obtained Bachelor's and Master's degrees at Stanford, having switched to economics from political science because he had realised that "most governmental problems are economic".

White was politically active at Stanford, organising a collective letter from students urging Robert LaFollette to run as a progressive third party candidate in the 1924 presidential election (US Senate, 1955: 2541–2542). He retained a life-long commitment to leftist ideas, shared with his wife and most of their close friends. He drafted proposals for the Democratic Party election campaign in 1940 that included universal old-age pension and unemployment insurance systems (White, 1940: 5). One of his last letters offered his support to Henry Wallace in his 1948 left-wing third party presidential candidacy (US Senate, 1955: 2560).

He set out on an academic career, first at Harvard where he combined lecturing with his doctoral studies, receiving his PhD for a thesis on French exchange rate policy and collaborating with the Canadian-born economist Laughlin Currie scheme to combat the Great Depression that formed the cornerstone of Roosevelt's New Deal (Currie *et al.*, 2002 [1932]). The proposals predated publication of Keynes's *General Theory* by four years. In 1934, along with Currie and several other promising economists, White accepted a summer contract to work on monetary policy at the Department of the Treasury in Washington. He spent the next thirteen years in public service, and was never to return to academia.

White's star rose rapidly in the Treasury. He was appointed director of monetary policy under Treasury Secretary Henry Morgenthau, and became part of a small policy-making inner circle. Consistent with his earlier collaboration with Currie, White was outspoken in supporting public works, deficit expenditures, interventionism and progressive taxation to ensure more equitable income distribution (White, 1935).

The international political and economic situation was deteriorating rapidly. White was set to work designing international economic policy, notably attempting to strengthen the Chinese economy as a bulwark against Japanese expansionism. His memo on this proposal mentions his belief, repeated later in the Bretton Woods blueprint, that countries could cooperate "irrespective of their political differences" (US Senate, 1955: 1456). Morgenthau and White next turned to strengthening Latin America, proposing a Bank of North and South America that would make credit available for economic development; this was the first mention of a plan for an international bank (White, 1939). The project never got off the ground, but the planning laid the theoretical groundwork for White's later proposal for a World Bank.

The 1939 Hitler–Stalin Pact risked isolating the United States. White continued to propose an accommodation with the USSR despite Stalin's apparent lack of interest in negotiating with the West, emphasising that Russia's ideological propaganda against the West should not be compared with the Axis menace. After Hitler reneged on his pact with Stalin and invaded Russia, White's star continued to rise; he was appointed Assistant to the Secretary, and involved himself in the most political of economic files, including proposals aimed at splitting Japan from the Axis. This project came to naught; Japan bombed Pearl Harbor on 7 December 1941 and the United States immediately entered the war. Strategic economic manoeuvres were no longer as important.

Bretton Woods, Keynes and the end of empire

The US administration adopted White's plan with minor changes and forwarded it to Britain's John Maynard Keynes, the doyen of world economics of the era, for discussion. Keynes had also grasped the catastrophe of war as an opportunity to build a more effective system of global economic governance. In 1940, the Axis powers had promised to institute upon their victory a "New Order" that would replace the capitalist anarchy of the interwar years with a managed international economic system based upon the pre-eminence of the Reichsmark, stable exchange rates, and an exchange clearing system (Einzig, 1941: 23–34). Approached by the Ministry of Information to review a rebuttal to the German position, Keynes found that "about three-quarters of the passages quoted would be quite excellent if the name of Great Britain were substituted for Germany or the Axis" (Keynes, 1980 [1940]: XXV, 1–2). The problem was not what the Germans were promising but what they would actually do. Thus, Britain needed not to reject the German argument but to "do it better and more honestly" (Keynes, cited in Van Dormael, 1978: 7). Keynes took key elements of the German plan and used them as a foundation for his proposal for a clearing union that was to become a core responsibility of the new International Monetary Fund. His early draft also proposed that the new institution would loan European countries money to pay for essentials in the process of post-war reconstruction (Keynes, 1980: XXV, 10–11).

Keynes's and White's post-war plans had similarities but also fundamental differences (Skidelsky 2000; DeLong, 2000). Essentially, Keynes, despite his liberal political views, sought to restore the colonial order in the post-war era. His proposals closely reflected British interests – he wanted the post-war plans to privilege generous aid to Britain and to leave in place trade barriers such as the system of imperial trade preference. On the other hand, White, with Franklin Roosevelt's support, was determined to destroy the old colonial system. The American New Deal liberals found the colonial system offensive and had no intention to subsidise its reinvigoration,[3] nor were they prepared to return to a global power distribution based on the British domination of trade facilitated by imperial preference policy. Finally, the United States was not going to set up a system it underwrote but from which other nations could draw with minimal economic supervision; otherwise, the Americans would be, in effect, paying for reconstruction of the British Empire.

Keynes was uninterested in the World Bank idea. He could not see its benefit to Britain, although once it was clear that Britain would not be able to extract directly from the Americans the aid it wanted in the war's aftermath, he supported the Bank at Bretton Woods, and ended up chairing the conference committee drawing up the Bank's Articles of Agreement. In contrast, the Bank was a core element in White's plan from the beginning; in 1943, he had told the American Economic Association, "Only an international agency organised by the governments of the world can assure the supply of capital needed for reconstruction at rates of interest and amortisation which will not unduly burden the balance of payments of the borrowing country" (White, 1943: 383).

The second major difference between Keynes and White concerned the structure of post-war institutions. Keynes preferred an agreement between Britain and the United States which would then be imposed on the rest of the world (Kapur *et al.*, 1997a: 62). Only grudgingly did Keynes recognise the possibility that Russia, as the third corner of the war alliance, might be added as a third "founder state" of the clearing union. He strenuously objected to the broadening of participation in Bretton Woods to encompass the whole world: "Twenty-one countries have been invited which clearly have nothing to contribute … . The most monstrous monkey house assembled for years" (Keynes, 1980: XXVI, 42). In contrast, White was determined to include rich and poor countries alike, and insistent on Russia as a key partner. His notes make repeated reference to the dangers of an excessive gap between wealthy and poor countries, which he believed was the main cause of political instability and war. He repeatedly emphasised that the key post-war relationship would be between Russia and the United States with Britain occupying a secondary but still important place, whereas Keynes agreed on a high profile for the USSR only on military-strategic grounds.

Despite the presence of a number of developing countries as well as the Soviet Union at the 1944 Bretton Woods conference, the United States and the United Kingdom were the decisive actors. Although Keynes publicly endorsed the development aspect of the new Bank's mandate, he emphasised that "the field of reconstruction from the consequences of war will mainly occupy the proposed Bank in its early days" (US Department of State, 1948: 1, 85). In general, he was sceptical of the idea of lending to nations, prophetically warning that "countries that lend, are only able to keep the borrowing nations in play by always re-lending" (Keynes, quoted in Harrod, 1951: 566).

Contrary to post-developmentalists who claim that the West invented the idea of underdevelopment and imposed it on the Third World, representatives of poor countries and colonies at Bretton Woods were vocal about the need for development of their territories to be a high priority of the new international system, and of the Bank in particular. Mexico, for example, emphasised that development should eventually prevail as the major goal of the Bank, and that "capital for development purposes in our countries is as important for the world as is capital for reconstruction purposes" (US Department of State, 1948: 2, 1170–1171), while an Indian representative who unsuccessfully demanded that the International Monetary Fund's charter should "mention specifically economically backward countries" saw his proposal reflected instead in the World Bank charter (US Department of State, 1948: 2, 1180–1181). Colombia, Egypt and Cuba, among others, also made development-oriented statements (US Department of State, 1948: 2, 1186; 1194, 1239).

International interdependence was the raison d'être of the conference, and the Americans, in particular, interpreted this as referring to the community of nations as a whole, not just the advanced countries. President Roosevelt, in his opening speech at Bretton Woods, emphasised that:

> Economic diseases are highly communicable. It follows, therefore, that
> the economic health of every country is a proper matter of concern to all

its neighbours, near and distant. Only through a dynamic and soundly expanding world economy can the living standards of individual nations be advanced to levels which will permit a full realisation of our hopes for the future.

(US Department of State, 1948: 1, 71)

Secretary of State Henry Morgenthau elaborated that: "Prosperity, like peace, is indivisible. We cannot afford to have it scattered here or there among the fortunate or to enjoy it at the expense of others" (US Department of State, 1948: 1, 81).

White shared these perspectives, and indeed probably inspired some of them.[4] He believed that the World Bank "must not be a rich man's club. The poorest and smallest countries must be represented in the decision-making process" (Oliver, 1971: 5).

The Bretton Woods agreement, signed by forty-five nations on 22 July 1944, included detailed plans for the World Bank and the International Monetary Fund, as well as a commitment to create an international trade organisation; the American Congress did not approve the latter organisation and a global trade organisation was not created until 1995. Despite many changes in the world economy and politics since 1944, this institutional economic structure, along with the United Nations, remains the cornerstone of the world system.

Downhill from Bretton Woods

The multilateral system created at Bretton Woods was designed in a spirit of naïve internationalism. The Rooseveltian liberals dreamed of cross-ideological fraternity:

> countries with widely divergent economic systems participated in preparing the Agreements for the Fund and the Bank. The United States is indubitably a capitalist country as Russia is a socialist one. Yet both agree not only on the desirability of promoting monetary stability and international investment, but on the means required to realize these ends. And this for a very simple and satisfactory reason – it is to the advantage of each to do so. As an impenitent adherent of the capitalist system, which in the crucible of war has once again shown its ability to deliver the goods, I am firmly convinced that capitalist and socialist societies can coexist, as long as neither resorts to destructive practices and as long as both abide by the rules of international economic fair play.
>
> (Morgenthau, 1945: 191)

This vision faced crisis almost as soon as the words had flowed from Morgenthau's pen. Roosevelt died in April 1945, and was replaced by his vice-president, Harry Truman, from the conservative wing of the Democratic Party. Truman's rival, Henry Wallace, New Deal agriculture secretary, vice-president from 1940 to 1944, secretary of commerce from 1945, and leader of the party's progressive wing, was dismissed in September 1946 for attacking the President's confrontational attitude towards the Soviet Union. Wallace ran unsuccessfully for president against Truman on a left-wing third party slate in 1948. Internationally, the peace almost immediately revealed the implausibility of the Great Alliance continuing beyond the defeat of the Axis powers. The Soviet Union imposed its authority in Central and Eastern Europe according to the terms of the Yalta agreement, a civil war broke out in Greece between pro- and anti-Communist factions, and the Communist Party appeared close to gaining power in France and Italy. Truman's harder line on the Soviet Union (Rees, 1971: 319) presented an insurmountable problem for White, who believed that:

> The major task that confronts American diplomacy – and the only task that has any real value in the major problems that confront us – is to devise means whereby continued peace and friendly relations can be assured between the United States and Russia.
>
> (White, 1945b: 4)

White's strenuous promotion of American support to the USSR as part of the anti-Nazi coalition became a source of suspicion (Rees, 1971: 104–113). His well-founded belief in Chiang Kai-Shek's corruption was now seen as treachery. His contribution to Morgenthau's de-industrialisation plan for the defeated Germany was held up as evidence of a desire to enfeeble the West against the Soviet menace (Penrose, 1953). White's leftist views, which had been fashionable only a few years before, were reconstructed as treasonous. It was only a matter of time before he was to be accused of spying for the Russians; most of the senior New Deal policy officials suffered the same fate. An entire generation of liberal policy makers, including almost all the key figures in the creation of the Bretton Woods institutions and the United Nations, were sullied by such allegations. No substantial evidence has ever been found implicating White (Boughton, 2000, 2002, 2003; Boughton and Sandilands, 2003). Nevertheless he was quickly dismissed under a cloud. Keynes lobbied hard but unsuccessfully for him to be given the top IMF job of managing director (Van Dormael, 1978: 302). He was nominated to the second-top position as the United States' representative, only to be asked to resign the next year at the urging of FBI chief, J. Edgar Hoover, who objected both to his Jewishness and his supposed disloyalty (Craig, 1999: 410). White worked as a consultant for the Mexican government and a Jewish charity for the next year, when he was asked to testify before the House Un-American Activities Committee (HUAC) probing Communist infiltration into government.

Despite having a heart condition, White was refused an hourly break in his testimony. He had a heart attack on the train home to New England and died three days later, aged 56. Keynes had died two years earlier, not long after the disappointing Savannah, Georgia meetings that launched the IMF, where it became clear that the United States would not permit genuinely multilateral economic institutions. Instead, there would be "an ad hoc system dominated by the United States, with rules that were dictated more by cold war political realities than economic benefit or international cooperation" (Gavin, 1996: 187). The Bretton Woods system seemed stillborn although, as will become clear, the genetic code of global management with which it was imbued at its foundation has continued to drive the Bank towards transnational initiatives.

Russia's retreat to isolationism

White went to great lengths to build ties between the Soviet Union and the United States. These culminated in his initially promising but ultimately abortive efforts to involve Russia in planning and implementation of the post-war economic system.

As noted, the fundamental difference between White and Keynes lay not in the fundamentals of economic theory, but in the nature of a post-war system. Keynes hankered for a return to the era of imperial preference, and a central role for Britain, while White was determined to end imperial economics and found a new economic system underpinned by the two superpowers.

White does not seem to have had great faith in Communism as an economic or political system. His initial proposal for the Bank and IMF is leavened with references to the need for "healthy development of democratic institutions" (White, 1942: 1–12). In his testimony to HUAC, he responded to questions about his colleague Silvermaster's alleged Communist leanings that, "he never struck me as a Communist; he was an able economist" (HUAC, 1948: 882). In handwritten notes written at the end of his life, White criticises both Marx and "American businessmen" for categorising economic developments as inevitable (White, 1948).

White did, however, feel positively towards the Soviet Union, along with many in his intellectual generation: "in the 1930s it was possible to approve of both the USA and the USSR" (Hobsbawm, 2002: 388). His sympathy towards Russia was probably motivated by three factors: a degree of Russophilia derived from his and his wife's family roots; a cautious interest in Soviet economic planning; and a possibly naïve but undoubtedly fervent belief in the role of the USSR as a bulwark against Fascism. This last factor was certainly the strongest. White's Jewish East European roots undoubtedly and understandably contributed to his near-vitriolic dislike for National Socialism; in his parents' native Lithuania, 85 per cent of the country's 168,000 Jews were murdered in the Holocaust (Gordon, 1992). He regularly pressed for better treatment for Russia and lobbied for a US–USSR alliance, with the overriding motive of forging a strong anti-Hitler alliance and combating appeasement (White, 1942a).

As the war ended, White worked closely with Morgenthau on plans to partially de-industrialise post-war Germany and to support Russian reconstruction. In 1944, he prepared at Morgenthau's request a proposal for a multi-billion low-interest loan that Russia would use to purchase American equipment, designed to continue the two countries' collaboration after the war. Negotiations went on for more than a year, but the idea fell victim to the emerging Cold War after Roosevelt's death (White, 1945a). Although the Russians had originally expressed interest, and indeed had requested $10 billion rather than the $5 billion proposed by White, they changed tack as the Cold War intensified, claiming alternately that the idea was blackmail and that it was intended to address overproduction in the United States (Craig, 1999: 295–296). White's advocacy of the loan was later presented as evidence of his disloyalty to America, though his papers evince only an intense hatred of Nazism and desire to continue the anti-German alliance (White, 1945b).

The "loyalty" or otherwise of White, his colleagues and indeed the 1930s intellectual milieu in general has been the subject of various academic and popular assessments over the years, but less attention has been paid to the other side of the coin: the Soviet Union's decision not to participate in the post-war global institutions and retreat behind a metaphorical and ultimately physical wall. It was this decision, as much as any made in the West, that converted the World Bank and IMF into vehicles for the propagation of a singularly American vision of the world. Only in the late 1990s, after the collapse of the Soviet Union, did grassroots pressure and the growing economic muscle of large developing countries begin to raise a flicker of the heterodoxy in the international institutions that had been central to White's vision.

The Soviet Union's decision to turn its back on the global system was made despite significant efforts on the part of White and others in the administration, including Roosevelt himself, to include the USSR in planning for the post-war system. In 1943, the Americans made numerous formal and informal approaches to the Russians, asking for their participation in the first rounds of talks on the proposals for a post-war economic system (Acsay, 2000: 257–260).

The Soviet ambassador Litvinov was convinced Russia should actively participate (Phillips, 1992: 171). However, Moscow dragged its feet and debates involving thirty countries on the White and Keynes plans, as well as a variety of alternatives proposed by Canada and other countries, were concluded without Soviet input. The final proposal, modelled on the White Plan, was sent to Moscow for comment in late 1943, but the Soviets were more interested in short-term bilateral loans.

Russia was offered about 10 per cent of the voting power in the IMF, well in excess of its global economic weight (Mikesell, 1994: 22), further indication of the Roosevelt administration's desire to create a genuinely multilateral system. The Russians responded with a series of bad-faith demands including exemption from the requirement to provide information about the USSR's gold, currency and foreign trade positions, and exemption from IMF scrutiny of changes to currency exchange rates. Subsequently, they expressed the same demands to the World Bank. Since these points were central to the functioning of a multilateral economic system, White declined to cede ground. Significantly, he did propose that "the Fund shall make no recommendations requiring changes in the fundamental nature of the economic organisation of the member countries" (cited in

Acsay, 2000: 269–270), thus explicitly acknowledging the legitimacy of different economic models.

White's vision attracted important support within the Soviet Union. Eugene Varga, the most prominent Soviet economist, wrote an article reproduced in the American Communist Party's newspaper that clearly privileged White's plan over that of Keynes, while again rejecting international scrutiny of the rouble exchange rate (Blum, 1959: 248–250).

After further foot-dragging by the Russians, the United States reached a crunch in its timetable to have Congress approve the Plan and then proceed with the Bretton Woods conference in June 1944. White lied to Soviet Foreign Minister Molotov and told him the British had agreed to proceed, and that the Russians' support was needed to bring the proposals to the US Congress for approval. Molotov agreed that the USSR's general approval of the initiative could be communicated to facilitate Congressional support for a multilateral initiative and the participation of smaller countries at Bretton Woods. Nevertheless the Soviet Union continued to reject the same key aspects of the Plan. Although the Soviet Union sent representatives to Bretton Woods, they played only a secondary role, almost as observers. By the time the institutional and financial structures of the organisations were put in place a couple of years later, the Cold War was already under way and the Soviet Union did not participate. Several of the Central and East European countries under Soviet occupation did join, but their requests for reconstruction assistance were turned down and they pulled out by the early 1950s. Evidently, however, it remained feasible for non-capitalist countries to participate in the institutions, as White had intended; after Yugoslavia under Tito split from the Soviet bloc in 1948, the country joined the Bank and IMF, and became a privileged client of the Bank, accessing loans on a number of occasions.

Legacy of the White era

White's purging and that of countless other progressives in all the post-War transnational institutions marked a fundamental retreat away from the truly global economic and political system they had struggled to create. As I will discuss in the next section, with Russia's retreat, there was no counterbalance to American government pressure for the institutions to reflect US foreign policy interests. The Bank and IMF both languished in the shadow of the Cold War and became intellectually dependent on contemporary American political and economic thinking, with its overweening fear of the Red Menace.

The tragedy of Harry White is not so much that his central role in creating the Bretton Woods institutions has been largely concealed by those very institutions (Murphy, 2007), because after his departure they very quickly reneged on his vision of a more egalitarian global order. As his daughter puts it, "the present incarnations of the progressive institutions imagined by my father are perversions of their original purposes" (Pinkham, 2005). The tragedy is rather that the Left to which he committed his life has ceded the discourse and the institutions of globalism to elite managerialism. Rather than seeking to transform the World Bank and its sister institutions into the kernels of a genuinely inclusive global system, most leftist Bank critics, like George Monbiot, seek to weaken or even destroy them. Doubtless unwittingly, they copy the fateful error of the Soviet Union, described earlier in this section.

It might thus appear that the internationalist vision was irrevocably lost with the onset of the Cold War and the McCarthyite purges. However, the Bank's globalist path, albeit shorn of its egalitarian core, continued even during the Cold War era, as will be seen in the latter part of this chapter. Chapters 3 and 4 will describe a fuller re-emergence of an international managerialist vision in the discourse of Joe Stiglitz and Jim Wolfensohn, coinciding with a sharply managerialist turn in governance practices in much of the world, particularly manifested in Third Way political movements. Consistent with the historical institutionalist approach discussed in the introduction to this chapter, the global imaginary is institutionalised within the Bretton Woods institutions' mission. Although they are obviously impacted by external events and forced to take account of the opinions of the US and other wealthy-country large shareholders, the World Bank and the other globalising economic institutions tend towards an authentic globalisation and cannot be written off simply as imperialist agents. What they are not, however, is genuinely committed to a more equal and a more democratic world. The naïve phase of global managerialism did not survive the demise of Harry White.

Figure 2.1 Harry Dexter White (left) and John Maynard Keynes at the Bretton Woods Conference, 1944 (photo: IMF).

From Bretton Woods to the Great Society: the United States and the World Bank, 1944–1981

The Roosevelt administrations were the high point of America's global vision in the twentieth century, although multilateralism remained a focus of the American public service elite long after 1945. While the underlying globalising emphasis of US foreign policy has been interrupted by waves of populist isolationism, these interludes typically ended abruptly as security issues arose, necessitating the forging of broader alliances.

At Bretton Woods, considerable debate had surrounded the financial arrangements to underpin the Bank's operations. Membership of the Bank and the International Monetary Fund were tied so that states could not enjoy the benefits of one organisation without incurring the obligations of the other. Voting rights in the Bank were dependent on the amount of capital committed. The US commitment of about one-third of the Bank's capital gave it about one-third of board votes. The capital commitment figure is somewhat misleading, however, as countries only had to deposit a small proportion of their subscribed capital in convertible US dollars or gold. The net result of the convoluted subscription arrangement was that the great majority of the Bank's initial capital came from the United States. On the Bank's official opening day, of the $714 million in usable funds, $571 million, or 80 per cent, came from the United States (Mason and Asher, 1973: 105–112).

The Bank was authorised to make loans up to the amount of its subscribed capital, but in the early years only the United States provided more than 2 per cent of its subscription. At the outset, Bank funds were to be used as collateral for funds to be raised in the financial markets, but this provision proved cumbersome and the Bank soon began loaning directly to nations. Another complication was that currencies were not readily convertible in the first years after the war, and thus money had to be raised in US dollars, the only funds exchangeable throughout the world. US dollars could only be raised on the US financial market.

Between the wars, a number of countries had defaulted on loans taken from private banks, and in the aftermath of a worldwide conflict that had arisen at least in part from the failure of international institutions, there was understandable scepticism about the stability and creditworthiness of a bank based upon international collaboration. It was critical to the financial success of the institution that the public face of the organisation reflect the United States' underwriting of the operation. In practice this meant an American Bank president (Kapur *et al.*, 1997a: 911), a practice that has been followed ever since.

While the decisive influence of the United States in the Bank's structure and initial leadership can be explained by these objective factors in the post-war environment, the decision to locate the Bank and the Fund in Washington, DC demonstrated the Americans' less altruistic side. The major European countries would have preferred the Bank headquarters to be located outside the United States but were prepared to accept New York because of the presence of the world's major financial market (Gwin, 1997: 198). However, the United States refused to compromise, having secured the support of many of the poorer countries that did not want to offend their major hope for aid and capital. This set a pattern in which the United States' actual decision-making weight far exceeded its nominal voting weight (Culpeper, 1997: 25). The United States also secured an effective veto over amendments to the Bank's Articles of Agreement, which required 80 per cent of the members' votes. In 1989, when the US share became diluted through increases in the subscriptions of other countries, and was about to fall below the 20 per cent veto threshold, the United States secured a change to the Articles of Association to reduce the veto to 15 per cent of votes (Kapur *et al.*, 1997a). The United States' desire to retain its veto has forced it to contribute more resources as the Bank grows, or limit Bank growth by refusing to allow others to contribute more resources, in turn risking the Bank's (and thus to some extent, the United States') pre-eminent role in the political economics of development.

It was 1946 before the Bank hired Eugene Meyer as its president and opened its doors, and the organisation was almost immediately plunged into internal conflict. The Bank's president reports to the board of executive directors, made up of representatives of the major vote-holding blocs; the largest national shareholders have a dedicated seat on the board, while others combine their votes to share a seat which may or may not be circulated between the bloc members. Meyer clashed with the US executive director, who wanted to force the Bank to make a loan to Chile for political reasons. Meyer won the showdown, setting an important precedent: the Bank would not simply be a conveyor belt for United States government interests. However, the conflict prompted Meyer to retire after less than a year in office. His replacement, John McCloy, was a prominent member of the Republican establishment, but also a confirmed opponent of isolationism (Bird, 1992: 133).[5] McCloy had refused the job until he received assurances of US government non-interference in the loan process and board non-involvement in World Bank hiring and day-to-day management, and that he, not the US government, would select the US executive director. His nominee, Eugene Black, was also put in charge of bond operations, and later became Bank president (Gwin, 1997: 199–200). While the United States "traditionally" names the Bank's president, he is subject neither to supervision by the US government nor to close scrutiny by the multinational board (also dominated by the United States). Thus, the Bank can pursue its globalising mission with some protection from short-term political pressures.

The next major challenge was the fallout from growing tension between the United States and the USSR. The Cold War, brewing for at least a year, became overt in 1947. The United States, which had been adopting a hard line over reconstruction assistance for Britain and other European countries, made an about face and adopted the Marshall Plan. The Plan provided Europe and Japan substantial concessionary funds for reconstruction, helping to ensure that they remained in the American camp, and isolating the Soviet Union within its Yalta-defined sphere of influence. The Plan's resources were far greater than the Bank had available, and its terms much more favourable. McCloy supported the Plan but insisted that it be housed separately from the Bank, as its political objectives would jeopardise the Bank's credibility as a borrower on the financial markets. He also insisted that the Bank not be used as a means to channel emergency food aid. These decisions further distanced the Bank from direct US government political influence (Bird, 1992: 292–294). The Marshall Plan marginalised the Bank's role in European reconstruction, and the organisation began focusing its attention on Third World development.

During the Cold War, numerous incidents demonstrated the Bank's contradictory position as a multilateral organisation in which the United States wielded a disproportionate share of power. In 1947, Poland sought assistance to develop its coal industry. The Bank carefully researched Poland's request, and McCloy even visited the country, concurring with his staff that it seemed a good investment and eligible for Bank financing, an opinion shared by the British government (Mason and Asher, 1973: 170–171). But Poland, although still governed by a multi-party coalition, was under Soviet domination. In the new atmosphere, the United States could not countenance Bank resources going to a country in the Soviet camp. McCloy had to cut off negotiations with Poland, which resulted in the country's withdrawal from the Bank in 1950, followed in 1954 by that of Czechoslovakia, which had also been unsuccessful in obtaining a loan, probably for political reasons.

McCloy left the Bank in 1949 to head US-occupied Germany, and Black was promoted to the presidency, facing the same dilemmas of retaining multilateral credibility while respecting American hegemony.

Both semi-official Bank histories detail numerous cases where politics intervened in decision making. Yugoslavia's 1948 defection from the Soviet bloc warranted the country receiving a World Bank loan because, according to Black, it was "very important that Titoism succeeds". Black also noted that, "Tito seemed more interested in the Bank's endorsement than in the funds", an early reference to the Bank's unofficial role in elite endorsement (quoted in Kapur *et al.*, 1997a: 103).

Nicaragua, run by the corrupt Somoza family, was one of the biggest developing country borrowers, despite having only one million inhabitants. The country provided a base from which American-trained troops left in 1954 to overthrow Jacobo Arbenz, the left-populist leader of Guatemala, and it was also the base for the abortive US-sponsored Bay of Pigs invasion of Cuba in 1961. In contrast, Guatemala received a Bank loan only after Arbenz's overthrow.

Bank policy towards Iran in the early 1950s was also politically influenced, though British interests predominated rather than those of the United States. First, at Britain's urging, the Bank rushed through a loan to prop up a pro-western government (Meeting of directors, 14 June 1950, cited in Kapur *et al.*, 1997a: 104). Then it halted negotiations on further assistance after the nationalist government of Mossadegh nationalised the British-owned oil concession (Mason and Asher, 1973: 173). The Bank then broke its own rules against making non-project loans, granting a $75 million general purpose loan to the pro-western post-Mossadegh government of Shah Pahlavi (Kapur *et al.*, 1997a: 105). The Bank made another programme (rather than specific project) loan to Italy in the early 1950s, again spurred by the political urgency of "postwar fears of a communist electoral victory" (Kapur *et al.*, 1997a: 134).

The establishment of the International Development Association (IDA) under the Bank's umbrella in 1960 provided a form of concessionary funding "between a loan and a grant", giving even the poorest countries the possibility of access to Bank money and expertise. The IDA was an American administration idea, linked to its growing worry that Communists were on the verge of taking power in a number of developing countries, a concern that had deepened considerably after Castro's takeover of Cuba in 1959. It was also a response to long-standing developing country demands for a multilateral economic development fund (Weaver, 1965: 11). The Americans preferred such a fund to be located at the Bank rather than at the United Nations as the developing countries had proposed. Thus, the Bank continued to reflect at the same time the desires of developing country governments to participate in a global development agenda, and the United States' overbearing influence on that development agenda. Nevertheless, the establishment of the IDA is further refutation of the post-developmentalist claim that the development paradigm was imposed on poor countries; it may have been imposed on poor *people*, but it had the strong support of poor people's *governments*.

George Woods, the Bank's president in the early 1960s, signalled the globalising normative vision underpinning the IDA: "An important difference between economic development in the twentieth century and past times is that today the rich nations have accepted a measure of responsibility for the progress of the poor" (Woods, 1966: 207). The IDA provided countries with money at near-zero interest rates, grace periods of up to ten years, and amortisation as long as forty years. Depending on market interest rates, the effective grant element can rise above 85 per cent (Mason and Asher, 1973: 399). Bank officials had another reason for supporting the IDA; several large developing countries, India in particular, were close to their hard loan borrowing limits based on their ability to repay. IDA loans would enable them to continue borrowing, and to continue repaying. One disadvantage of the IDA was that interest-free loans could obviously not be financed on the bond markets; the new arm of the Bank required regular infusions of funds from the developed countries, and this resulted in much closer scrutiny of Bank activities, particularly by the US Congress.

During the 1960s, the Bank was pressured by the United States administration to internationalise the Kennedy–Johnson administrations' domestic War on Poverty. Johnson's appointment of Kennedy intimate and former Defense Secretary Robert McNamara in 1968 institutionalised a highly committed but technocratic anti-poverty approach. For McNamara, the Bank was a tool to defeat Communism by addressing the ills that gave rise to Communist sympathies: "unless there is visible progress toward a solution [of less developed country poverty] we shall not have a peaceful world. We cannot build a secure world upon a foundation of human misery" (McNamara, 1978 presidential address, cited in Head, 2001). During his thirteen-year reign, the Bank grew rapidly, building up project loan portfolios all over the developing world.

Outside regions strategically important to the United States, there was little discrimination based on recipient countries' political economy. The Bank lent substantial resources to Nyerere's Tanzania, including assisting his project of *ujamaa* (village socialism).

> President Nyerere has given the country a clear sense of direction with the long term perspective of a socialist society … We are inclined to give Tanzania an excellent performance rating and recommend a maximum Bank Group effort to assist the country in its pursuit of development objectives.
>
> (World Bank, "Country Program Note: Tanzania",
> 12 February 1973, cited in Kapur *et al.*, 1997a: 394)

The Bank was generally tolerant of government ideologies and policies. For example, a 1972 coup in the small West African state of Bénin brought an "Afro-Marxist" military dictatorship to power that established close ties with Kim Il Sung's North Korea and attempted to collectivise agriculture; the World Bank continued to make project loans to the country until the end of the "Marxist" period in 1989[6] even though the country's economic management was not only antithetical to the free market, but corrupt and catastrophically incompetent (Gbado, 1998). Apart from a disastrous effort in the late 1960s to influence Indian economic policy through a policy-linked loan, almost resulting in the downfall of the Indira Gandhi government, the Bank's policy impact remained limited by its self-imposed restriction to project financing until the late 1970s.

McNamara continued his predecessors' careful manoeuvring between acknowledging US hegemony and retaining the institution's multilateral credibility. He bowed to US Congress pressure not to lend to Vietnam (Woods, 2000: 138), but ignored US objections to a loan to the leftist government of Guyana that had nationalised US interests and apparently failed to provide proper compensation (Gwin, 1997: 255). McNamara also continued large-scale concessionary lending to India despite opposition from the United States and others (Kapur *et al.*, 1997a: 298, 1154). Most significantly, he pressed ahead in negotiating the People's Republic of China's adhesion to the Bank despite vehement opposition from elements in the US government.

The World Bank and the new agenda of neo-liberalism

Until almost the end of McNamara's presidency, the main American domestic challenge to the Bank's activities was isolationism that coalesced particularly in the right wing of the Republican Party. Isolationism has long been a popular political platform in the United States, but has always been at odds with the interests of large American corporations that have long been active throughout much of the world. However, by the 1970s, the long post-war economic boom was grinding to a halt and the counter-cyclical, welfare-state economic policies on which Bretton Woods was founded no longer seemed effective in staving off economic downturns.

The stagnation of Keynesian economic thought provided an opening for a new capitalist discourse, centred on the ideas of Friedrich von Hayek and the so-called Austrian School. In 1944, while White and Keynes were planning the new managed world system, Hayek published *The Road to Serfdom*, calling for individualism and arguing against planning, collectivism and socialism. Hayek's viewpoint did not find mass appeal until the policy and intellectual void of the late 1970s. The new right-wing ideology came to full fruition with Thatcher and Reagan's ascendancy, stressing an aggressive ideological promotion of capitalism, abandonment of the notion of peaceful competition with the Soviet Union, and rejection of the welfare state.

Paradoxically, the free marketeers' conquest of global economic and social policy was the culmination of years of assiduous planning. In 1947, Hayek and a number of his acolytes from the University of Chicago, the London School of Economics, and fellow Viennese émigrés (including Ludwig von Mises and Karl Popper) formed the Mont Pèlerin Society (MPS), an exclusive invitation-only society dedicated to promoting what is now known as neo-liberalism (Cockett, 1994: 109).

In the immediate post-war era, the idea of subjugating the state to the market had very little currency on either side of the Atlantic. Economists and politicians alike were more concerned about establishing an international order that could avoid the destabilising market failures of the interwar era. The feasible alternatives were either carefully managed capitalism or outright socialism. The adherents of the MPS were prepared, however, to take the long view.

Private organisations facilitating and promoting elite networking and problem-solving on an international scale were not new. In the early twentieth century the US banker J.P. Morgan had sponsored various networks aimed at identifying economic and political governance problems and proposing solutions, as had Cecil Rhodes on the other side of the Atlantic. However, the Bilderburg Conference, the Trilateral Commission and the Club of Rome were largely pragmatic with the simple goals of maintaining order, liberal capitalism and elite control. By contrast the MPS was unabashedly ideological. Truth was not constructed through dialogue, it pre-existed (van der Pijl, 1998: 129). Over the next thirty years, the MPS and its connected thinktanks (including the Institute for Economic Affairs in Britain and the Heritage Foundation in the United States) laid a foundation for the counter-revolution in economics that profoundly altered the trajectory of global development. While the MPS was generally associated with the political right, this identification was not total. The relative political autonomy of the MPS enabled it to achieve a broader influence on policy. Indeed, some of the earliest, most ardent and effective implementers of neo-liberalism had roots in the erstwhile political left, for example New Zealand's Labour government, which was captured in the early 1980s by a small group of Hayek-influenced politicians and bureaucrats (Halimi, 1997).

While Hayek was the doyen of grand neo-liberal political economy, the University of Chicago economist Milton Friedman developed the monetarist theory that provided a specific policy alternative to Keynesianism. Friedman argued that Keynesian counter-cyclical economic policy led to inflation; his policy prescription centred instead on tight control over money supply to promote economic stability. He also called for a reduction in the state's role, measures to control capitalist monopoly, and, especially, limits to the power of trade unions (Cockett, 1994: 109–115). Friedman was a founder of the MPS and headed the society from 1970 to 1972.

International development proved fertile ground for neo-liberals. Oil price shocks in the late 1970s forced many developing countries to appeal to donor countries and the international financial institutions for help, just when neo-liberal economists, particularly Milton Friedman, were attracting broad interest (Murshed, 2003).

Towards the end of McNamara's presidency, the Bank began re-examining its lending approach. Many projects had given disappointing results, and frequently it seemed that poor macroeconomic policies contributed to failure. But it was a dual shock outside the control of developing countries that pushed them to the wall, and propelled the Bank to take a complete change of direction. The first was the Islamic revolution in Iran, which cut off a significant proportion of American oil supplies, and created a worldwide market panic that drove prices to unprecedented levels. The second blow came when the United States Federal Reserve, then led by the monetarist Paul Volcker, responded to the inflationary impact of rising oil prices by raising interest rates (Volcker, 2000). A number of countries, notably in Latin America, were caught in an impossible squeeze. They had pursued ambitious protectionist and import-substitutionist policies in line with development economics orthodoxy (typically with the Bank's approval), and overextended themselves with easy private credit (often ignoring the Bank's warnings). When the Iranian crisis struck they were hit by three simultaneous blows: high fuel prices, spiralling interest rates, and credit tightening (Kapur *et al.*, 1997a: 495–505).

McNamara's concerns about poorly performing loans and the sudden debt crisis were largely pragmatic, but his vice-president, Ernest Stern, and others at the Bank believed that, rather than focusing on state-driven domestic growth through protection of nascent import-substituting industries, developing countries should aim for export-led growth. This would require substantial changes to the policy mix. Under internal pressure to respond to the deteriorating situation of many of the Bank's clients, McNamara announced the Bank's willingness to provide support to countries undertaking "structural adjustment" to reorient their economies towards exporting (Kapur *et al.*, 1997a: 506). The Bank would provide three- to five-year loans to help countries restructure their economies; the money would be used to help finance the resultant balance of payment deficits.

McNamara retired in 1981, and most of his senior management team left with him. McNamara's replacement Tom Clausen selected Anne Krueger, a prominent neo-liberal ideologue, as chief economist. Krueger soon became the dominant force in the Bank.

The Bank's board of directors, made up of national government representatives (but dominated by the western powers in general and the United States in particular), grudgingly agreed to permit programme lending to support structural adjustment, a major but supposedly temporary change in the Bank's modus operandi. As noted earlier, previously the Bank had lent only for specific investment projects, such as infrastructure development. Originally, structural adjustment lending was to account for no more than 15 per cent of the Bank's annual lending portfolio, and was to be available only to countries that had autonomously decided to undertake pro-market reforms. However, both the percentage limit and the proscription on "buying reform" were soon violated, and structural adjustment became the centrepiece of both Bank and IMF policies (Kapur *et al.*, 1997a: 449–512), Eventually both were encapsulated within a one-size-fits-all set of policy nostrums known as the Washington Consensus.[7] During the 1980s, thirty-eight sub-Saharan African countries administered a total of 257 structural adjustment programmes, with fourteen countries each administering ten or more (Cheru, 1999: 16). The structural adjustment period set in motion a growing divergence between the Bank's activities and anything that could be viewed as traditional banking activity. The Bank had always had influence over government policy, proportional to the size of the projects it funded, the importance of projects to the overall national budget, and the fungibility of the project resources to be provided. Nevertheless, by and large, the scope for the Bank's policy intervention had remained morally and rationally circumscribed within the range of policy options having a direct bearing on the success of its specific projects.

In contrast, structural adjustment policy lending established a neo-colonial relationship in which the local elite was required to carry out the policy edicts and adopt the philosophical standpoint of the international financial institution lender, now taking the colonists' place. While many critics have noted the questionable relationship of domination and subservience inherent in the policy lending framework, policy lending also corrodes developing country elites' leadership responsibility and undermines elite/citizenry interdependence in favour of a global elite/local elite relationship. The new breed of monetarist economists, who came to dominate the Bank during the structural adjustment period, were articulate and generally accurate raconteurs of the moral hazards inherent in state control of the economy. However, they were less prescient in identifying the moral hazards caused by forcing governments to adopt policies in which they did not genuinely believe (Gervais, 1992).

Conclusion

The Bank's formative years have been depicted through an account centred on Harry White's ideological perspectives and vision for the global system. This serves to recapture the early history of the Bretton Woods system and the World Bank in particular, in the face both of the Bank's own accounts that diminish the trans-ideological global agenda inherent in the organisations' founding documents and agreements, and those of many radical globalisation critics, who, as has been discussed in Chapter 1 above, construct globalisation as a spatially unidirectional process entailing the construction of an imperial-type global order against the will of the entire population of developing countries. The result of these currently dominant interpretations of Bank history is to portray a stark duality of globalisation alternatives: either accept the World Bank managers' sanitised history that obscures the early vision for a heterodox global economic order, or reject the globalisation project in its entirety in favour of already-tried-and-discredited autarky (dependency theory) or fantasy regression into the natural lifeworld (post-developmentalism).

Not only were alternative and less peremptory globalisations possible within the Bretton Woods system, this was the founders' intent. White's personal political and economic management views, which clearly illuminate both his domestic and international policy advocacy, reflected his faith in a managed global system with room for both capitalist and socialist national economies. The anti-imperialist nature of the early Bretton Woods vision is confirmed by White's determination, and that of the Roosevelt administration *in toto*, to destroy the system of imperial preference that Keynes continued to defend. While Robert Cox portrays this as merely asserting the United States as a new global hegemon, White's insistence on the US–USSR partnership shows that within the US Treasury, at least, the project was globalisation rather than imperialisation.

White's abortive efforts to involve Russia in the Bretton Woods system were pursued with bravery and eventually at great personal cost. Russia's failure to grasp the opportunity to participate in the post-war global economy was another crucial historical juncture, where the path taken led inexorably towards economic and political isolation, and the ultimate discrediting of socialism. The lessons from this disastrous decision have not been learned by today's radical critics of globalisation (Murphy, 2007).

I have portrayed White in a sympathetic light; his major contribution to the post-war order has been unfairly tarnished by anti-Communist and racist elements in the United States, as well as leftist "anti-globalisation" critics such as Monbiot, whose critique is bolstered by asserting that the Bretton Woods institutions have never been anything other than American pawns. However, White's internationalism, opposition to colonialism, support for social democratic economic models and tolerance for socialism do not necessarily imply a particularly democratic impetus. Like most progressives of his era, his preferred governing modalities involved state-driven planning, albeit within a democratic political structure. The managerial bent of the Bretton Woods institutions today reflects these predilections.

Following the occlusion of the Rooseveltian internationalist vision with the onset of the Cold War, the United States continued to play an important and often decisive role in the Bank's early life. Not only was the Bank a largely American vision, the bulk of its capital came from the United States, and the Bank's presidents have all been American. The Bank was strongly impacted by

American Cold War imperatives, and examples of US interference in Bank policy decisions during this period are legion. At the same time, the United States did not always get its way and successive Bank presidents, though invariably part of the American establishment, have emphasised the principle of Bank independence.

During the 1970s, however, the Bretton Woods currency system unravelled and the Keynesian orthodoxy was challenged by monetarism, the first wave of market fundamentalist ideology that soon came to dominate economic thought in the West. The advocates of neo-liberalism enlisted the Bank in implementing structural adjustment programmes in numerous countries, reversing the development paradigm in favour of a free market, export-oriented approach. While critical analysts have justifiably focused their attention on the extraordinary negative impacts of these new policies on popular living standards in the developing world, the more significant long-term feature of this paradigm shift was in institutionalising the right of global institutions to impose homogenous economic policy worldwide.

The Bank's relationship with the United States during the post-war era cannot be captured within a dualist interpretation: whereby either the Bank is a globalising institution or it is an instrument of US foreign policy. The World Bank has sometimes been one, sometimes the other, and often both. As Woods (2000: 135) points out, "if the United States had control over the organization, or indeed was perceived to, the Bank would be of little use to the United States". In a global economy, powerful nations require multilateral institutions to achieve their objectives. The World Bank provides intellectual and moral justification for a world order which undoubtedly tends to serve the interests of the United States. It helps to shape global economic and social policies in the interests of major corporations, the majority of which are still based in the United States. The World Bank and the rest of the global institutional order pool the costs of addressing global economic and social problems, and can limit the exposure of the United States to direct conflict with elites from lesser powers. But the World Bank, and other global institutions, come with more than a monetary price tag for the United States. Although it can often find ways to bend rules to serve its interests, in the end the multilateral institution must have credibility. Even at the peak of its power in the 1950s and the 1960s, the United States could not always get its way at the Bank. The global vision of the Bank's founders is inscribed in the organisation's name, its mission and its activities.

The creation of the Bank and the rest of the Bretton Woods system was the first critical step towards global managerialism. The second step was the dramatic expansion of the Bank's activities and anti-poverty imaginary in the 1960s through the creation of the International Development Association and the internationalisation of the War on Poverty. Structural adjustment, which converted the Bank and IMF into disciplinary overseers of global economic governance, marked the third step towards global managerialism. The next chapter will explore the fourth critical step: the expansion of global managerialist ambitions into the spheres of social policy and political governance.

3 The Poverty Bank

This chapter is concerned with the most recent critical juncture in the World Bank's development as a global managerialist institution. From the mid-1990s the Bank has abandoned the rhetoric (if not, as will be seen, the policy reality) of structural adjustment, in favour of an approach emphasising comprehensive development and a focus on poverty reduction. Once again, interpretations of what has been happening at the Bank differ. Many critics argue that the changes in the Bank's practices do not alter the fundamental "neo-liberal" orientation of the organisation. This argument is based mainly on the Bank's continuing emphasis on "fiscal prudence". From a global managerialist perspective, I argue that a focus only on the economic content of the Bank's activities overlooks a substantial change in the Bank's orientation. Where the Bank had previously sought to influence economic policies, now it aimed its sights also at social policies, through a focus on what it calls "poverty reduction". As part of this new policy orientation, the organisation adopted the Millennium Development Goals, a trans-institutional initiative to improve the quality of life in a wide range of indicators ranging from health, education and gender equity to environment and governance. Far from representing merely a sprinkling of angel dust on the heavy pudding of structural adjustment, the "poverty turn" reflects a more intrusive managerialist orientation than structural adjustment.

From the perspective of an emergent transnational elite, neo-liberal economic policies were essential in breaking up the national-level class alliances that delivered independence in the former colonies, and held national economic and political power in the former socialist bloc countries. However, although the continued proscription of national alternatives to the global political economy is a *sine qua non* of global managerialism, the managerialist society is built not on "free markets" but on an ever broadening managed hegemony. As soon as the period of neo-liberal ideological fervour had passed, the organisation set about expanding its mandate, and simultaneously building bridges with its critics, through the poverty turn.

The four-step progression in global managerialism presented in the last chapter thus represents not an abandonment of one mode of managerial intervention by another, but the organisation's intervention in cumulatively wider domains. In general, each new domain of intervention is added to previous activities rather than replacing them, as shown in Figure 3.1.

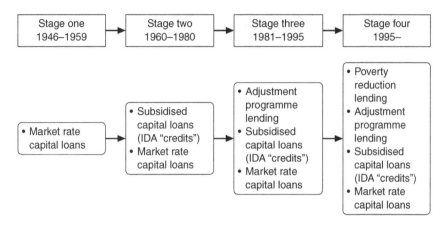

Figure 3.1 Expanding domain of global managerialism, 1946–present.

This chapter begins with a discussion of the emergence of "the Poverty Bank", emphasising the concertive control management techniques that were integral to the Bank's new orientation. The chapter then examines the Millennium Development Goals, a joint social policy initiative of the OECD, the World Bank, and the United Nations Development Programme (UNDP). It is argued that, while the MDGs have managed to rally almost all shades of international opinion behind them, they are based on a highly managerialist approach that evades fundamental questions of global power distribution. From p. 67, the discussion with (post)Marxism on the nature of contemporary managerialism is rejoined. I analyse the position of the political economists Ben Fine and Paul Cammack, who argue that Stiglitz and the Bank's "poverty turn" represent little more than window-dressed neo-liberalism. Finally, the (negative) position of the US administration towards the poverty-reduction focus is discussed. Its determined opposition to the Poverty Reduction Strategy Paper (PRSP) underlines the emergence of a real distinction between unilateralist American neo-liberalism on one hand, and an increasingly assertive global managerialism on the other.

The poverty turn

During the 1990s, the structural adjustment agenda became increasingly imbued with an anti-poverty focus. By 1992, the Bank's staff operational manual emphasised that poverty reduction was the benchmark for measuring success (Kapur *et al.*, 1997a: 51). The rhetorical shift intensified with the arrival of the charismatic Clinton nominee James Wolfensohn as Bank president in 1995, and Joseph Stiglitz's appointment as chief economist in 1997. By 1999, when the Bank adopted PRSP methodology, all the Bank's activities were to be tied to the ultimate objective of reducing poverty.

The perspectives underpinning the PRSP originated in the Bank's Comprehensive Development Framework (CDF), announced in January 1999. The CDF combines a technocratic concern with "coordination" and "comprehensiveness", carried over from the structural adjustment period, with a new emphasis on social outcomes, "country ownership" and "inclusivity" through the involvement of subject populations and civil society organisations: "We cannot adopt a system in which the macroeconomic and financial is considered apart from the structural, social and human aspects, and vice versa" (Wolfensohn, 1999: 7). As will be discussed in the next chapter, this discourse is consistent with the Third Way politics of British New Labour and the Clinton New Democrats.

Starting from the belief that "there is much too little coordination of effort, much too much suspicion between participants and in many cases, a simple absence of a framework to coordinate and bring together under government guidance an agreed set of objectives and effective and accountable programmes", Wolfensohn proposed that each country should have a development matrix that would give all the actors in development a "framework of information which can ensure openness, a basis for coordination of effort, and for judgment of the effectiveness of programmes and strategies" (see Figure 3.2). On the horizontal axis, Wolfensohn identifies fourteen factors in development, divided into four groupings including structural (e.g. good, clean government and a social safety net), human (e.g. education and health systems), physical (infrastructure such as roads and sewage systems), and specific strategies (such as

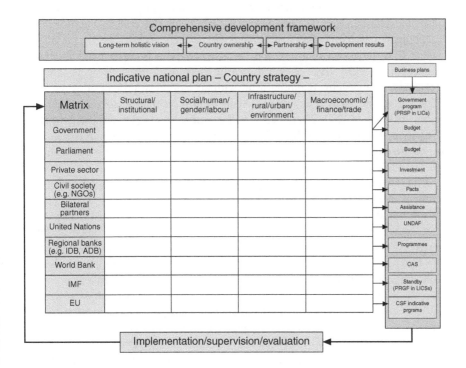

Figure 3.2 The CDF matrix (source: World Bank (2000)).

urban, rural, and country-specific issues, for example drug trafficking in Bolivia), while on the vertical axis of the matrix would be the various "players" in development: government, multilateral and bilateral development agencies, civil society organisations, and the private sector. The matrix "is a tool for the governments and people of the countries we serve. It is they who must own the programmes, not us, and it is they who must set the pace" (Wolfensohn, 1999: 23).

The CDF is an approach of great complexity, with a plethora of subsidiary activities feeding into the overall long-term development plan:

> the matrix and annexes can and should be kept up to date in real time. The matrix will be a summary management tool. But behind each heading there will be Annexes for each subject area, containing a substantive description and far more detailed listings of short and long-term goals, programmes, their present status, timing, cost and progress.... For each of the annexes, specialists would meet under the guidance of the government or minister concerned perhaps setting forth the programme for the next one to three years within a ten to twenty-year framework.
>
> (Wolfensohn, 1999: 23–24)

Perhaps aware that his approach could be criticised by the Bank's many remaining free-market fundamentalists, Wolfensohn is at pains to note that this "is not a return to central planning. It is a holistic and strategic approach to development based on country ownership and partnership".

The CDF reflects a return to the "systems" approach popular among Bank planners in its glory days during the early McNamara years. However, under McNamara, the systems planning dealt with an individual project or at most an industrial sector. Now it involved a state's entire economy, social sector and polity. As Cooke (2002: 23) puts it, "as the matrix headings make clear, what is being managed is not a work organization, but a nation state, which is required to prioritize and taxonomize its activities according to the Bank's matrix to its satisfaction".

A major problem faced by structural adjustment had been that developing country governments would sign on to the programme in order to access funds, and then find ways to bend it to meet their own needs (Gervais, 1992). At its most basic, therefore, the country ownership mantra was probably a Bank gambit to avoid subversion of the CDF project. Country ownership, however, also fitted with the new, participatory approach that was sweeping not only the Bank but the entire international development community, driven in large measure by the increasingly powerful civil society sector. Country ownership also reflected the importation into the Bank's managerial skillset of the concertive control strategy discussed in Chapter 1 above.

As would be expected in a concertive control strategy, the contents of the CDF were not really negotiable, nor was country ownership a choice. The word "must" appears forty-five times in Wolfensohn's thirty-five-page document:

The framework should not become a straitjacket ... But over time, all the requirements within a holistic framework *must* be addressed if there is to be stable, equitable, and sustainable development ...

Countries *must* be in the driver's seat and set the course.

(Wolfensohn, 1999: 8, 10; italics added)

In addition to country ownership, the Comprehensive Development Framework emphasises coordination, meaning "alignment of external support to the country's strategy, reducing wasteful competition among donors, and promoting learning, selectivity, transparency, and accountability at country level" (World Bank, 2000b). In short, the Bank would be the gatekeeper for all international development assistance, and would use that power to discipline developing country states. This same management approach was developed and expanded by the Bank in the poverty reduction initiative, discussed below.

The CDF was initially adopted by twelve countries as a "pilot", but in September 1999 it was effectively incorporated within the even more audacious and comprehensive PRSP process: "The PRSP will, in effect, translate the Bank's Comprehensive Development Framework (CDF) principles into practical plans for action" (World Bank, 2000a: 3).

The PRSP represents the Bank's largely successful attempt to enrol the IMF, developing countries, multilateral and bilateral development agencies, and NGOs behind a single development agenda. While the Bank asserted that this would benefit developing country governments by avoiding conflicting policy conditionalities, the fundamental purpose of Bank coordination, as in the CDF, was to limit developing countries' ability to play their creditors off against each other, thus strengthening the Bank's hand in imposing its policy agenda.

The poverty reduction process was to be country-driven, results-oriented, comprehensive, partnership-oriented, and based upon a long-term vision (World Bank, 2003c). Governments would develop an interim strategy (I-PRSP), to include "a description of the nature of the poverty problem and existing government strategies to tackle it, along with a timeline and process for preparing a full PRSP in a participatory fashion, and a three-year policy matrix and macroeconomic framework". The full PRSP would follow within a year of the I-PRSP's completion. The I-PSRP step was introduced because "Many countries are currently not in a position to fully complete the key steps to develop a PRSP" (World Bank, 2002). I-PRSPs were often carried out quickly and with limited "participation", which could be postponed to the full PRSP process. The interim PRSP also gave the Bank and other donors the opportunity to request significant changes before a "final" PRSP was written. In Cambodia, for example:

after the first draft of the PRSP was released, the World Bank's "hands off" policy came to an abrupt end. They sent in 50 pages of comments, and sent a staff member from Washington to help restructure and re-write the document.

(NGO Forum on Cambodia, quoted in Overseas
Development Institute, 2003b: 11)

Many poor countries already had some kind of anti-poverty action plan (Booth, 2001: 5), and were lukewarm about starting another process. Thus, for the PRSP system to succeed, the incentives for participating had to be irresistible. This was achieved by enlisting the IMF as a partner. The Fund's Enhanced Structural Adjustment Facility (ESAF), a key revenue source for the poorest countries, was renamed the Poverty Reduction and Growth Facility (PRGF) in honour of the PRSP. Acceptance of the PRGF's policy conditions, largely unchanged from ESAF, was a requirement for receipt of any IFI support through the PRSP (Cammack, 2002: 45–50). Thus, in order to access the World Bank's IDA funding, even for specific projects such as electrification or irrigation schemes, countries had to accept IMF surveillance of their economies and satisfy the IMF as to the probity of their fiscal and monetary management, ceding a significant amount of policy control. Another carrot and stick was the enhanced Heavily Indebted Poor Countries (HIPC) initiative through which the Bank and the Fund, and major creditor countries, agreed to reduce unsustainable debt loads, provided countries participated satisfactorily in the PRSP process. Other donors were thus drawn into PRSP conditionalities.

The PRSP was an offer poor countries couldn't afford to turn down; by 2004, about seventy countries had or were developing PRSPs. As always, the rigour with which Bank discipline was exercised was inversely related to the power and importance of the borrowing country. The Bank's dream of extending the PRSP framework to middle-income countries that borrow from the Bank at market rates through its core IBRD[1] operation remains unfulfilled.

Although "country ownership" is the first PRSP principle, the Bank left nothing to chance as to the actual contents of each PRSP. It produced a two-volume Sourcebook totalling 1,280 pages, describing in infinitesimal detail the Bank's expectations in the areas of macroeconomics, social policy and the role of the private sector, as well as several hundred pages of guidance on how to ensure participation in the PRSP process, the elements of good governance, community-driven development, and the importance of gender inclusivity (World Bank, 2002a). The *Sourcebook* contains disclaimers that it is

> not intended to be prescriptive, nor does it aim to provide a definitive solution to the difficult issues that countries face in putting together a poverty reduction strategy. It is intended only to be suggestive and to be selectively used as an informational resource.
>
> (World Bank, 2002a: II, 3)

As a final fail-safe, each PRSP has to pass a Joint Bank–IMF Staff Review, underlining the increasing integration of Bank and IMF disciplinary practices. These Reviews typically find that the country's work provides an "adequate" or "acceptable" framework for reducing poverty (thus qualifying for resources), but emphasise the importance of following the globally interchangeable macroeconomic policies laid out in the PRSP. The PRSP's social objectives are usually rated as laudable but too ambitious given the limited resources available, costings are criticised as insufficiently detailed, and the report emphasises that success will depend on the pursuit of structural reforms including the reduction of the size of the civil service, and prioritisation of basic services in education and health at the expense of industrial investment and higher education expenditures. These "defects" are to be addressed in the mandatory annual progress report to be provided to the institutions.

Often, foreign consultants are funded by the Bank or other donors to help write the PRSPs. In Albania, "The PRSP was drafted by a consultant funded by DFID [Department for International Development, UK], with involvement of the Ministry of Finance" (Overseas Development Institute, 2003: 7), and in Bangladesh, observers noted that much of the document was drafted by two consultants and that "little attempt had been made to integrate the PRS into existing government systems". In Cambodia, NGOs complained about the Bank "bringing in international consultants to prioritise the PRS and restructure the document according to the World Bank's comments" (Overseas Development Institute, 2003b: 5).

In Tajikistan, the Asian Development Bank (ADB), a regional multilateral bank, paid for a team of foreign and local consultants to prepare the I-PRSP draft. Then the ADB hired another international consultant to write the final full PRSP draft – "he had worked a long time for the World Bank".[2] Unsurprisingly, a USAID-funded international finance consultant to the Tajikistan government warns, "don't assume that the PRSP is central to the government's plans". The government's planning is based on its own fifteen-year development plan, and the PRSP is not integrated into the country's annual budget. Because of the disconnect between the "country-owned" PRSP and the government's actual policies, donors are reluctant to increase aid to Tajikistan.

National government officials often visit Washington to "present the draft PRSP and discuss the thrust of the strategy with Bank and Fund staffs", prior to validating the document through in-country consultations (IMF/IDA, 2002: 3). These business class trips are paid for by the IFIs.

African PRSP documents are remarkably homogeneous in content (Murphy, 2003: 34–37; Marshall and Woodroffe, 2001; Craig and Porter, 2003; Cheru, 2001). In Kyrgyzstan, an external review of the I-PRSP noted it did "not differ much from a classical Structural Adjustment Strategy" (Leblanc, 2000: 4).[3] A Cambodian NGO group remarked that: "From a content point of view, the Interim PRSP appears more heavily influenced by World Bank/IMF dialogue than by Cambodian dialogue" (ANGOC, 2001).

Similarities between various PRSPs do not necessarily come about through direct Bank instructions. Developing country officials are well aware of the Bank's expectations, and the PRSPs are written accordingly, an issue raised by the European Union during the 2001 PRSP review: "PRSP's may reflect more what Governments and civil society perceive as *donors' wishes* than what they really see as priorities for poverty reduction" (European Commission, 2001: 86; original italics). Cheru (2001: 12) quotes an unnamed Ugandan official:

We do not want to second-guess the Fund. We prefer to pre-empt them by giving them what they want before they start lecturing us about this and that. By so doing, we send a clear message that we know what we are doing – i.e. we believe in structural adjustment.

Such personal distancing from the institutions' project presents a difficulty for the Bank and IMF in the CDF/PRSP era of "country ownership". The official's perspective demonstrates the institutions' failure to adequately socialise this actor in their corporate goals, suggesting that the Bank's corporate culturism (Willmott, 1993) strategy remains only partly realised.

In recent years, the Bank has made great efforts to build a positive image, through strategies including a major expansion in both the quantity and scope of its "external affairs" (communications) activities (Kapur, 2000: 45; Kapur, 2002: 60), sponsoring quasi-independent initiatives that broadly support its corporate vision (Stone, 2000), expanded assumption of its "convening agency" through the systematic enlisting of other development actors to endorse and implement a common agenda (Cammack, 2001), and hiring developing country bureaucrats and elected officials to staff positions in the Bank.

Despite the rhetoric of country ownership, there are numerous signs that this remains little more than window-dressing. Documents are often written in English even when the supposed "country-owners" of the process don't understand the language, exposing the dominance of headquarters and the myth of devolved ownership:

> The I-PRSP was drafted in English and a Khmer copy was not released to the public before the document was passed by the Council of Ministers in October 2000. SEDP [Small Enterprise Development Project] II was also drafted in English and a Khmer translation was not released until July 2001 .... As a result, the plans are being analysed and discussed by foreigners while most Cambodians are not able to access them at all.
>
> (ANGOC, 2001)

Similar examples are related from Thailand (Hildyard *et al.*, 2001: 58) and Nicaragua (Sanchez and Cash, 2003: 11). Even when documents are produced in the official state language, for example in French in Niger, this is typically the language of the educated elite, while the majority of the population, including almost all the poor to whom the Bank is devoted, remain excluded.[4]

PRSP/MDG: economic and social objectives in contradiction?

The policy management strategies underlying the PRSPs can be divided into two: the macroeconomic framework and the social goals. The social goals have increasingly become aligned with the Millennium Development Goals (MDGs), a set of eight objectives and eighteen development indicators derived from the final declaration of the United Nations' Millennium Summit in September 2000 (United Nations, 2000).[5] Macroeconomic goals remain frozen in the philosophy of structural adjustment: export-oriented growth, reductions in the size of the public sector, and privatisations.

It is not surprising, therefore, that the macroeconomic and social components of the PRSP are often at odds. Economic actions are mandated that deepen poverty and make realisation of the PRSP's social objectives impossible. One area that frequently causes conflict in developing countries is utility services. Public utilities, and water in particular, are health necessities. It has been known since at least 1842 that lack of clean water and absence of sewage systems are directly correlated with mortality (Hanley, 2002). Thus one of the eighteen programmatic targets of the Millennium Development Goals is to halve the proportion of the world's population that does not have access to safe drinking water and basic sewage systems. At the same time, Bank and IMF economic ideologists firmly believe in full cost recovery for utility services, and utility companies' transfer to the private sector. However, in most PRSP countries the poor cannot pay the full cost of their utilities. Therefore, privatisation combined with disconnection for non-payment (the only effective sanction) inevitably results in loss of service. However, citizens invariably believe they have a right to basic power and safe water. There are numerous failed privatisations, as international companies lured into a new market are then forbidden to raise rates to a profitable level, or attempt to raise rates only to be met by civil unrest (Phillips, 2003: A2). Progress in the poorest countries on achieving the MDG target on water and sanitation has been almost non-existent. In sub-Saharan Africa between 1990 and 2004, the proportion of the population with access to potable water and basic sanitation rose from 32 per cent to 37 per cent; at this rate the target of 66 per cent coverage that the MDGs say should be met by 2015 would not be reached until 2095, eighty years behind schedule.[6]

There is general critical agreement that the macroeconomic policies of PRSPs are imposed by the World Bank and the IMF, overshadowing the remainder of the PRSP's strategies. Considerable evidence can be marshalled to support that argument; there is a remarkable level of consistency in PRSP macroeconomic strategies.

The Niger PRSP's summary of its macroeconomic objectives succinctly describes the expected economic strategy:

> further broaden the tax base, better canvass tax payers and households, enhance tax collection and strengthen the fiscal administration; control and restructure current expenditure; effectively implement public expenditure, reviews recommendations in the health, education and rural development sectors; improve the management of public debt, including domestic and external areas; and rehabilitate and modernise public finance management.
>
> (Government of Niger, 2002: 85)

The Joint IMF/World Bank Staff Assessment of Niger's PRSP noted positively that the Niger PRSP was built on a "macroeconomic framework ensuring

economic and financial stability while promoting sustainable and robust growth",
and concluded the government was on the right track and thus deserving of continued concessional financing (IMF/IDA, 2002: 5).

A review of Tajikistan's 2002 PRSP reveals almost identical priorities:

> achieving a stable economic and financial environment through a wide range
> of measures, notably in the areas of fiscal and monetary policy ... and ensur-
> ing increased allocations of public resources to social sectors – education,
> health and social protection – through improved revenue performance,
> careful management of external debt and other means.
>
> (Government of Tajikistan, 2002: 17)

Given that a former Bank employee had written the Tajikistan PRSP's final
draft, it is not surprising that the Joint Staff Assessment (JSA) approved of the
macroeconomic framework; however, the JSA's emphasis on hard budget constraint at the expense of the PRSP's social objectives reveals the essential inco-
herence of the strategy. Although the PRSP points out that "unemployment and
underemployment rates in Tajikistan are high, and this is a basic source of
poverty", the JSA insists that "downsizing the public sector should form part of
the reform package" (Government of Tajikistan, 2002: 14). The Asian Development Bank representative in Tajikistan (whose agency had funded the former
World Bank consultant who wrote the PRSP) remarked that, "it would be crimi-
nal to reduce the size of the public service while there is nothing else for people
to do". Despite the discordance, the ADB is listed as one of the four "key multilateral partners" in the implementation of the PRSP (Government of Tajikistan,
2002: 8).

Marshall and Woodroffe (2001) analysed sixteen early I-PRSPs and PRSPs
(all but three were from sub-Saharan Africa), and found that the core macroeconomic policies proposed in the PRSPs were identical across all countries. These
involved: emphasis on economic growth (with very optimistic growth rates);
macroeconomic stability through strict government expenditure controls and
enhanced revenue collection; deepening of structural reforms including reduction of the size of the public sector; privatisation of public enterprises; emphasis
on international competitiveness and reduction in corporate taxation; and, liberalisation of internal and external trade.

Sanchez and Cash (2003) examined the PRSP process and contents in nine
countries, including three in Latin America, three in Asia, and three in Africa.[7]
They concluded that: economic growth, not poverty reduction, was the main
goal of the PRSPs; non-governmental organisations were excluded from
economic policy discussions; "with a few notable exceptions",[8] the PRSP's economic proposals were simply a reformulation of neo-liberal economic policies
found in the structural Adjustment Programmes that PRSPs replaced. Privatisations were emphasised in the PRSPs analysed; trade liberalisation and market
access were part of many of the PRSPs, and equity issues were generally
avoided.

The Nordic countries established a monitoring group to assess the progress and outcomes of the PRSPs in seven countries, including three African, three Latin American and one Asian country.[9] Their review questioned the extent to which liberalisation and privatisation are tied in practice to poverty reduction, and noted that the "IMF is not particularly conscious about the social impact of economic policies" (Danish Ministry of Foreign Affairs, 2003: viii). Real power often seemed to lie in Washington; neither the Bank nor the Fund gave more than theoretical consideration to income distribution and its role in poverty; in none of the countries was there any effort to track the impact of the PRSP on inequality. Indeed, in Nicaragua, the outcome of the PRSP was likely to be the transfer of resources from a poor to a better-off region (Danish Ministry of Foreign Affairs, 2003: 26, 18).

DFID strongly advocates the social programming aspects of the poverty reduction approach and has called for a rebalancing of PRSP to ensure social objectives are as important as economic. In its submission to an internal Bank taskforce on the first two years of the PRSP programme, DFID castigated the Bank for not thoroughly integrating the new comprehensive social and economic approach into its actual programming. Excessive emphasis was being placed within PRSPs on macroeconomic stability, and the macroeconomic policies proposed seemed neither innovative nor flexible. It was often unclear how anticipated economic growth would actually improve the living standards of the poor. In Mozambique and Tanzania, for example, growth was dependent on expansion of extractive industries, although these are believed often to have a perverse effect on poverty, and there was no indication of how mining industry growth would translate into reduced poverty (DFID, 2001: 120).

MDGs and managerialism

The MDGs have near-hallowed status in development discourse, due partly to the fact that they have been adopted by the United Nations General Assembly and therefore represent a collective commitment of developing and developed countries alike. In fact they are only a modest variation of the International Development Targets (IDT), a 1996 initiative of the developed country cartel, the OECD (White and Black, 2004). Prior to the International Development Targets, international development commitment was measured primarily through inputs, and particularly the generally unrequited commitments by the international community to set aside a proportion of GDP for international development. The shift away from such input measures and towards results-based indicators such as the MDGs is part of a worldwide shift towards managerialist approaches.

During the 1980s and early 1990s, the primary vehicle for public sector reform was through New Public Management (NPM), whose various approaches mainly aim to mimic market signals to drive more efficient public service delivery. Apart from an overall predilection for privatisation and reducing the size of government, NPM involves converting public services into a series of quasi-markets with the intention of introducing competition. The World Bank was and remains an enthusiastic supporter of NPM. Although NPM may have originated in development administration (Caiden, 1991), its transnational adoption was consciously driven by bodies such as the OECD's Programme on Public Management and Governance (PUMA), and spurred by the neo-liberal revolution initially associated with the Thatcher government in Britain and Lange's New Zealand Labour administration, whose dramatic policy shift away from social democracy was in turn influenced by senior government officials who had spent time at the IMF and World Bank (Kelsey, 2000; Goldfinch, 1998). Despite the highly contested nature of the neo-liberal reforms in those countries, officials from Britain and New Zealand were then contracted by the Bank, the IMF and the regional development banks to proselytise in developing and developed countries about their success. NPM has nevertheless enjoyed at best modest success in changing governance practices in developing countries (Manning, 2001).

By the early 1990s NPM was joined by results-based management (RBM) as a key tool for upgrading development efforts. RBM was popularised by Osborne and Gaebler (1992) and became a bible of the new Clinton administration. It was adopted as a management tool by the World Bank in 1993, and became a centrepiece of the New Labour administration that took power in Britain in 1997; in fact results-based management was a key part of the New Labour election manifesto that year. The New Labour fetish for RBM reached extraordinary proportions: "Units, task forces and review groups, commissars of modernisation on every subject from silicon breast implants to social exclusion, proliferated ... . The government had more targets – over 6,000 on one count – than Stalin" (Rawnsley, 2001: 292).

Not surprisingly, therefore, the UK government's DFID international development arm was instrumental in promoting the International Development Targets and subsequently the Millennium Development Goals as a centrepiece of international development activities. It was joined in this mission by the United Nations Development Programme, then headed by Mark Malloch Brown, a Briton who had previously been a political communications consultant and World Bank vice-president, and close confidant of New Labour leaders, and who became a British cabinet minister in 2007.

The Bank's relationship with the MDGs has changed significantly. At the outset, the Bank downplayed them. However, as the MDGs gained favour among donors and within developing countries, the Bank enlisted the IMF in an effort to capture part of the action; the two agencies have appointed themselves monitors of global progress towards the goals (World Bank, 2006), producing an annual progress report, although the UN has stubbornly refused to give up control and continues to produce its own progress reports. Competition between the Bank and other transnational institutions is discussed at greater length in the next chapter.

Despite their evidently "developmentalist" character, the MDGs have received surprisingly little criticism, even from the post-developmentalist school. Some civil society representatives have raised the issue of "the limits of poverty discourse" exposed in the goals' evasion of the economic distribution issues underlying global poverty and inequality (Khor, 2003), and one commentator has questioned the policy conditionality generated by the international financial institutions' adoption of the MDGs as part of the PRSP framework (Barton, 2004).

Radical Bank critics Cammack (2002) and Kothari and Minogue (2002) obliquely criticise the MDG thrust through the proxy of other programmes. Cammack describes the World Bank's 1990 anti-poverty proposals to provide basic social services to the poor including primary health care, nutrition and primary education as part of a "systematic programme for the establishment and consolidation of capitalism on a global scale [starting with] the conversion of the world's poor into proletarians" (2002: 127–128). Kothari and Minogue refer to the 1996 OECD Development Committee proposals for anti-poverty targets – as noted, almost identical to the MDGs – as proof of "the continuing dominance of the neo-liberal paradigm within development" (2002: 10), a perspective that they inexplicably fail to extend to the – nearly identical – MDGs.

This reticence of even radical critics to directly challenge the MDGs means they are usually taken as given. Civil society organisations expend great energy lambasting wealthy countries' failure to provide the international development funding said to be needed to meet the goals (Pettifor and Greenhill, 2003). This approach perfectly fits the Bank's agenda, and is part of a pattern of civil society incorporation into global managerialism that will be explored in Chapter 5 below (World Bank, 2004).

As noted in Chapter 1 above, a key feature of contemporary managerialist practice is the shift away from hierarchical management models towards concertive approaches. In the transnational field, this shift is particularly important, because hierarchical structures through which formal disciplinary authority can be exercised do not in any event exist. The discussion of the processes leading to the adoption of the MDGs has provided a very cursory sketch of how managerialist ideas or discourse emerge, and are adopted and enriched through transnational elite networking.

The MDGs have been imbued with immunity from criticism through their endorsement by both developing country governments and even radical civil society and academic critics. In part, this is because the content of the Goals themselves, including targets such as reductions in infant and maternal mortality, and universal basic education, would be accepted by most people as highly desirable. This does not mean, however, that the Goals strategy is beyond reproach. Martin Khor (2003a) notes that most of the MDG outcomes are largely dependent on the overall global economic environment in which developing countries operate, an environment that even moderate critics of the global order find inequitable. However, the technocratic, target-based nature of the MDGs excludes all broader questions of political economy. The construction of organisational problems so as to exclude fundamental questions of power distribution is highly indicative of contemporary managerialism.

Further criticism of MDGs comes from possibly unexpected sources. The United States administration, which is strongly influenced by political ideology rather than managerialist discourse, is sceptical of both MDGs and PRSPs, preferring an authentically neo-liberal growth-focused approach, as will be discussed later in this chapter. Perhaps more surprisingly, the World Health Organisation (WHO) has mounted a rearguard action against its agenda being subsumed by the MDGs (Horton, 2002), reserving particular criticism for DFID, which it is claimed has made continuing financial support for WHO conditional on its prioritising MDGs at the expense of other activities. WHO argues that its role as guardian of the world's health requires that it should not restrict itself to specific "targets", but should remain free to act in case of emergent issues, such as the risk of avian influenza crossing the species barrier.

Stiglitz and the poverty agenda

While various forms of market purism continued to predominate in economics faculties, particularly in North America, by the late 1980s the implementation of neo-liberal structural adjustment was coming under increasing overt and covert attack in both developed and developing countries. Economic reforms turned out to be a lot messier than cloistered ideologues might have supposed, except perhaps in Chile where the free market restructuring took place under the sheltering umbrella of a brutal military dictatorship. In plural systems, entrenched interests effectively subverted key aspects of structural adjustment (particularly preserving various forms of market capture, even if now under a "private" rather than "state" rubric), so that the net outcome, while undoubtedly different from the starting point, bore little relation to the original vision. This problem was most evident in the post-Soviet states, where wholesale liberalisation of property rights allowed the elite to capture markets, strip assets and destroy the existing economies without investing in any alternative. While the ideologues continued to insist that these failures happened because their directions had not been followed faithfully enough, an ever greater number of policy advocates cast around for more nuanced approaches that could take into account institutional environments. Institutional economics enjoyed a resurgence, albeit shorn of Veblen's moral-critical dimension. The obvious success of state-led development in the East Asian countries, spearheaded by Japan but followed by Korea, Malaysia and China, posed a particularly strong challenge to structural adjustment orthodoxy; and during the 1990s, the structural adjustment agenda became increasingly imbued with an anti-poverty focus. By 1992, the staff operational manual of the Bank emphasised that poverty reduction was the benchmark for measuring the Bank's success (Kapur *et al.*, 1997a: 51). The rhetorical shift accelerated with the arrival of the charismatic Clinton nominee James Wolfensohn as Bank president in 1995, and another Clinton insider Joe Stiglitz's appointment as chief economist in 1997.

Joseph Stiglitz's arrival at the Bank marked a definitive rupture with free market fundamentalism. Stiglitz had made his name developing a theory of information asymmetry which explained why markets in practice failed to operate efficiently (Stiglitz, 2002: xi). Without challenging the orthodoxy that markets are in principle the most desirable system for allocating resources, Stiglitz and his followers argue that markets can only operate efficiently when all the participants have equal access to information, which is typically not the case in real life. Thus, the state must intervene to ensure equitable access to information. Although the core of what Stiglitz calls "informational-theoretic" economics appears to be a relatively mild critique of capitalism, and is accordingly dismissed as such by leftist political economists, his policy conclusions are far-reaching. Because markets cannot operate in a vacuum, they always exist in implicit or explicit partnership with the state. There are many fields where market imperfections mean that the state must assume a predominant role; for example, in supporting not merely universal basic education, which even neo-liberals generally favour, but in sustaining advanced training and research. Market liberalisation and privatisation are theoretically desirable, but in practice require a regulatory infrastructure, and both industrial protectionism and capital market controls are temporarily necessary in developing countries to permit nascent industries to grow. For developed countries, a variety of different models for sharing social and economic responsibilities between the state and market are possible, ranging from the "purer" system in the United States to the social welfarism of Scandinavia; in recent writings, Stiglitz makes it clear that he is more sympathetic to the latter (Stiglitz, 2002: 217–222). Stiglitz's approach forms the foundation of what has become known as the post-Washington Consensus, in which a variety of interventions are proposed through development policy, to help level the informational playing field between different market actors in developing countries, and ensure that functioning and transparent institutional structures are in place so that resources are distributed equitably, whether directly through services or through market access.

Stiglitz, previously a senior member of the Clinton administration, combines academic legitimacy with passionate advocacy, and strident denouncement of neo-liberal orthodoxy. In both policy and personality, the Wolfensohn–Stiglitz team fitted easily into the Third Way wave that swept America and Britain as well as other assorted Anglophone and non-Anglophone countries during the 1990s. Within three years, Stiglitz was purged from the Bank, having apparently gone too far in his public denouncements of the IMF (Fine, 2001: 17). Nevertheless, this was a case of victory in defeat; Stiglitz was awarded the Nobel Prize for economics in 2001, an indication that he had won the (policy) popularity contest. Despite Stiglitz's departure, the "holistic" approach to development has gained momentum. Although many of the Bank's economists recruited during the neo-liberal Washington Consensus phase would doubtless prefer the simpler world of economic adjustment, the Bank's leadership continues to pursue an ever broader range of managerial initiatives and alliances, all the while insisting that "[t]he Washington Consensus has been dead for years" (Wolfensohn, 2004).

In popular development circles, Stiglitz has achieved the iconic status reserved for fallen heroes. Freed from the constraints of policy responsibility,

Stiglitz's rhetoric became more radical, and he has increasingly flirted with the popular "anti-globalisation" movement. Nevertheless, he has not avoided criticism from left political economy. Ben Fine, associated with the neo-Marxist economic journal *Capital and Class*, questions the authenticity of Stiglitz's radical mantle. Fine's concerns are several: Stiglitz's insight into information asymmetry is merely a logical extension of the various market imperfections that neo-liberal economists have long acknowledged, if not incorporated into their practical policy advocacy; Stiglitz is blind to power imbalance that is foundational to inequality; and he only engages critical political economy to use it as ammunition against neo-liberal orthodoxy: "[i]t is little exaggeration to suggest that reference is made to this critical literature simply as a means to support the new consensus, both pillaging and reducing it to the new consensus through its own single-minded information-theoretic framework" (Fine, 2002: 14).

Paul Cammack, a British Marxist political economist, conflates the Washington and post-Washington Consensus under the title of neo-liberalism, albeit "second phase", a categorisation he believes applies not only to the post-Washington Consensus, but also the British Third Way and its intellectual founders such as Anthony Giddens (Cammack, 2003b: 19). Cammack notes the extension of IFI disciplinary authority through mechanisms such as the Comprehensive Development Frameworks and the Poverty Reduction Strategies, capturing the post-Washington Consensus as a new moment in the system of global management, a point Fine also makes but does not develop: "the new consensus can be understood as strengthening and extending the scope of permissible intervention in recipient countries" (Fine, 2002: 15). However, Cammack undermines the specificity of this insight by continuing to refer to the long-abandoned adjustment-era 1990 *World Development Report* as the touchstone of the Bank's poverty analysis, and insisting that Stiglitz-backed anti-poverty policies such as the CDF and PRSP serve mainly to enlist Third World workers into the wage labour logic of global capitalism (Cammack, 2002: 38).

Both Cammack and Fine limit the significance of their insights into the Bank's global managerialist practices by requiring them to fit into a predetermined deep-structural model of neo-liberal capitalism. Without denying their assertion that underlying structuring processes can be present, or that exploring hidden structuring phenomena can contribute to understanding human existence, I argue that these structures exist in dialectical relationship with presenting discourse.

For example, if a prominent economist such as Stiglitz says that the world order is unjust or dysfunctional, the theoretical rationale of such a statement may be less relevant than its impact on the hegemonic discourse and the conditions of possibility of alternative ways of seeing the world, which in turn impact the theoretical and political structuring phenomena. The presenting discourse in Stiglitz's 2002 bestseller, *Globalisation and its Discontents*, is particularly interesting when analysed in this light. The themes Stiglitz repeats are by and large constitutive of Third Way discourse. Globalisation is inevitable because of technological advances in physical and virtual communication (2002: 9). In principle, globalisation is good because it allows knowledge to be shared across societies, improving quality of life generally (2002: 224). However, globalisation's fruits have not been shared fairly, and the global rule-making process has made life worse for much of the world's population (2002: 216, 9). The principles underlying the Bretton Woods system were good (2002: 11), because markets often do not work well and "result in mass unemployment", and thus "there was a need for collective action at the global level for economic stability". However, these original goals were perverted by the Cold War and triumphalist market fundamentalism after the Communist system collapsed (2002: 25, 98). Keynes's belief in the crucial role of the state in economic stability and growth is fundamentally correct (2002: 249–250), and he "would be rolling over in his grave were he to see what has happened" to the IMF. Governments, and by extension the international financial institutions, have an essential role in "ensuring social justice"; "there is broad agreement that government has a role in making any society, any economy, function efficiently – and humanely" (2002: 218). To realise its potential, the global system must be democratised both by more equitable distribution of voice within global institutions and by greater institutional transparency (2002: 225–230).

While Stiglitz does not use the term "class" as an analytical category, Fine's claim that he avoids discussions of power is dramatically wide of the mark. One of Stiglitz's recurring themes is how the West, and particularly the United States, has misused its dominance of international institutions to enforce unfair global rules (2002: 64).

Whatever his objectively revealed place in the deep structure of the capitalist order, Stiglitz's "truth effect" derives from his repeated propagation of two key perspectives: there is a need for a system of global governance, correctly understood by the Bretton Woods founders as having broadly human rather than narrowly economic objectives; and differing and potentially conflictual interests should be explicitly managed rather than left to some mythical hidden market mechanism.

Stiglitz has made two theoretical contributions that challenge the economic fundamentalisms of left and right. His theory of asymmetrical information is consistent with Habermas's theory of communicative rationality. While his and Habermas's belief in the possibility of rationally informed decision making is naïve and effectively refuted by Foucault's demonstration of the ubiquity of power, this is nonetheless a considerably more sophisticated approach to power than the economic conveyor-belt approach to which Cammack and Fine resort. Most importantly, Stiglitz situates the ownership, if not the definition, of knowledge as a central power locus. Further, his understanding that the nature of the global system is economically indeterminate (susceptible to conscious alternatives) and thus subject to "management" places the political explicitly at centre stage and out of the deadening grasp of both deep structure and the hidden hand.

Nevertheless Fine's observation that Stiglitz "is seeking not only to set the agenda but also to incorporate dissidence" (Fine, 2002: 16) has a ring of truth

(Stiglitz's bestseller includes a sticker that can be removed and presumably affixed to some symbol of market fundamentalism, surely a first for a Nobel Prize-winning economist), and is at the same time perfectly in line with the incorporatist tendencies of global managerialism and Third Way thinking.

Poverty reduction and the American superpower

Given the assertions by various critics, discussed in Chapter 2 above, of American hegemony in the globalisation process, it might be thought that the PRSP must be a creature of the American administration. Nothing could be further from the truth. The United States has long vacillated between suspicion of and outright opposition to multilateral development initiatives, particularly the PRSP and the MDGs.

In the PRSP's early implementation phase during the Clinton administration, the United States Agency for International Development (USAID) deputy chief and partisan Democrat Harriet Babbitt warned that: "we have not reached the conclusion in the United States that the various multilateral-driven frameworks will necessarily replace the need for bilateral country strategies" (Babbitt, 2000).[10] The unilateralist American position hardened under the George W. Bush administration. As an example, in 2001, USAID sent a relatively junior official, the acting Deputy Assistant Administrator for Africa, to the World Bank's high-level meeting reviewing the first two years of PRSP implementation. His comments expanded on overall US concerns about the PRSP. USAID would permit its missions to participate in PRSPs if they wished, but questioned whether PRSPs were really country-owned, felt that PRSPs overemphasised the state's role in development as opposed to that of civil society and the private sector, noted that there was insufficient emphasis on growth and too much on health and education, opposed linking budget support to PRSP implementation as "deleterious to PRSP acceptance", and concluded that the United States would not in the foreseeable future move towards a coordinated, multilateral development assistance strategy (Smith, 2002).

A 2003 US summary of its position avoided the key issue of harmonising US development assistance with other countries, but repeated the complaint that "PRSPs generally encourage donors to support social services to relieve the symptoms of poverty rather than supporting economic growth to address the fundamental causes of poverty" (USAID, 2003).

The United States has consistently rejected "poverty reduction" as a legitimate international development goal throughout the Clinton and George W. Bush administrations: "the Agency makes a fundamental distinction between a direct poverty reduction strategy and its own sustainable development strategy" (Buckles, 2002: 85).[11] The disagreement on this issue between the United States on the one hand, and the rest of the developed countries and multilateral institutions on the other, has generated an instructive debate. In 1999, as part of the Bank-driven shift to prioritise poverty reduction in international development, the OECD Development Assistance Committee (OECD-DAC) launched a study

comparing donor poverty reduction policies and practices in the OECD countries, the United Nations and the Bretton Woods Institutions. Of the twenty-five
countries and institutions, only the United States, France, the IMF and Portugal
did not have poverty reduction as an international development goal. The United
States' failure to focus on poverty reduction was attributed to the American
public's dislike of welfare, with which poverty reduction programming seemed
too closely associated (OECD, 1999: 2).

The IMF was soon recruited as co-sponsor of the entire PRSP process, and
Portugal and France also fell in line and adopted poverty reduction as their
guiding priority in development programming. The US response went in the
opposite direction, entrenching and justifying its opposition to the poverty reduction focus. While the OECD went on to establish "guidelines" that subsumed all
development activities under the mantra of poverty reduction (OECD, 2001),
USAID produced research to justify subsuming poverty reduction activities under
the mantra of economic growth. The agency's senior economist drew on internal
research in growth and poverty reduction in five developing countries (Crosswell,
2000, 2003), as well as an empirical analysis of global growth and inequality
data, to present a comprehensive ideological critique of the concept of targeted
poverty reduction: "most of the world's poor are poor because they live in the
poorest regions and countries" (Crosswell, 2000: 8), and thus "poverty reduction
largely become[s] a matter of overall country development" rather than a matter
of improving intranational income and wealth distribution (Buckles, 2002: 86).
The studies concluded that neo-liberal growth strategies including market and
trade liberalisation, and privatisation, resulted in strong economic growth with
little impact on the GINI[12] income inequality coefficient, while state-led development efforts led to stagnation; the poor were better off as a result of market-led
growth.

Thus, Crosswell believes, "the disturbing tendency in the UN and the World
Bank to urge donors and recipients to program directly towards the separate
[Millennium Development Goal] targets and indicators" (Crosswell, 2003: 11) is
indicative of the international community's shift away from the growth-focused
development emphasised in the 1980s and early 1990s, and towards what he
identifies as a return to statist developmentalism practised, and discredited, in
the 1970s. He finds it, "remarkable that discussions of poverty reduction strategies after 1996 made absolutely no reference to experience and lessons learned
in the 1970s" (Crosswell, 2003: 7).

Although Crosswell's identification of the PRSPs with 1970s state-led developmentalism exaggerates the "anti-market" tendencies in the PRSP process, his
research does point out the ideological differences between the state–market
partnership ideology underpinning the PRSP, and the unadulterated neo-liberalism
dominant in the Bretton Woods institutions during the 1980s which remains the
official American position. Crosswell's observation about PRSP advocates' refusal
to engage in serious analysis and debate about the merits of contrasting development approaches is also pertinent. Indeed, after OECD-DAC's observation of
America's non-conformism with the poverty reduction agenda in its initial survey

of development agencies, DAC documents avoided the question of differing perspectives on poverty reduction, or even implied that the United States was "on-side" in the project, when it clearly was not:

> Canada/CIDA, Denmark/Danida, Germany/BMZ and USAID are changing their monitoring and performance management systems. These changes are geared to finding the right "fit" between these agencies' enhanced commit-ment to poverty reduction, partnership and policy coherence – and their formal structures, systems and processes.
>
> (OECD, 2001: 93)

Refusal to acknowledge fundamental differences, efforts to incorporate diver-gent and even opposed perspectives in an artificial consensus, and, con-sequently, the closure of debate and the delegitimisation of dissent, are central characteristics of the global managerialist praxis.

Conclusion

This chapter has explored the World Bank's adoption of poverty reduction as its core policy objective. The "poverty turn" is revealed as an ambitious effort to extend the Bank's policy influence within developing countries, and to mobilise other countries and multilateral institutions behind this initiative. The Bank's Poverty Reduction Strategies, and their forerunner, Comprehensive Develop-ment Frameworks, do not, however, replace the structural adjustment pro-grammes that first imposed a policy framework on developing country governments. Continuing neo-liberal economic policies remain crucial to the Bretton Woods institutions' policy domination over developing countries, espe-cially once the PRSP/MDG social agenda is added to the disciplinary policy mix; Cuba among other countries has demonstrated that poverty reduction and advanced human development can be achieved by pursuing entirely different strategies from those mandated by the international institutions. The extension of the international institutions' governance authority in the post-government global arena depends on achieving what Foucault called "governmentality": the exclusion of radical alternatives and the reduction of the scope of debate to the technical details involved in perfection of the current order.

Poverty reduction policies are imposed by the Bank and IMF through lending conditionalities, mobilisation of the international multilateral and bilateral donor community, enlisting the international NGO community, and crucially through "country ownership", a vehicle for incorporating local elites into the global man-agerialist agenda. Examples from PRSP development in several countries docu-mented that country ownership is a chimera – like structural adjustment, the policy solutions in PRSPs are a set of prescriptions designed in the Bank head-quarters in Washington. There is often a disconnect between the social and eco-nomic components of PRSPs, as the shrinking of the public sector, fee-for-service policies, and privatisations invariably included in the economic part of the PRSP preclude the universal access to health and education mandated by the PRSP's social agenda.

Up to this point, the analysis presented in this chapter is broadly consistent with other critical perspectives on the Bank. The latter part of the chapter, however, focuses on areas of divergence. The first of these relates to the Millennium Development Goals. With very few exceptions, the MDGs have been welcomed by all development actors. Those, such as post-developmentalists, whose philosophical position should render them opposed to such instrumental indicators of human achievement, have been silent. Despite being presented as a consensual global initiative, the impetus for the MDGs derives from the OECD group of developed countries. MDGs are an iteration of results-based management, a managerialist methodology introduced into the public sector by Third Way management gurus, as an adjunct to, rather than a replacement of, the neo-liberal New Public Management. The RBM approach inherent in the MDGs shifts focus away from broader questions of social equity that underlie poverty in the developing world, towards the technical solutions needed to accomplish the narrowly framed development targets. A maelstrom of convening and concerting efforts have been whipped up to achieve the Goals, to the discomfort of some agencies such as the WHO, pressured to drop its broad global health surveillance in favour of focusing on three diseases named in the MDGs.

The chapter went on to discuss critical perspectives on Joe Stiglitz, the public face if not the architect of the Bank's shift towards broad-based policy intervention. (Post)Marxist political economists essentially dismiss Stiglitz's contribution as window-dressing for neo-liberalism. I have shown, however, that the practical implications of Stiglitz's critique of purely neo-liberal policies are quite far-reaching, particularly his insistence on a broad economic and social policy role for international institutions in managing global development. The political economists' fixation with Stiglitz's failure to make a clear theoretical break with mainstream economics distracts them from the real impact of his discursive assault on neo-liberalism in the international institutions and his insistence on the development of a consensual, managed and socially sensitive global order. These are the hallmarks of global managerialism.

The chapter's final section addressed the orientation of the Americans towards the World Bank's poverty turn. Here, the distinction between neo-liberalism and the managerialism of the Poverty Bank are most clear. The Americans, dourly committed to neo-liberal economic development, have steadfastly resisted PRSPs and MDGs in favour of old-fashioned emphasis on economic growth. Their criticisms are not without substance. The countries, particularly in Asia, that have focused on (their own) growth strategies rather than World Bank social programmes, have achieved by far the biggest improvements in human development indicators in recent years. Transnational managerialism is a smoother form of governance than the pincer effect of American supply-side economics and the overt bullying of the structural adjustment era, but it is by no means evident that the outcome for ordinary people in developing countries is any more pleasurable.

4   The Managerial Bank

The last chapter concluded that the Bank's anti-poverty strategy is somewhat misplaced because poverty is *symptomatic of the absence of power*, rather than a fundamental problem in itself. The most important critical frame of analysis is thus not the technicalities of policy alternatives, but the construction and development of power relationships, a subject of which the Bank steers well clear in its development research and public pronouncements. This chapter will focus on how the Bank manages to secure its own power.

In common with all large organisations, the Bank manages its internal and external relationships in order to further its institutional agenda. I will examine some of the key discursive "nodal points" around which the Bank organises its activities, including "convening power", the "Knowledge Bank" and "participation". The internal processes of institutional expertise construction are also examined, as well as the strategies the Bank employs in its dealings with organisational competitors, and the broader managerial commonalities shared by the World Bank and the international Third Way political current.

The role of language or discourse as a primary vehicle in the construction of power in human relationships is a prominent theme in CMS, as discussed in Chapter 1 above. There has been a tendency for discourse analysts to represent power as a *sui generis* and pervasive property of discursive interactions, a perspective drawn from a reading of Foucault and associated with the post-structuralist school of thought. This approach causes inattention to the role of discursive hegemony as a social structuring tool, and thus leads to a naïve if not complicit disregard for the material foundations and results of such hegemony. The consequences in terms of critical social analysis are often extreme; one leading "critical" management thinker has gone so far as to suggest that imprisoned asylum-seekers are as able to construct and project their identities as their state gaolers (Hardy, 2003). Some contrasting "critical realist" work has been done on discourse analysis, which has the merit of taking into account the economic dimension of the discourse/materiality relationship (Fairclough, 2001), but often suffers from a uni-directional economic base/discursive superstructure approach derived from economic determinism. This chapter will show that, for the World Bank, materiality, structured power and discourse are intertwined and act upon each other. The Bank's success in hegemonising its poverty reduction discourse allows it to control the material flow of aid to the developing world, both directly and through "convening power". However, the anti-poverty discourse is itself grounded in the Bank's institutionalised power that arose out of the Bretton Woods agreement of 1944, in turn a product of the Allies' physical victory in the Second World War. Confidence in the superiority of the Bank's thinking is inculcated in staff and summed up by the "Knowledge Bank" moniker. Neither the Knowledge Bank nor even poverty reduction would carry much authority if the Bank were not itself materially well endowed and thus able both to hector and to seduce its audiences.

Policies and power relationships

One of the findings from the preceding chapters that discussed the history of the Bank was that the key feature of the transformations in the Bank's identity was the organisation's ever expanding horizon of interest, rather than its shifts in ideological colour. In the recent past, the critical juncture marked by the adoption of structural adjustment was decisive because of the Bank's metamorphosis as policy lender into the role of comprehensive economic "adviser" and concessional lender, as well as the international community's judge of countries' economic probity, rather than because of the organisation's adoption of neo-liberal economic ideology.

Poverty reduction strategies deepened and extended this increasingly intrusive and disciplinary role played by the Bretton Woods institutions, which now included defining the appropriate "social" orientation of governments. Poverty reduction's most significant new feature, however, was its capacity to mobilise a far wider coalition of support in favour of the Bank's activities. This coalition includes the Bank's twin, the IMF, almost all bilateral donors, and most international development NGOs. The incorporative strategy is a defining feature of contemporary managerialism, and is the transnational iteration of "Third Way" politics. The commonalities between contemporary Bank discourse and the Third Way will be assessed towards the end of this chapter (p. 91).

The international financial institutions' judgement of a country's economic and social (and to an increasing extent, political) management has impact far beyond the resources provided by the institutions, which are not always substantial.[1] The IMF has a reputation as provider of "surveillance" on national economies, and private sector country ratings services and investment analysts consult its data as a matter of course. The Bank's authority, on the other hand, depends on cultivating an external reputation and internal culture as the pre-eminent managing institution of international development. The Bank's ideas or discourse are translated into practice both directly, through various types of interchange with developing country governments, and indirectly, through its capacity to project the authority of its discourse in conjunction with external organisations and networks.

At the simplest level, contact with the Bank either through negotiations or as a staffer expands the organisation's reach in the developing world. Bank adviser Arnold Harberger speaks of:

the upgrading of member country personnel through a) the apprenticeships that many of them serve as staff members of the Bank and Fund, b) the direct lessons, learned by government personnel in member countries through dealing with missions from the two sister institutions, and c) the similar but rather more specific lessons that member country cadres have learned by going through the Bank's process of project evaluation at the various stages of a project's development.

(cited in Krueger, 1998: 1997)

Harberger, a prominent neo-liberal and Mont Pèlerin Society member, claims that at one time four of the Bank's six regional economists had been his students (Harberger, 1999). He designed the key elements of the economic restructuring programme introduced in Chile after Pinochet's 1973 military coup, and he is proud that a number of his students assumed senior positions in the dictatorship's administration.[2]

There is a substantial interchange between many developing country administrations and the World Bank. The Bank is an attractive location for high-flying national officials, not least because its salaries are many multiples more than could be earned in a developing country administration. Movement also occurs in the opposite direction. Two prominent examples of the close interchange between the Bank and government in Africa are Nicephore Soglo of Bénin and Ellen Johnson Sirleaf from Liberia. Soglo, a France-trained economist and nephew of the country's former military ruler Christophe Soglo, served in increasingly senior positions in the country's Finance Ministry in the 1960s and 1970s, eventually becoming finance minister. He left Bénin to work for the World Bank during the 1980s, returning to become the country's first president after democratic transition in 1991. Ellen Johnson Sirleaf, Liberia's current president, has similarly shifted between the World Bank and her country's government several times. Sirleaf also worked for the American-headquartered multinational bank Citibank, as well as for the United Nations Development Programme. A much larger number of senior and mid-ranking officials regularly exchange between national government and the Bank and other transnational institutions.

The direct exchange of personnel between the transnational institutions, national governments and the private sector is an important feature of the creation of a global elite, and parallels the phenomenon noted by Wright Mills in his study of the American power elite. However, successful implantation of transnational policy norms depends on a much broader sway of Bank ideas than would be possible merely through personnel exchange. This is achieved through the construction of discursive hegemony.

Convening power and the "Knowledge Bank"

The Bank uses a series of discourses to project its image and self-image. "Convening power" describes its capacity to convene different agents to "coordinate" country strategies, built upon the Bank's involvement in overall economic management through SAPs, CDFs and PRSPs. The advent of the "holistic" CDFs and PRSPs provides wider opportunities for convening than did straightforward economic adjustment programmes. The strategic importance of "convening power" to the Bank is reflected in the term's ubiquity in Bank discourse; it appears in several hundred different documents posted on the Bank's website, and is particularly prominent in analyses of the Bank's "comparative advantage" in prospective issues for Bank intervention.

Nick Stern, the Bank's chief economist from 2000 to 2003, who came to the Bank from the European Bank for Reconstruction and Development, and left to become chief economist at the British Treasury under the Blair government, regularly emphasised the importance of convening power: "we can see the IFIs, and particularly the World Bank, as having a power of 'convening' that arises from their special ownership structure and goals (Stern, 2002: 184)".

Former External Affairs Vice-President Mats Karlsson places the convening power at the centre of the Bank's raison d'être:

> I believe that the World Bank combines rare qualities that would have to be reinvented or found elsewhere if they did not already exist. It has an international convening power and a unique role as catalyst, convener and coordinator, which helps leverage both its own resources as well as those of other development partners in official capacities and, increasingly, the private sector.
>
> (Karlsson, 2000)

Given the Bank and IMF's integrated work, for example in approving PRSPs, and the much lower profile adopted by the Fund, the Bank has become the dominant public voice of global economic governance. Its success in building alliances with numerous civil society groups is based in part on marketing its convening power. Figure 4.1 is a World Wildlife Fund (2003) slide describing the key "competitive advantages" the Bank and WWF bring to their strategic alliance.

The Bank also devotes substantial resources to constructing and marketing its expertise as the "Knowledge Bank", developing prodigious quantities of research and analyses on subjects ranging from economic theory to empowering rural women. While much of this output has limited direct policy impact – particularly in social development where other actors typically have superior practical expertise – the Knowledge Bank concept helps staff assume an aura of competence and authority and thus confidence in the legitimacy and importance of their convening role. The Bank aims to institutionalise its knowledge-broker role through the Development Gateway, a nominally independent organisation largely funded by the Bank that posts development research and information on the internet. The Bank's internal evaluation of this initiative noted approvingly that "[t]he convening power of the Bank has mobilised resources and empowered the Development Gateway to share technology innovations globally"

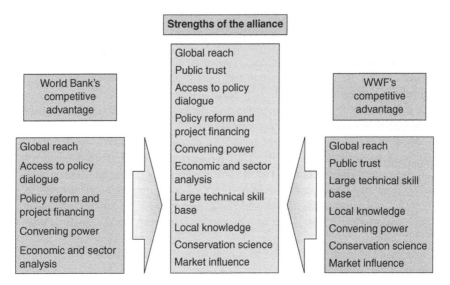

Figure 4.1 World Wildlife Federation and World Bank alliance (source: World Wildlife fund (2003)).

(Walker, 2003: 16). Conversely, the initiative has drawn extensive criticism from civil society groups who claim that it is an attempt to monopolise discussion on development issues (Wilks, 2001), and that the Bank is concealing the extent of its involvement and control of the initiative (Bretton Woods Project, 2001).

Convening power supports the Bank's global managers in their objective of replacing nationally generated economic and social planning with centrally conceived acronymic programmes to be implemented worldwide; SAPs and PRSPs are at the pinnacle of these pervasive strategies but numerous other Washington-designed sectoral programmes are forced on client countries. Some countries resist the rebranding of their existing programmes. For example, The Gambia established a Strategy for Poverty Alleviation (SPA) five years before the PRSP, and insisted that the new anti-poverty programme demanded as an IFI funding conditionality after 1999 be named SPA II. Nevertheless, Bank and other bilateral donors invariably describe SPA II as The Gambia's PRSP. In other cases, such as Uganda, the IFIs "permit" existing anti-poverty strategies to be considered as "equivalent" to a PRSP and thus the country is not required to repeat the process in order to access concessional funds. This is considered generally undesirable, however, as a country's own ideas about how to look after its citizenry are naturally inferior to those provided by the Bank. Bank staff's internal discourse frequently constructs developing country governments as "hopeless", "backward" and "without a clue", thus justifying imposition of one-size-fits-all policies designed in Washington.

In the fluid environment of developing global governance, where formal legis-
lative authority is minimal, convening is an important – and undertheorised –
activity. Its effectiveness is based largely upon the self-confidence of Bank
officials in their legitimacy as global managers. This self-confidence is built upon
the effective internal articulation of corporate managerial identity, a form of the
corporate culturism (Willmott, 1993) discussed in Chapter 1 above.

Participation

Participation is another key word in the Bank's pantheon. "Participation and
civic engagement" merits its own team and section of the Bank's website, offering an "interactive learning guide" on CD-ROM, "brown bag" lunch sessions,
"toolkits", and "sourcebooks" on participation. Various Bank policies mandate
use of participatory processes at all levels of its work.

Despite then Bank President Lewis Preston's 1994 claim that the Bank's
interest in the subject was "not new", the "Bank-wide Learning Group on Participatory Development" established in December 1990 (World Bank, 1994: 51)
uncovered only a single reference to participation prior to 1990, and no Bank
research on the subject prior to 1987. As has been noted, the Bank's founders
did not even consider citizen participation in the Bretton Woods institutions. In
its final report, the Learning Group admitted that although the Bank "has always
interacted with governments and a limited number of stakeholders [it] has not
systematically sought the broad-based participation required by its objective of
helping its borrowers achieve sustained poverty reduction". While holding fast
to the Bank's shibboleth and defensive fall-back position that its main clients are
governments, the Learning Group developed an action plan that called for all
lending and country diagnostic projects to identify and involve stakeholders.
The report specifically identifies "poor people" as being key stakeholders in
Bank development activities (World Bank, 1994: 2–3).

In June 1995, the Bank produced its *Sourcebook* on participation, indicating
that the theme had truly arrived in its life. James Wolfensohn's appointment the
same month added further momentum to the participatory turn. Early the next
year, the *Sourcebook* was reissued complete with upgraded graphics and a fore-
word from the new Bank president, who took the opportunity to claim that he
always consults a range of stakeholders when visiting country operations, and
commends Bank staff who are "pioneering participatory approaches in the
Bank's work" (World Bank, 1996a: ix). The *Sourcebook* contained inspiring
stories of Bank engagement in grassroots collaboration across the world, contrasting the "old" Bank with its "external expert style" to the new Bank where consultation and listening are merely prerequisites for learning, and where it is the
stakeholders themselves who "invent the new practices and institutional arrangements they are willing to adopt" (World Bank, 1996a: 5). The Bank claimed that,
as poor people become stronger and their voices are heard, it must move away
from "welfare-oriented approaches and focus rather on such things as building
sustainable, market-based financial systems" (World Bank, 1996a: 8), a happy

coincidence given that this is what the Bank would have recommended without the benefit of the poor people's input.[3] This transaction reflects the new challenge in Bank operations, central to all of the discourse of inclusivity. Countries, clients, even opponents must be engaged, empowered, participate, and own the development process, but the outcome must not threaten the predetermined policy initiatives already designed by the global managers.

Although the Bank's interest in participation was by no means groundbreaking, it did precede the widespread criticism that the Bretton Woods institutions endured from the late 1990s, which often centred on claims that they imposed policies and conditionalities on poor people and countries. This suggests, in turn, that the shift to participation was not the result of popular pressure, as civil society advocates are wont to claim, but rather part of a broader managerial reorientation. To some extent, the Bank was pushed into a participation mode by its developed country members; much of its early work in the field was driven by financing and technical support from the Swedish and German international development agencies, another sign of an international shift in management style during the 1990s. *Participation*, along with the other key Bank words discussed in this chapter including *country ownership* and *collaboration*, as well as the emphasis on *convening methods* in internal management, are all aspects of the privileging of pseudo-democratic practices, which has become a trans-ideological principle of governance discourse in the post-Soviet era, and central to the politics of the Third Way, which will be discussed later in this chapter.

The Bank's shift towards participation earned plaudits from development observers, as a welcome move away from the traditional Bank focus on megaprojects conceived without adequate consideration of the impact on local populations. Participation was initially less popular with developing country governments, who feared that their traditionally exclusive relationship with the Bretton Woods institutions would be diluted. However, it was soon realised that a large, if different, infrastructure would be needed to support this new Bank scheme; many senior officials left poorly paid positions in national civil services to take relatively well-paid posts running NGOs funded by the Bank and bilateral donors and mandated to animate the participation of the poor in Bank-sponsored projects.[4]

Northern-based NGOs also generally supported the philosophy but not always the Bank's practice of participation. Civil society input into the joint IMF/World Bank review of the PRSP in 2001 acknowledged and welcomed the opportunity to take part in discussions on the development of the PRSPs. The international NGO Action Aid complained that as the PRSPs reached completion, input dried up; input was generally restricted to the "softer" social aspects of the PRSP such as health and education, but there was minimal openness to discuss macroeconomic policy; and the participatory process broke down completely when it came to negotiating the financial instruments that were to finance the poverty reduction strategy (IMF/World Bank PRSP Comprehensive Review (hereafter Review), 2002: 2–3). Catholic Relief Services repeated some of these concerns but emphasised that donor funding from all sources should be coordinated and implemented through the PRSP process (Review, 19). Christian Aid felt participation had too often been superficial and circumscribed, that people in developing countries should be given training so that they could follow and participate in macroeconomic debates, and more grants should be offered to "facilitate deep and representative participation" (Review, 31). A network of southern NGOs headed by Jubilee South complained that while people were invited to participate in drawing up the PRSPs, it was always understood that this had to be in a context of, "the neo-liberal free market 'growth' framework guiding the 'broad economic policies'" (Review, 114).

More fundamental questioning of the participation project is found in Cooke and Kothari's (2001) edited collection, *Participation: The New Tyranny*, written from within the CMS tradition. The editors argue that "tyranny is both a real and a potential consequence of participatory development, counterintuitive and contrary to its rhetoric of empowerment though it may be" (Cooke and Kothari, 2001: 3). They posit two core arguments: that participatory methods tend to crowd out and devalue existing decision-making processes; and that the group methods used tend to reinforce the voices of the powerful and exclude the marginalised – the exact opposite of the rationale for participation. As an extreme example, in the same volume, Hailey (2001) cites historic examples of participatory methods being used as part of pacification strategies during colonial conflicts.

Henkel and Stirrat (2001) deconstruct the discourse of participation, comparing development's abandonment of the "expert stance" and adoption of participatory methods to the rise of Protestantism as a decentralised and grassroots (participatory) alternative to the centralised (expert stance) Catholicism. The twist in Protestantism is that freedom from the authoritarian church is secured at the price of assuming a personal moral responsibility to practise the faith, or, as Henkel and Stirrat extrapolate, to engage in the participatory empowerment project. Engagement implies acceptance of the outcomes of the process, "participation as an administrative or political principle eases authoritative force, in turn placing responsibility on the 'participants'". Thus, participation "is a form of governance – in fact the ultimate modern form" (Henkel and Stirrat, 2001: 179). In Chapter 5 below, this argument is extended to show how the Bank and global civil society elites share a common interest in constructing "participatory democracy" as preferable to representative democracy, thus legitimising simultaneously their own global governance credentials and disciplinary intervention in national social policies.

Each year, the Bank organises hundreds of "dialogues" on key Bank themes, involving national politicians, civil society and bilateral partners, and judiciously selected Bank critics. These sessions are usually led by the Bank's External Affairs staff, but for important events, the mechanics of constructing consensus are contracted out to specialised freelance "facilitators". Riz Khan, former television news anchor for both CNN and the BBC, who moderated the main session at the Bank's May 2004 Shanghai "Scaling Up Poverty Reduction" event, is a leading practitioner of this art.

In the aftermath of the 1999 Seattle protests during WTO meetings, and the 11 September 2001 terrorist attacks which led to the cancellation of the 2001 annual World Bank–IMF meetings planned for Washington, "managed dialogue" has become a favoured global managerial approach to the organisation of large-scale elite fora. From 1999 onwards, Khan organised and chaired numerous sessions including the Council of Europe's Global Forum for Poverty Eradication (1999), a session on the education MDGs at the Bank–IMF annual meeting in Washington (2002), the 6th Annual Business Week CEO Forum in Beijing (2002) and promotional interviews for the 2nd International Islamic Finance Conference in Dubai, held in conjunction with the World Bank/IMF annual meetings (2003). In Khan's interview with the United Arab Emirates' finance minister and chief organiser of the Bank–Fund meetings, Dr Mohammed Khalfan Bin Kharbash gave an insight into why the Bank and other international organisations are increasingly choosing the Gulf dictatorships as agreeable locations for big international meetings:

> We in Dubai 2003 are very ready to listen to NGOs, to people coming here with a voice to share with us their views, concerns, and ideas. I think this is a legitimate gathering of all people concerned. But let me be clear. We are not here to be tolerant to people seeking harm for harm's sake. That will not happen at all.
>
> (General Council for Islamic Banking
> and Financial Institutions, 2003)

Organisational myths

Like many contemporary large organisations, the Bank prides itself on its internal collegiality, teamwork, and resemblance to a large family. Although the organisation is headed by a president who is, "by tradition, a national of the largest shareholder, the United States",[5] with a senior management team including four managing directors, the chief economist, and the general council, who in turn preside over twenty-four vice-presidents each with a geographic or thematic responsibility, it is the internally received wisdom that the organisation is "flat" and non-hierarchical.

The Bank emphasises and invests in building internal cohesiveness. Strategies include orientation materials, a plethora of internally advertised awards for staff having made special contributions ("spot awards", "awards for excellence"), an intranet site that repeats currently emphasised messages, an internal communications team, videoconferenced international staff meetings, and continual repetition in internal channels of touching stories highlighting the Bank president's charismatic leadership.

The Bank has various mechanisms to address internal conflicts. There is both a mediation team and an Ombudsman's office to which staff can refer if they are dissatisfied with their treatment, although the mandate, powers and independence of these officers are sharply circumscribed, and the Bank is exempt from national labour and human rights legislation. The Bank relies heavily on contingent labour, but makes this a virtue through its numerous special contingent employment programmes including internships and young professionals programmes. Given the generous, typically tax-free remuneration paid by the Bank, there is a strong incentive to accommodate to or indeed incorporate the organisation's values.

Bank orientation materials aim to instil in staff a sense of mission and moral superiority. In 2004, a large glossy poster hanging on the wall above this author's desk while he was working as a consultant in the Bank's London office was headed with the Bank's current top slogan, "Our dream is a world free of poverty". Below was a row of alternately chastening and inspiring photographs of life in the developing world; in the middle of the poster were reproductions of newspaper articles extolling the Bank's work and letters from national officials thanking the Bank for its interventions. Then came frames detailing the Bank's mission statement and the qualities of its staff:

Guiding principles:

* Client centered
* Working in partnership
* Accountable for quality results
* Dedicated to financial integrity and cost effectiveness
* Inspired and innovative

Values

* Personal honesty, integrity, commitment
* Working together in teams – with openness and trust
* Empowering others and respecting differences
* Encouraging risk-taking and responsibility
* Enjoying our work and our families

Bank information documents almost invariably carry inspiring pictures of poor people working together to resolve their problems. Figure 4.2, a photograph of "a focus group meeting in a rural area in the Republic of Yemen", appears opposite the Bank's mission statement on the first page of the introductory manual given to new staff and visitors. This gives a somewhat misleading picture of Bank work: of its several thousand employees, half are based in Washington, DC, and most developing countries only have a small Bank office, typically situated in luxurious premises in a desirable neighbourhood of the capital city, protected by understandably rigorous security. The country-based team's work generally involves: rounds of meetings with senior government officials and other multilateral and bilateral donors; frequent travel to headquarters and regional Bank meetings; participation in Bank, government and other donor meetings, often at resort hotels; and an occasional sortie into the countryside to visit a project, timed to ensure return to the capital city and home comforts on the same day, given the generally low standard of accommodation outside the capital city in developing countries.

Figure 4.2 A focus group meeting in a rural area in the Republic of Yemen (source: World Bank (2003) *A Guide to the World Bank*, Washington, DC, World Bank, p. 2).

Internationally based Bank staff have diplomatic status and sport special vehicle licence plates exempting them from the daily police harassment typical in most developing and transitional countries. Bank offices are connected to headquarters by satellite communications and thus staff rarely suffer the typical developing country frustrations of dealing with dilapidated telephone systems. In summary, Bank staff, even when physically located in a developing country, have only a tangential connection with the daily lives of the subject populations.

Bank country-based offices are visited by a never-ending parade of Bank staff and consultants who travel from Washington and other developed countries to impart specialised expertise, a process greatly simplified by the existence of pre-packaged solutions to address equally pre-diagnosed maladies.

Bank staff going "on mission" are advised to approach travel in developing countries with extreme caution. There is a special office at the Bank geared to providing safe travel information; for example, staff are advised to carry a special medical kit to avoid infection with reused needles in the event of their having to receive emergency treatment from underfunded national health services. Staff travel by business class on most missions, but, unlike IMF staff, they are not permitted to charter aeroplanes to avoid developing country airlines. When discussing conditions in a developing country with Bank staff, it is commonplace to be regaled with anecdotes derived entirely from observations made in a five-star hotel in the capital city. When raising the question of luxurious Bank staff travel and insulation from developing country realities, this author was smartly rebuked by a young consultant: "this is the World Bank, it would not be appropriate to expect staff to live at the same level as the developing country's poor".[6]

The Bank and the shifting global power balance

The Bank's strategy of incorporating potential opponents is demonstrated in its approach to the distribution of global power. The Bank's leadership believes the current domination of global decision making by the G8 countries is not sustainable, and presents a risk to managerial control. The sheer scale of loans held by large semi-industrialised countries in the global South such as China, India, Indonesia and Brazil is so important that the organisation cannot risk alienating these countries' elites. The Bank could not afford default; more pertinently, its future financial health and independence are linked to continuing and expanding its loans to these countries, many of which are made through the full-interest IBRD arrangement, thus generating cherished untied revenues that can be used to fund the expansion of Bank activities into new domains and allow it to act quickly to position the organisation in emergent global governance arenas, as in the aftermath of the 2003 Iraq war.

Major developing country elites are well aware of their strong position. One politician from India's governing coalition described the country's relationship with the Bank:

> We have an excellent relationship with the Bank. It is one of the best sources of funding for us. From time to time the Bank starts to get a little pushy about the things it wants us to do, structural adjustment, privatisation, etc. But when that happens, we simply tell them that we are thinking of pre-paying a large tranche of loans, which would save us lots of interest. They usually stop talking about policy changes then.[7]

The Bank has gone to extraordinary lengths to enlist the socialist Brazilian President Lula da Silva as an ally. Lula was given top billing at the Bank-organised 2004 conference in Shanghai on "Scaling Up Poverty Reduction", where the Bank highlighted China and India's recent success in reducing poverty levels, which it ascribed to the classic Third Way agenda of market liberalisation and social inclusion, or "growth with equity" (World Bank, 2004a). President Wolfensohn's efforts to build and sustain alliances across the political spectrum were redolent of New Labour's approach in Britain: "The political discourse of New Labour is inclusive and consensual – it tries to include everyone, there are no sharp divisions, no 'us' versus 'them', no enemies" (Fairclough, 2000: 34).

During 2003 and 2004, the Bank stepped up its discourse in favour of a more inclusive global management system. In his keynote address in Shanghai, Wolfensohn endorsed Lula's call to restructure global governance to provide a more equitable balance between developing and developed countries:

> I remember very well in Evian, where I had the privilege of attending the [G8] summit, and President Lula entered the room, and in a typically self-effacing way said how proud he was to be with the leaders of the G-8, but that maybe next year President Hu of China, Prime Minister Vajpayee of

India, or his successor, the President of Nigeria, the Prime Minister of South Africa, and himself, maybe they should be the G-8 because they represented the five billion out of six billion on the planet. And he pointed to this new balance that is needed in our world.

(Wolfensohn, 2004)

In his speech, Wolfensohn continued to touch on the key themes in recent Bank discourse; the need for "engagement" with the poor, the fact that we need to learn from them, that they are "rich in capacity". Of course, in order to realise their capacity, they need the Bank's help with "the structure and the approach", "infrastructure" and "resources".

In a passage that should astonish those who interpret Bank activities as simple neo-liberalism, Wolfensohn congratulated China on its long-term, centrally planned approach to development, noting that the country has lifted hundreds of millions of citizens out of poverty in the past twenty years:

We've had ten five-year plans. The government is now looking at the 11th five-year plan, and it is consulting widely. And as the Premier noted, the poverty reduction strategy of years ago, the seven-year strategy, now succeeded by another five-year strategy.

Reflecting global managerialism's obsession with size and technology, Wolfensohn is above all impressed by scale, such as China's project that brought "three million people ... from the tops of the mountains into the valleys". The Bank's initiatives must be equally grandiose. So when it was planning the Shanghai conference, it conducted a survey of "60,000 poor people in 60 countries", summarised a hundred case studies, took elite participants on eleven field trips throughout Asia, and organised twenty videoconferences. And the conference message is that the Bank knows what to do and how to do it, but needs to begin doing it on a scale befitting global managers.

feeling good about individual projects is not enough. The challenges that we face are just too big. It's not ten schools. It's 10,000 schools. It's not five bridges. It's 5,000 bridges. It's not 100 people. It's millions and billions of people.

The Bank leadership's rhetoric of empowerment, inclusivity and grassroots development appears incongruously linked with the celebration of five-year plans and mass mobilisation. However, Fairclough also notes the same tendency to marry incompatible concepts in New Labour rhetoric in Britain, where leaders regularly reel off lists of concepts, "connected only in the sense that they appear together" (Fairclough, 2000: 28).

Sublimating incompatibilities into a content-free "consensus" that leaves the power of execution in the right hands requires exceptional communication skills. Devesh Kapur's churlish comment that "in recent years, the bank's research budget has been roughly equal to its public relations expenditures" (2000: 45) misses the point that *communications are more central to the Bank's success than programme content.*

As discussed earlier, the Bank directly or indirectly organises a plethora of consultations, workshops, seminars and other assorted "learning events" each year. Although the Bank describes its learning events as promoting "dialogue", they typically involve the recitation of points of view without dialectical interaction. Through airing all possible perspectives without engaging with them, the Bank claims to have "taken into account" various points of view, while retaining freedom of action that would have been constrained by the outcomes of a genuine conversation.

Staying ahead of the game: the Bank and other "development partners"

The international development community is a crowded neighbourhood, with multilateral, bilateral and non-government agencies competing for attention and resources. The Bank's extensive use of convening authority requires it to maintain positive relationships with other development organisations, while simultaneously manoeuvring to extend its influence and authority. This strategy is underpinned by a justificatory and categorising internal discourse.

Other international organisations sometimes pre-empt the Bank in launching successful global programme brands. As discussed in the last chapter, the most important of these currently within the Bank's bailiwick are the Millennium Development Goals, a UN initiative to reduce poverty and its symptoms by 2015. The Bank was initially lukewarm about the MDGs, but as their momentum gathered pace, it changed strategy and presented the PRSPs as implementation vehicles for achieving the MDGs. The Bank then attempted to seize ownership of the project by appointing itself monitoring agent of progress towards the MDGs, producing an extensive report released during the joint Bank–Fund annual spring meetings in 2004, a strategy described by an IFI watching organisation as an "audacious grab to consolidate their roles as judge and jury of countries' policies" (Wilks, 2003). The progress report repeats the Bank's current key messages: the Millennium Development Goals are in danger of not being met, because developed countries are not delivering the massive required amount of development aid, while too many developing countries lack the "capacity" (e.g. elite competence) to effectively use assistance. Further, there is inadequate "coordination" of bilateral financial and technical assistance, which would be best channelled through multilateral institutions, and specifically the Bank (Development Committee, 2004).

The Bank has attempted to incorporate and subvert other international development initiatives. A recent example is the Education for All (EFA) campaign, a UNESCO-led project to ensure universal, quality education at all levels. While the MDG education goals focus on achieving universal basic education and gender equality, EFA seeks to improve access and quality of education at all levels (UNESCO, 2002). Publicly, the Bank supports EFA, but its whispered internal wisdom is that UNESCO lacks the competence to effectively coordinate the campaign, and that EFA's goals are too broad. In its public discourse, the Bank elides EFA into the education MDGs, and devotes almost all its attention to the question of universal basic education, to which it mainly attaches the goal of gender equality. In its regional and country practice, the Bank consistently argues for the transfer of funds away from the secondary sector to pay for basic education (Mingat, 2002; World Bank, 2002b: 9). EFA is further subverted by the joint Bank–Fund Fast Track Initiative (FTI), which aims to marshal bilateral development resources and allocate them to "fast track" countries: those that have produced "realistic" plans for universal education that include large class-room sizes and restricted salaries for teachers. A case study of the impact of EFA in developing countries is discussed in the next chapter.

The politics of development goal setting is only one facet of the Bank's relationship with the UN. Formally, both the Bank and the IMF were founded by United Nations resolutions, and thus are theoretically accountable to the UN General Assembly. In practice, the Bank and Fund are almost completely independent of the UN, although Bank staff travel on UN diplomatic passports, and at the country level sometimes participate – half-heartedly – in UN coordinating committees under the chairmanship of the UNDP. The creation in 1960 of the IDA, which offers heavily subsidised loans, places the Bank and UNDP in more or less direct competition as providers of development expertise and resources.

Although right-wing critics view the UN as the kernel of communistic world government (Lindsey, 1996), it is actually beholden to its member governments in both its policy-setting processes and in-country work. The Bank, however, is sufficiently free of shareholder government control to have at least partially achieved a transnational character. Although the United States casts a long shadow over the organisation, the Bank's central PRSP policy is pursued despite American scepticism, and the Bank repeatedly, if impotently, criticises developed countries for their inadequate development assistance and unfair trade practices.

In the nascent system of global governance, the Bretton Woods institutions and United Nations agencies each have areas of competitive advantage. The former have more financial resources than the latter, and, even more significantly, their resources are mainly internally generated through loan repayments, and can be allocated at the discretion of Bank management. In contrast, the UN agencies are continually seeking nation state and charitable contributions, an increasing number of which are tied to specific initiatives. UN member nations, and particularly the United States, have regularly withheld funds to force UN policy change. The discipline that wealthy countries can impose on the United Nations is limited, however, by the UN's "one country, one vote" structure, and also by the veto power of the Security Council member countries. Further, some smaller and medium-sized developed countries, especially the Scandinavians, consistently support the UN with untied contributions far in excess of their per capita obligations, thus providing the organisation with some independence from the United States, the largest contributor. The net result is that while the UN enjoys a certain moral superiority vis-à-vis the Bretton Woods institutions, these, however, have more money, and because they are formally governed through shareholders' relative financial weight, enjoy greater confidence from wealthy country administrations.

The Bank's strategy, therefore, is to align itself with the United Nations' moral standing, while simultaneously quietly doubting the UN agencies' ability to deliver effective programming, due to both lack of funds and absence of disciplinary authority over developing country governments. Despite its surveillance and disciplinary functions, the Bank is welcomed by developing country administrations because its resources, even though generally in the form of loans, are substantial, disburse rapidly, and are typically tied to very broad policy objectives, providing opportunities at best for independent policy setting and at worst for large-scale misappropriation (Stiglitz, 2002: 133–165; Wedel, 1998).

Relationships between in-country Bank and UNDP representatives are often superficially cordial but fundamentally strained. The UN often finds itself mounting a rearguard action to defend its development objectives in the face of generously funded and conditionality-imposed Bank initiatives, knowing that even if UN projects achieve ascendancy, the Bank is able to co-opt the UN initiative and conflate it with its own strategies, as has occurred with the MDGs. In internal discourse, Bank staff tend to depict the UNDP and other UN agencies as never "bringing money to the table", too beholden to developing country governments, "hung up" on formalities and philosophic purity, and generally incapable of implementing practical projects. Conversely, UN agency staff frequently criticise the Bank's use of its resources and its disciplinary role as a "bully pulpit" to impose a narrow ideological agenda. The extent to which the Bank leads the relationship with the UNDP is reflected in the fact that the last two UNDP administrators, Mark Malloch Brown, and Kemal Dervis, are both former long-term Bank officials.

The Bank's relationship with the IMF, its Bretton Woods "twin", warrants its own study. Briefly, the conjoined twin metaphor is genuinely appropriate, as the two organisations are joined at the hip, both geographically (their headquarters are next door to each other in Washington) and in daily activities. As noted, the Bank and the Fund must jointly sign off a PRSP before a country can receive concessional funding. As both organisations have adopted an increasingly interventionist stance towards developing country governments, they regularly interact "in the field". Nevertheless, their policy viewpoints diverge significantly. The IMF, despite by tradition being headed by a European, is tied closely to the US Treasury and generally wedded to neo-liberalism. Even after Stiglitz's departure, the Bank has continued to appoint post-Washington Consensus chief economists, including Britain's Nicholas Stern and current incumbent and institutional economist François Bourguignon. By contrast, in 2001 the Fund selected former (1982–1986) Bank chief economist and devout neo-liberal Anne Krueger as deputy managing director. Her appointment was designed to please the Bush administration, which shares her market fundamentalist views and scepticism about the merits of poverty reduction (Smalhout, 2001).

An examination of Krueger's discourse highlights the important differences between Wolfensohn's Third Way approach and the aggressive neo-liberalism favoured by the US Republican administration. Krueger regularly makes head-lines with tough talk, for example, in 2002, threatening Argentina with "serious consequences", including the cancellation of social programme assis-tance, if it failed to keep up payments on its unsupportably high debt (BBC, 2002a). In a 2003 speech on the merits of globalisation, she remarked that "it really does make sense to pause before condemning conditions in the so-called 'sweatshop' factories in developing countries", argued against legislation in developed countries to help ensure developing country workers are paid a "decent wage", and implicitly opposed laws against child labour (Krueger, 2003).

Critics sometimes dismiss the Bank and IMF's divergent rhetoric as little more than a "good cop, bad cop" routine, but leading Bank and Fund staff clearly believe they have conflicting perspectives on matters of principle as well as personality. During a stint in academia between leaving the Bank in 1986 and joining the Fund in 2001, Krueger wrote an extended article on the future of the Bank and the IMF, calling for the Bank to end lending to middle-income coun-tries, largely eliminate project funding, and focus on support for structural adjustment in the world's poorest countries, carefully differentiating "between countries where reforms are serious and stand a reasonable chance of success and those in which window dressing is used as a means of seeking additional funding" (Krueger, 1998: 2009). Above all, she warns of the "major danger" in the Bank seeking to be "all things to all people".

Stiglitz brought the differences with the Fund to a head with increasingly provocative denunciations of the IMF for worsening the Asian and Russian crises in the late 1990s. Wolfensohn eventually fired Stiglitz, supposedly at the US Treasury's behest (Fine, 2001: 17), although he still receives numerous invi-tations to speak at Bank events.

The Bank's relationships with bilateral development agencies such as Britain's Department for International Development (DFID), the US Agency for International Development, and the EuropeAid office of the European Union are complicated by the twin imperatives of cooperation and competition. While the Bank is the world's largest single provider of development aid,[8] bilateral donors together provide more than 80 per cent of the world's aid. To enable the Bank to exercise managerial control over developing world governments, it needs to co-opt bilateral aid agencies into its discourse. At first glance, Wolfensohn's Bank achieved astonishing success in this regard. Only the Americans among the OECD countries retain a critical distance from the PRSP; all other countries have promised to align their aid to PRSP priorities. The Bank has also forged some genuinely close relationships with larger bilateral funders; Britain's Third Way government and the Netherlands both regularly offer Bank initiatives sub-stantial moral and financial support. On the other hand, the United States and

France in particular pay little or no attention to the Bank's wishes unless these coincide or interfere with their own strategic objectives.

As with the UN agencies, therefore, the Bank aims simultaneously to co-opt and to diminish its bilateral development partners. It rarely misses the opportunity to point out how much more "efficient" it would be if bilateral resources were channelled through the Bank, while seeking resources and endorsement for its programmes from those same bilateral agencies. The influencing process is bi-directional, however. European governments, in particular, have established a number of "trust funds" within the Bank, to be allocated for specific purposes reflecting those countries' development priorities. These funds generally encourage more inclusive policy making, and implicitly encourage the Bank to move towards greater emphasis on social objectives rather than neo-liberal economic restructuring.

As discussed, the Bank's relationship with the United States must be differentiated from those with other developed countries because of America's global dominance and its coolness towards multilateralism. The United States' confrontational foreign policy under President George W. Bush presents a major challenge to the Bank and to global managerialism more generally. The rupture in developed country consensus over American military adventurism is the first significant setback in the global governance agenda since the collapse of the Soviet bloc. The Bank has tried to satisfy the Americans by quickly manoeuvring itself into a coordinating role for reconstruction assistance in Iraq and Afghanistan, while repeatedly bemoaning the draining of development assistance funds into military and reconstruction purposes.

> Looking ahead, there is some concern that additional flows could be significantly influenced by donors' strategic agendas, such as the war on terrorism and conflict and reconstruction in Afghanistan and Iraq. It will be important to ensure that such strategic objectives do not crowd out development aid.
>
> (Development Committee, 2004: III.11.2)

The World Bank, inclusivity and the Third Way

The World Bank is not unique in pursuing a concertive managerialist style. This approach has become the defining contemporary governance mode. In the political sphere, the Third Way movement pioneered this "post-ideological" managerialism. This section of the chapter will explore some of the parallels and interconnection between the Bank and the Third Way, thus underlining this book's argument that global managerialism is a widespread phenomenon responding to the transnational elite's governance needs in an era of globalisation.

From its beginnings, Third Way discourse has embraced the globalisation project. Whether in Anthony Giddens's breathless account of the promise and perils of globalisation (Giddens, 2000), the Clintons' "global village" metaphor, or Tony Blair's "no country is immune from the massive change that globalisation brings" (Blair, 1998), the Third Way movement has consistently argued that globalisation is inevitable, that no country can stand in its way, and that we must quickly learn how to win in the global village. These perspectives mirror those of the World Bank.

I have already emphasised that global managerialism cannot be conflated with the pursuit of economic neo-liberalism. The "short, sharp shock" (Leys, 1985) of the ideologically fixated neo-liberalism of the 1980s – the structural adjustment and Thatcherite era – may have been "necessary" in bringing a rapid end to the welfare state approaches in the West and nationalist development strategies in developing countries. However, the popular premise of neo-liberalism, that the state in contemporary society can be "rolled back", is a myth; the supposedly natural operation of the hidden hand of the market is achieved only by constructing protective scaffolding that defines, denaturalises and domesticates the exchange process (Polanyi, 1944; Campbell and Lindberg, 1990). As the global economy transcends national boundaries, a transnational economic framework must be built, no matter the dominant economic paradigm. It does not follow that the framework is merely an iteration of that paradigm, as neo-Marxists like Cammack (2003a) seem to assume. While neo-liberalism needed global economic governance institutions to broaden its domain, it does not follow that global managers need neo-liberalism. Just as neo-liberalism has been found wanting as a motivating ideology in national contexts, so its narrow focus and appeal also hamper the development of global managerialism.

Thatcherism, emblematic of neo-liberal political practice, defined itself by what it was against and, in its derisive dismissal of "wets", prided itself on its opposition to shabby compromise. Mrs Thatcher's cachet was built on the premise that the possession of power and conviction was sufficient to justify action even in the jaws of ferocious opposition – "this lady is not for turning". But when this aggressive strategy became bogged down in various protracted struggles, such as over the poll tax, most of the British business community abandoned the Conservatives in favour of the Third Way's inclusive style. After many years in the political wilderness, the British Conservative Party has enjoyed a resurgence in support since 2005, but this rebound is directly tied to its shedding of Margaret Thatcher's and her acolytes' confrontational rhetoric in favour of the studied inclusiveness of new leader David Cameron, the "Prince of Hearts" (Walden, 2006). France's right-wing president Nicolas Sarkozy, elected in 2007, has also abandoned the traditional patrician étatism of his Gaullist predecessors in favour of open admiration for the "flexibility" of Blairism (Chrisafis, 2007), a move paralleled by the French left's candidate, Ségolène Royal (Arnold, 2006). The same phenomenon has been observed as far afield as Taiwan (Lee, 2005) and South Africa (De Beus and Koelble, 2001). There appears to be a generalised spread of Third Way concepts and governance style.

The Bank underwent a similar transition as it moved from structural adjustment to poverty reduction discourse: a change in communication styles of the organisation's leading personalities as stark as that between Thatcher and Blair. Anne Krueger, chief economist from 1982 to 1986, fulfilled the Bank's Thatcher role, while Wolfensohn's appointment in 1995 and Stiglitz's in 1997 epitomised the ascendance of Third Way discourse. Stiglitz and Wolfensohn are, of course, directly connected to the Third Way movement. Wolfensohn was well known as a "Wall Street Democrat" prior to his appointment to the Bank, was a Clinton nominee for the Bank presidency, and is a consistent donor to the Democratic Party and its various election causes, including Hillary Clinton's election campaigns in New York State. In the ten years between 1996 and 2006, Wolfensohn and his wife Elaine together donated over $100,000 to political causes, all but $2,000 of which went to the Democrats and liberal political campaigns. Prior to working at the Bank, Stiglitz was chair of President Clinton's Council of Economic Advisors. Stiglitz donated $24,100 to the US Democratic Party and its candidates between 2004 and 2006, and nothing to the Republicans.[9] In 2005, Wolfensohn was replaced as Bank president by Paul Wolfowitz, one of the architects of Bush's confrontationist foreign policy. However, Wolfowitz was poorly accepted by both the Bank's staff and developing country leaders, and had very little impact on the Bank's policy trajectory between 2005 and 2007. He was forced to resign in 2007 as a result of a scandal about preferential treatment for his companion and fellow World Bank employee Shaha Ali Riza. He was replaced by the less controversial former US trade negotiator Robert Zoellick (Adams and Clark, 2007).

Wolfensohn strongly supported Tony Blair's 2004–2005 "Commission for Africa", which called for the standard World Bank-endorsed mixture of increased development aid, dismantling of trade barriers, and improved African governance, the latter through ensuring compliance with international governance norms. Like Wolfensohn's poverty reduction approach, the Commission's report emphasises the need for a "comprehensive" development framework (the word comprehensive appears fifty-four times in the report), and the "coordination" of all the different development actors to ensure policy consistency (Commission for Africa, 2005). The Commission's work was directed by Nick Stern, the former Bank chief economist who has returned to the UK government.

Apart from the direct personal links between the Bank leadership and both American and British Third Way political leaders, there is a striking commonality of discourse. The key organising concepts that have been discussed in this chapter, such as participation, convening power and partnership, are used extensively in Third Way discourse. The managerialist and depoliticising character of New Labour's public management reforms has been noted by several writers. Like Cooke and Kothari (2001) on the World Bank, Maile and Hoggett (2001) emphasise New Labour's use of versions of participatory democracy as a "therapeutic" alternative to electoral democracy. Much as James Burnham had proposed in his 1941 *Managerial Revolution*, Third Way managerialist participation is aimed at "including" citizens and securing policy feedback: "*[p]olitical* processes are being reshaped as *management* processes" (Maile and Hoggett, 2001: 513; original italics). The public displays of participation arranged by Third Way governments are consciously or unconsciously manipulative, as is the Bank's anti-poverty programming discussed in the last chapter, because the core policy directions have always already been decided.

Third Way discourse is characterised by the accretion of apparently incompatible concepts, with no mediating mechanisms; McLennan (2004: 486) cites the examples,

> no rights without responsibilities, ecological modernization, philosophical conservatism, countering exclusion at the top as well at the bottom, equality of worth/opportunity but by no means equality of outcome, the social investment state, positive welfare, cosmopolitan nation, responsible capitalism, flexicurity, and so on.

There is a remarkable similarity, of course, with the World Bank in its poverty phase, where poverty reduction plans equally promised competition and security, free trade and support for small producers, marketisation of public utilities and universal coverage, etc.

New Labour and the World Bank share a fondness for "consultation" in which marketing and dialogue are collapsed into a single process. At the Bank, consultation functions are located within the External Affairs vice-presidency, with dialogue managed by the Bank's marketing personnel. Consultation processes are used to distribute and market Bank positions, a strategy also used by New Labour, where for example the 2004 "Big Conversation" not only helped gauge party activists' disaffection with Labour leaders over the Iraq war, but also served as a vehicle to market a new "get tough" policy on nuisance public housing tenants (Travis, 2004: 1).

Ideology and sociology of the new managerialism

At its most cynical, the Third Way approach thus involves political manoeuvres, including marketing masquerading as dialogue, and the creation of a "big tent" that allows opponents to be marginalised or, better still, harnessed to carry out some part of the agenda. Whatever the motivation, however, Third Way thinking at the national and transnational level has had a substantial impact on the character of democratic debate. Fairclough describes the advent of Third Wayism as the "closure of political discourse" through the "hybridisation" of left and right perspectives (2001: 210). The closure that is achieved is fundamentally unsatisfactory, however: the different perspectives that are brought together are never sorted, analysed, and accepted or rejected. For Fairclough and other critical realists, there *is* a deep structure underlying this apparently incoherent juxtaposition of political perspectives: the capitalist neo-liberal agenda. From their perspective, which parallels Fine's (2002) and Cammack's (2003a) analysis of the Poverty Bank, the Third Way is little more than a sophisticated or smoother version of neo-liberalism. Even Stuart Hall, who was responsible for some of the early Third Way theorising, argues that, "[t]here is a *dominant strategy or logic* at work here, and fundamentally it is *neo-liberal* in character" (Hall, 2003: 13; original italics).

In contrast to this critical realist position, I propose that the specificity of Third Way and Poverty Bank discourse is precisely its absence of deeper meaning. Jodi Dean (2005: 56) implies the same of what she calls the era of "communicative capitalism":

> Matters aren't represented – they don't stand for something beyond themselves. They are simply treated in all their particularity, as specific issues to be addressed therapeutically, juridically, spectacularly or disciplinarily rather than being treated as elements of larger signifying chains or political formations.

The managerialist objective is *not to waste precious time* arguing about philosophy, but *to resolve the problem*. There is a continuity between this approach and that of the "old" managerialism. Burnham's *Managerial Revolution* (1941) emphasised the superior capacity of managerial society to resolve intractable human problems: unemployment could be solved in five years at most, he asserted, if only the right technical approach could be adopted. Likewise, Third Way and Poverty Bank discourse demands universal enrolment in a comprehensive, problem-solving action plan. Paradoxically, policy content is often thin, or contradictory, but there is no room for divergence in the global managerial order.

An example of how the World Bank enforces its policy whether or not it is desirable is its ranking of countries according to what it calls "governance indicators". These indicators are simply a measure of the extent to which countries comply with "current thinking" (Kaufmann *et al.*, 2006). Current thinking is encapsulated in the integration of thirty-one measures developed by a range of international elite institutions ranging from development banks to private sector risk ratings agencies, conservative thinktanks, Ivy League universities and international NGOs (one measure from the French NGO Reporters without Borders, and three from the American government-sponsored Freedom House). The results are as a leftist cynic would expect: Cuba, with a life expectancy of 76 and a child mortality ratio of 7/1000, scores a governance rating of 19 out of 100. Senegal, with a life expectancy of 52 and a child mortality rate of 67/1000, scores 50 for governance (see Figure 4.3). These governance measures are used as a basis for determining eligibility for World Bank funding (though Cuba is in any event ineligible as one of the few non-members of the Bank). New Labour has introduced a parallel plethora of measures to assess "performance" of British public entities, from local government to the different levels of the education system; likewise, these involve a high level of disciplinarity, although typically the life cycle of each set of targets is not yet exhausted before a newer and more elaborate measurement regimen is introduced (Cochrane, 2000). Summarising, while the policy content of both national and global managerialist discourse is highly questionable, adherence is required, and those who place themselves outside the measured orthodoxy will, at best, be excluded from resources.

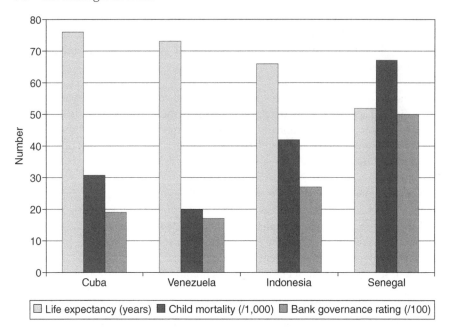

Figure 4.3 World Bank governance indicators: inversely correlated with human life indicators (source: http://info.worldbank.org/governance/kkz2005/govmap.asp).

In order to explain this phenomenon, it is necessary to go beyond both presenting and "deep structural" ideology and look at the sociology of this new managerialism. As Laughlin (2004: 20) points out, the end of the welfare state era in the 1960s coincided with the decline of traditional social classes, and the emergence of individualised, aspirational, consumerist society. The Thatcherite/structural adjustment period could be viewed either as the last revenge of traditional capitalist rule against the eroding bastions of socialism or as a transitional governance phase. Whichever way it is viewed, Fordism, developmentalism, and other collectivist bases for social organisation were destroyed (Aglietta, 1997). The social tensions unleashed during this period were, however, destabilising, and necessarily short term. It is emblematic of the shifting winds that Francis Fukuyama, the triumphalist right-wing ideologue of *The End of History* (1989), is now a virulent critic of neoconservatism and an advocate of managerialist "soft power" (Fukuyama, 2006).

The dissolution of the traditional class-based left and its re-emergence in various postmodern forms reflects the disintegration of economic class-based social stratification and a tendency towards multiple identifications centred on a variety of what Laclau and Mouffe (1985) call "nodal points", including Islam, gay rights, feminism, etc. Those critical thinkers who remain wedded to the ultimate primacy of the economic motor are restricted to historical romanticism leavened by ever rarer examples of contemporary "real class struggle" in action.

However, poststructuralists like Laclau and his supporters in CMS are wilfully blind in ignoring sociological developments on the other side of the barricades, a subject to which this book aims to make a modest but nonetheless distinctive contribution.

The fact that the working class is no longer a viable unified force does not mean that coherent elites no longer exist. Globalisation has certainly transformed the nature of elites, who are now increasingly internationalised. Further, as has been discussed, in Europe and further afield, class struggle neoconservatism has been replaced by the managed consensual approach of the Third Way. The impact of the earlier neo-liberal economic restructuring resulted not so much in rolling back the state, as the neo-liberals had promised, but rather in the intertwining of the state with the private sector. The privatisation of public utilities, the replacement of state capital financing with private finance arrangements, and the importation of private consultants' expertise (Craig, 2006) all result in extremely complex organisational interconnections, which naturally translate into extensive personal elite networks inside and across national boundaries (Wedel, 2004). The Third Way celebrates breaking down the traditional separation between government and private business (Bevir, 2005). Relationships that would have been considered improper under the rules of the old Weberian bureaucracy are now seen as innovative. Given that numerous negative evaluations have been made of the cost-benefits of the public–private partnerships, the motivation for such arrangements must be found outside objective economics. Cross-sectoral partnerships, like the discourses of participation, the subversion of political difference, and the marginalisation of opposition, are indicators and practices of a new managerial order. Global managerialism, as represented by the Third Way political movement and the World Bank's poverty reduction initiatives, represents a generalised shift away from ideology-driven claims to power. Authority in global managerialism rests upon the ability to hegemonise discursive space.

Conclusion

This chapter has described the Bank's managerial technologies, the corporate culturism that inculcates faith in the organisation's civilising mission and makes possible the exercise of convening power to enlist other organisations in the Bank's globalising projects. It has discussed how "participation" enlists participants in their own management, a corollary of the process of self-management uncovered by CMS. The Bank's managerialist discourse colonises and technologises commonsense terms such as "community" and renders development inaccessible to its recipients without its own professional mediation. CMS-inspired analysis has been used in this chapter to explain the Bank's internal and external dynamics. These CMS insights are applied beyond internal organisational life, reconnecting organisational theory with exploration and understanding of broader social structure.

The Bank is located within the global neighbourhood, and this chapter has shown how it alternately competes and collaborates with other transnational and development institutions to further a dominant position within the globalised terrain. The Bank's vision for an inclusive managerial system is discussed in detail in the next chapter, which also provides concrete examples of the Bank's efforts to incorporate international civil society into its agenda.

The chapter then explored the organic links between the Bank's global managerial discourse and the Third Way political movement. New managerialism, like its "old" ancestors, seeks to sublimate difference through construction of a "non-political", technical agenda to which all but "extremists" should subscribe. The World Bank's global managers administered structural adjustment programmes, and Third Way political leaders continued Thatcherite economic policies, necessary elements in definitively ending the "old class politics" and thus paving the way for a "post-ideological" order. However, stable managerial rule is founded on incorporation rather than direct confrontation, and thus the Bank is more naturally an ally of Third Way governments than those that privilege neo-liberal or neoconservative ideology, such as the George W. Bush administration. Finally, this chapter discussed new managerialism as a sociological phenomenon, presenting the rise of an elite unified in its predilection for, and benefits from, the management of transnational social and economic space.

5   The Bank, global social policy and civil society

Previous chapters described the broad lines of the World Bank's historical and ideological development, including its shift during the 1990s towards comprehensive poverty reduction, heralding a more expansive, comprehensive and intrusive version of global managerialism. This chapter traces contemporary global managerialism from theory into practice. The first section discusses the transnational elite thinking that lies behind the Bank's decision to build an alliance with civil society. The chapter then goes on to examine the Bank's overtures towards NGOs, as well NGO leaders' motivations for accepting an alliance with the Bank. The final sections of the chapter examine the Bank–global civil society alliance in action in the education sphere, through two case studies on the implementation of the MDG education initiative in Niger and in India. These case studies provide insight into the gap between the rhetoric of participation as pronounced through Bank–international NGO alliances at headquarters, and the reality of token or non-existent participation on the ground in the developing world.

The Bank, global managerialism, democracy and civil society

The World Bank plays a pivotal role in building a global managerial elite into a cohesive force. Pareto and Mosca's elite theory, discussed in Chapter 1 above, emphasises the importance to a ruling elite of recruiting new blood, as a means both to incorporate opposition and to rejuvenate and re-energise. In the past two decades, the "Third Sector" or "civil society" has emerged as a global power and its leaders have been incorporated into a variety of elite circles. The democratic legitimacy provided by civil society participation permits the Bank to extend its policy governance agenda far beyond its original economic brief.

The Cold War was portrayed in the West as a battle between democracy and totalitarianism, and although the democratic imperative in developing countries could be temporarily sacrificed on the altar of strategic necessity, once "democracy triumphed" (Reagan, 1989), the New World Order had to be built in the image of democracy. The new situation presented global managerialism with an opportunity to expand its sway over new terrain in the East, while it also made the position of developing and transitional country elites more precarious.

In order to participate in the new order, they had to display some plausible version of democracy, while simultaneously restructuring their economies and national class systems into the preferred model. The participatory techniques which the Bank promotes, as discussed in Chapter 4 above, are at once a toolkit for national elites to manufacture "democratic" consent for implementing the Bank's agenda, and a vehicle enabling the Bank to claim democratic legitimacy for its partnership with "civil society".

Burnham's (1941) prescient observation that limited or managed democracy would be more functional to developed managerialism than authoritarian rule is even more crucial in the era of global managerialism. The IFIs' transnational managerial agenda requires legitimation to justify global policy setting, counter radical critique, discipline potentially errant national elites, and further their institutionalisation as a cornerstone of global governance. Key tools in this legitimation are the construction of "participatory democracy" as the privileged version of democracy and the forging of an elite alliance with civil society to hegemonise this perspective.

While Wright Mills (1957) predicted the narrowing of the power elite into an ever smaller, more powerful, and closely defined group, CMS theorists have shown that consensual hegemony is built upon the absorption of managerial ideas into the general population's worldview, involving colonisation of organisational culture and blurred distinctions between managers and workers. It was posited earlier that these processes spill into the broader social arena. Thus, it was seen in Chapter 4 above that the World Bank's internal life includes extensive goal and role socialisation, and that this provides a foundation for its hegemony building in the transnational arena, achieved through building relationship, with state and quasi-state actors as well as with other transnational institutions and corporations. Effective hegemonisation of the broader social arena also requires at least the acquiescence of "the masses". This is achieved, formally, in liberal democratic-style societies through representative democracy, but this is only the final exercise in a legitimation process built on the hegemonic articulation of civil society. Thus, contrary to Wright Mills's predictions, in the global era civil society is not squeezed out, but instead plays a key role in endorsing or destabilising consensual elite rule within a (quasi) democratic framework. To construct a stable global order, elements of civil society leadership join with private sector leaders and senior bureaucrats from national governments and transnational institutions to form a global elite. In the next few pages I discuss how transnational elite thinkers conceptualise the cross-sectoral global governance partnership, and the steps taken by the World Bank to incorporate civil society leaders in such an alliance.

In the mid-1990s, a Yale-educated German researcher and consultant, Wolfgang Reinicke, began exploring and promoting the idea of "global governance without government", underpinned by conscious elite networks drawn from transnational institutions, national governments, business and civil society (Reinicke, 1997, 1998). Reinicke argues that these "global public policy networks" already exist in nascent form, and their role should be extended and formalised. Reinicke embodies this transnational cross-sectoralism; he has been a senior bureaucrat with the World Bank, a research fellow at the liberal American policy institute the Brookings Institution, an associate of a Canadian quasi-government international development thinktank,[1] and in 2007 heads the Germany-based non-profit thinktank, the Global Public Policy Institute, as well as a private company based in Switzerland.[2] Reinicke has assiduously used his various affiliations as channels to refine, rework and recommend his model to international financial institutions (Reinicke, 1996), elite networks (Reinicke, 1999), the United Nations (Reinicke and Witte, 2005), bilateral development agencies (Reinicke and Deng, 2000), civil society (Reinicke, 2004) and the private sector (Reinicke, 1996).

While Reinicke's work has been influential within relatively restrained international policy circles, Jean-François Rischard, a former World Bank colleague, has packaged an almost identical message and policy prescription in a more populist form. Rischard, a Luxemburg-born lawyer and former investment banker, worked for the World Bank for twenty-five years, rising to become European vice-president from 1998 to 2005 and its leading ideologist for the new global governance system. In *High Noon*, a 2002 bestseller, Rischard lists twenty global challenges not being adequately addressed by the current international system, and proposes a governance system (which he insists is not "global government") based on elite networks drawn from "knowledgeable" government bureaucracies, global business, and the NGO sector:

> to create for each of these twenty issues a global issues network … there would be people from three parties, government officials that really know the issue well … the second party that would bring in knowledgeable people from the private sector, big companies that know all the ins and outs … the third group of people would come from knowledgeable NGOs, the IUCN, the World Wildlife Fund, a lot of these big NGOs and networks of NGOs that have a lot of knowledge.
>
> (Rischard, 2002a)

Rischard asserts that the World Bank must take the lead in constructing this new system because the United Nations is "tanking" and other "old style" institutions such as "parliamentarians" are standing in the way, because, "their natural base is selfishly territorial" (Rischard, 2002a; 2004). Under Bank leadership, networks of top government officials, big business and big NGOs will analyse problems, and design and enforce solutions:

> These three parties would sit together and would give birth to a detailed analysis of the problem … what are the norms and standards we should impose on nation states, companies and all other players … the product of these networks would be very detailed norms and standards … . In a third stage these networks would become ratings agencies, essentially producing ratings tables of countries.
>
> (Rischard, 2002a)

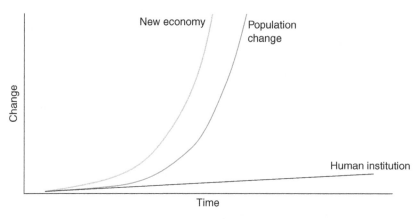

Figure 5.1 The growing global governance gap (source: Rischard (2001)).

Rischard's scheme is striking in its hubris. One reviewer describes it as "a completely non-accountable government-by-committee model" (Michael, 2002: 388). *High Noon* distils each of the twenty global problems – including issues as complex as education, poverty, and global warming – into a five-page discussion. Unverifiable and contestable assertions are cloaked in a pseudo-authoritative graphic format (see Figure 5.1).

Despite its shallow analysis, *High Noon* collected celebrity endorsements from a who's who of the global elite in the three networks of government bureaucracy (Pascal Lamy, the European trade commissioner), business (the CEOs of the *International Herald Tribune*, 3M and Motorola) and "global civil society". The chief executives of Civicus ("the world alliance for citizen participation"), Accion International and ActionAid all offered fulsome praise. Salil Shetty, then ActionAid CEO, commented that:

> Rischard's message is simple and compelling: We know what needs to be done to have a world with shared prosperity and a sustainable future. Can we get our act together to govern our affairs better in the new global context?[3]

The Rischardian elite networks are interlinked. As Wright Mills noted, business and global (and national) financial institutions have long exchanged personnel, but multilateral agencies now seek to incorporate the NGO elite. In 2004, Shetty took up a senior UN position coordinating the Millennium Development Goals, while Civicus is part-financed by the World Bank (Civicus, 2003: 26), and its CEO was a 2003 World Bank "Presidential Fellow".

World Bank engagement with civil society dates back several decades but became strategically important only in the 1990s. The overt rationale was the Bank's self-proclaimed shift away from the assertion of technical superiority ("expert stance") and towards participatory development, as detailed in Chapter 4 above. This new engagement coincided with the rise of Third Way political movements in the United States and the United Kingdom, and with the growing appeal of communitarian ideas, particularly those developed by Harvard University's Robert Putnam (1995).

Putnam's social capital theory argues that wealthy and healthy societies are built not only on financial and human capital, as neo-liberals claim, but also on largely intangible qualities of intra-societal networking, the sum total of which is described as social capital. While Bourdieu had already used this term, Putnam's version differs in several respects, notably in its isolation from any overall model of power in society, and its assumption that social capital is a simple social good (Murphy, 2003). These lacunae allow Putnam's theory to underpin the Bank's increasingly interventionist social capital-building development policy agenda, while excusing its avoidance of distributional issues.

The Bank's civil society work has expanded rapidly. In 2003, the organisation had approximately 130 experts working on civil society issues, including forty based in the Washington headquarters and the rest spread around seventy country offices. By 2004, President Wolfensohn claimed the Bank had 220 civil society specialists.[4] The organisation has a policy note on engagement with civil society,[5] encouraging staff to engage with civil society, and identifying information sharing, policy dialogue and operational collaboration as the three broad areas for contact (World Bank, 2000b). The document cautions, however, that many NGOs have "limited expertise in macro or specific economic issues", and its suggestions for NGO involvement in economic policy making are aimed at securing a veneer of participatory legitimacy: "During the preparation of the Zimbabwe country economic memorandum, a participating NGO helped to organize field visits and ensured that the mission had direct contact with the rural poor".

In 2003, the Bank launched an internal and external consultation on its relationship with civil society (World Bank, 2003). In its background paper, the Bank explains its vision of civil society and the value of engagement that has grown out of lessons learned about "the development effectiveness, poverty reduction, and risk management benefits of participation" (2003: ii). While theoretically acknowledging the distinction between broader civil society and formal non-governmental organisations, in practice the Bank conflates the two and constitutes collaborations with NGOs as "working with civil society". The main areas proposed for collaboration are facilitation, consultation and dialogue, and partnership. Facilitation, which means "encouraging" governments to work through civil society, has replaced "information-sharing" from the policy note mentioned above (World Bank, 2000b). The shift towards an increasingly proactive and interventionist comportment in developing countries is theorised as a reflection of "new models of public–private cooperation, transparency and oversight that give a greater role to CSOs in public life" (World Bank, 2003: 17), underlining NGOs' importance as vehicles for asserting global governance. This is further confirmation of the hypothesis put forward in Chapter 1 above on the growth of intrusive, evangelical global managerialism, this time through the medium of civil society.

As mentioned in the preceding chapter, the Bank's paper assumes developing country state incapacity, asserting that its work with civil society is "essential" if developing countries are to achieve the Millennium Development Goals, "promoting public consensus and local ownership for reforms", ensuring national state "accountability and transparency", and "helping to ensure that government funds are focused on citizens' needs, and are actually spent on the programs for which they were intended" (2003: 4, 7, 17). The Bank claims that involvement with NGOs has also encouraged it to "enhance the Heavily Indebted Poor Countries (HIPC) framework and link debt relief to countries' poverty reduction strategies". NGOs are thus enlisted to justify the Bank's imposition of a standardised economic and social programme on the poorest developing countries.

The paper proposes that additional Bank resources be channelled to civil society organisations (CSOs), particularly for service delivery in the light of state shrinkage (often caused by Bank-imposed structural adjustment programmes):

> CSOs have become important channels for delivery of social services and implementation of other development programs, especially in areas where government capacity is weak or non-existent. Economic and fiscal policy reforms in many countries have led to decentralization or even privatization of social service delivery, which can result in a larger role for CSOs.
>
> (2003: 16)

Engagement with civil society can provide "early warning" of potential hot spots of agitation that may "use up extensive Bank resources and ... endanger operations". Early warning will allow experienced Bank external affairs and civil society teams to "manage early and sustained dialogue" (2003: 32). The potential for political incorporation of civil society organisations through funding goes unspoken. The report does, however, imply that the Bank should try to drive a wedge between "radical" and "constructive" Bank critics: "[o]ften it is the analyses by generally constructive Bank critics which provide much of the intellectual credence to the messages carried by the more radical movements" (2003: 23). Finally, the report notes but implicitly rejects concerns that the growth of civil society political power can undermine traditional representative democracy.

The report omits one frequently practised Bank strategy: the direct creation and spinning-off of nominally independent organisations in which the Bank retains control through funding, hosting and/or staffing, ensuring their support for its work. Recent examples include the Development Gateway, a development information portal, and the Parliamentary Network on the World Bank. The Development Gateway was discussed in the previous chapter. The Parliamentary Network brings together parliamentarians interested in development issues. Despite its claim to provide a "critical eye" on the international financial institutions, its main purpose is to mobilise parliamentarians in favour of Bank initiatives, and specifically to pressure developed country governments to support the Bank's programmes. The organisation claims to be independent but its headquarters are at the World Bank's Paris office and a Bank staff member is listed as its contact person (Wilks, 2001; O'Brien *et al.*, 2000: 46; Rowden and Icama, 2004: 39).

Civil society responses to the Bank

Ann Hudock, a former senior USAID official now with a large Washington-based NGO, is one of an increasing number of civil society leaders participating in and simultaneously criticising Bank activities (see also Clark, 1998, 2003a). Hudock finds the Bank's interaction with civil society positive but inadequate. The Bank offers NGOs opportunities for collaboration with governments, resources for development projects, "information relevant to development strategies", and "impetus for governments to support a more enabling environment for NGO work" (Hudock, 1999: 49). She criticises, however, the Bank's tendency to engage southern NGOs as a substitute for dealing with genuinely grassroots civil society. The Bank's financial weight tends to distort relationships: "southern NGOs' responsiveness to donors rather than grassroots groups is the greatest threat to southern NGOs' ability to act as effective intermediaries, and to empower grassroots groups as part of civil society development" (Hudock, 1999: 86). Further, while the Bank engages NGOs in policy discussions, how significantly it is prepared to change its policies based on those discussions is questionable.

Overall, Hudock supports what Steve Commins, an American NGO executive who later moved to the Bank, calls a policy of "critical engagement" (1999, 57). Despite acknowledging power imbalances between the Bank and (especially, its southern) civil society partners, she agrees with key features of the Bank's analysis, including structural adjustment and minimal respect for national governments:

> NGOs are uniquely positioned to facilitate the development of a global civil society in which state behaviour becomes less central to collective choice. Most bilateral donors have realized that their development assistance has in some cases been thwarted by an inefficient and corrupt state, one which was overly involved in its economy.
>
> (1999: 58)

Hudock views southern NGOs as a direct alternative to governments as providers of employment to "displaced, educated, middle-class professionals. This may ease the burden of structural adjustment programs in which civil servants are made redundant" (1999: 89–90).

An apparently more critical perspective is offered by a number of northern campaigning NGOs, whose perspectives are drawn from radical developmentalism. These groups include the World Development Movement, as well as organisations like the Bretton Woods Project that focus on "watching" multilateral institutions. Watch organisations often collaborate with more traditional, service-oriented NGOs; for example, the Bretton Woods Project is based in ActionAid's London office.

Even these campaigning NGOs share some core principles with the Bank, including the development–underdevelopment paradigm, the need for "capacity-building" in the Third World, and above all the importance of increasing "aid". While they often disagree with the Bank on economic policy and on loan conditionality, they tend to support governance conditionality. Thus, the Bretton Woods Project argued that a "silver lining" to the 2005 appointment of Paul Wolfowitz was that he "may take a more principled stance on lending to autocratic regimes" (Bretton Woods Project, 2005: 1). Campaigning NGOs expend much of their energy on projects to increase the "accountability" of the IFIs; the accountability sought is primarily to organised civil society.

O'Brien *et al.* (2000), who focus on World Bank interactions with the women's movements and environmental social movements, also represent this more radical civil society perspective. In a chapter on women's movements, Anne-Marie Goetz (a University of Sussex development academic who later went on to assume a senior position with the UN women's agency, UNIFEM) claims that "[w]omen's movements project a vision of a new social order which is more radical than the social change projects of other 'new' social movements globally, in that the gender equality which feminists propose would fundamentally change current approaches to social organization" (O'Brien *et al.*, 2000: 32). Like Hudock, Goetz remarks that "there is increasing recognition of the 'comparative advantage' exercised by NGOs over state bureaucracies in delivering development resources to the poor", while acknowledging that this creates the potential for incorporation by the Bank of southern NGOs into a harmless service role (O'Brien *et al.*, 2000: 28, 58). Goetz is similarly conflicted about the tactic of some southern women's NGOs which use their connections with Washington-based NGOs to persuade the Bank to ensure "policy changes are imposed on Southern governments", citing one "positive example" of this practice from Mexico, while acknowledging the potential that this could, "undermine democratic or potentially democratic dynamics locally" (2000: 61, 62).

In his chapter on environmental NGOs and the Bank, Williams ties growing Bank/civil society engagement directly to a decline in the role of the state under neo-liberalism, noting that this process "shifts the relations between the international organization, governments, and civil society" (O'Brien *et al.*, 2000: 134). Williams repeats Goetz's conditional endorsement of civil society organisations using influence on the Bank to impose policies such as "environmental standards in development and trade" even when pursued "in opposition to the interests of Third World governments"; this can be justifiable because "it is a moot point whether the governments are truly representative of their peoples", a somewhat ironic perspective given Goetz's acknowledgement that (at least women's) NGOs "tend to lack a broad base of public sympathy – or a broad constituency" (2000: 157, 33).

In their joint summary, O'Brien *et al.* acknowledge that engagement in the Bank policy development process requires at least acceptance of "the general goal of liberalization" and that "the institutions' generalised principles of conduct are subject to debate, but relatively immune from revision" (2000: 224, 209). Civil society engagement with the Bank is nevertheless appropriate, because of the shift towards "complex multilateralism" in which "governance of the global economy cannot rest solely on an international – that is, inter-state foundation" (2000: 217). O'Brien *et al.* present the motivations of "global social movements" as entirely altruistic, seeking "some form of social protection and policy reorientation so that costs are not borne primarily by the weakest members of society" (2000: 219). They do not acknowledge the possibility, pre-figured in institutional theory, that NGOs operate from individual and organisational vested interests, which might encourage collaboration with the Bank even while this subverts the organisations' formal mandate (Selznick, 1949: 10–12).

A few NGOs have remarked that the Bank's fundamental economic policies are rarely open for discussion, and have questioned whether NGO involvement in Bank participatory exercises in setting poverty reduction strategies might undermine "representative democratic structures, imperfect as they may be": "The role of CSOs in the PRSP process has raised important new questions such as, What role should civil society play in policy formulation in relation to parliamentarians, local governments and national government agencies" (Rowden and Icama, 2004: 38–39).

A study sponsored by the German bilateral development agency GTZ noted that during the development of the World Bank's poverty reduction strategy papers, "the donor community initially focused entirely on the civil societies of the countries" and that a "one-sided concentration on civil society actors can undermine the legitimate basis of the parliaments" (Eberlei and Henn, 2003: 27).

There is strong resistance to this message in the NGO community; Civicus's Secretary General Kumi Naidoo "vehemently reject[s]" the claim that "citizen activism threatens to undermine democratic systems by 'short-circuiting' estab-lished procedures for democratic decision-making" (2003). He presents two main responses to criticism of lack of civil society accountability. The first is what he calls "perform or perish": civil society organisations are funded on a voluntary basis, and will fail through lack of resources if they do not perform adequately. Second, civil society organisations have established self-regulation mechanisms, disclosure and public reporting standards, and usually have volun-teer governing boards, all assuring accountability (Naidoo, 2003a).

Naidoo's argument for market accountability has several weaknesses. If civil society organisations are really only accountable to their financiers, they do not differ in any important respects from private corporations, and therefore could hardly demand the status of a separate and privileged organisational category. Further, in the development field, Naidoo's "market" for "purchasing" NGO activity is heavily skewed towards institutions, and specifically towards developed country governments. It is naïve to imply, as does Naidoo, that gov-ernments support NGOs only for the betterment of humanity and never to temper policy criticism (for example, of the poverty and dislocation caused by structural adjustment). Even if the government funder's reasons for supporting an NGO are entirely noble, that support still impacts the NGO's independence (Cooley and Ron, 2002). Given Naidoo's proposition that NGOs should also assume "quasi-regulatory or watchdog functions" vis-à-vis national and trans-national governance institutions from which they are likely to receive direct or indirect financial support, the market-driven "perform or perish" accountability mechanism is fated to degenerate into a system of elite interdependence and popular unaccountability, as seen in Rischard's "networks of global governance" model that Naidoo warmly praises.

Naidoo's second argument for NGO accountability through "[s]elf-regulation mechanisms" is also problematic. Few NGOs are actually enrolled in such voluntary schemes, and from Naidoo's comments about Bank accountability, it is clear that he would not consider World Bank self-regulation as an adequate substitute for independent (and popular) accountability; the same argument should apply to the NGO sector.

Naidoo's accountability discourse underscores the tensions between "representative" and "participatory" democracy. While nodding in the direction of the complementarity of the two, he makes sweeping criticisms of representative democracy: "the meaningful interface between citizens and the elected is minimal between election periods", "the [political] parties themselves are characterized by a lack of internal democracy or fail to address issues that citizens believe are important", and "the influence of monied interests in many political systems is also turning citizens away from traditional engagement in favour of new forms of participation". In presenting "participatory democracy" as an alternative to representative democracy, Naidoo offers the Bank a cherished fig-leaf. Through participatory processes involving civil society, it can redeem itself not only as a global democratic force, but also as representative of a higher form of democracy than that of elected national officials. Significantly, none of Naidoo's proposals for increasing Bank accountability includes instituting or expanding accountability to *any* elected institutions.

Global managerialism in action: education policy

The Bank's convening capacity to mobilise funds and partnerships allows it to capture other organisations' initiatives, shaping them to its own agenda. As noted in Chapter 4 above, the Bank has hijacked the broad seven-point agenda of UNESCO's Education for All (EFA) initiative, intended to increase access to education at all levels (UNESCO, 2000), and has distilled it into a narrow basic education programme.

One vehicle for achieving the Bank's education objectives has been the Fast Track Initiative (FTI), a project to recruit countries prepared to implement a global set of conditionalities, described as "policy benchmarks" or "indicative framework", in return for the promise of more basic education funding. FTI candidates, including Niger which will be discussed in the first case study, were required to prepare "credible" national plans to achieve universal primary education by 2015. The plans had to adhere to a rigid set of quantitative conditions, including set ratios of teachers' salaries to average salary levels, a pupil–teacher ratio of 40:1, 50 per cent of education spending to be allocated to the primary level, education spending to be 20 per cent of overall government spending, and – apparently unrelated to education policy – the restriction of overall government spending to between 14 per cent and 18 per cent of GDP (Development Committee, 2004: 3).[6] Initially, countries were "selected" by the Bank and Fund as having suitable policies that would "benefit" from the FTI, although it was eventually decided that participation should be self-selecting. Up to forty countries are expected to sign up, but they will all have to be "formally endorsed for incremental financial support". Through Education for All and FTI, the Bank has co-opted many international NGOs via an umbrella group called the Global Campaign for Education, which includes as key members Oxfam and the international teachers' trade union Education International (EI). EI launched the Fast Track Initiative together with the Bank (Wolfensohn and van Leeuwen, 2000).

The second case study on universal education presents a more subtle example of global managerialism and the influence of the Bank than that of Niger. India's commitment to universal basic education derives from the initial UNESCO-organised conference in 1990. India has not signed up to the Fast Track Initiative, and although its universal basic education programme is financed through Bank loans and other bilateral donors, this external influence has been heavily downplayed by the Indian government. Nevertheless, the programme follows the same model as in Africa, including the wholesale deprofessionalisation of teachers, and the manipulation of community participation to legitimise the top-down imposition of a programme whose outcomes remain questionable. The Indian case represents a genuine managerialist partnership between the Bank and national government policy setters.

Niger – at the sharp end of global managerialism

O'Brien *et al.* note that when "[m]uch of the policy dialogue with NGOs is carried out informally, e.g., the Tuesday Group meetings", southern NGOs are by definition excluded (2000: 134). The following case study from Niger explores this process in practice, showing how the Bank's centralised policy development framework inexorably percolates down to the implementation level, blending with "hard budget constraint" and congealing into rigid prescriptions preventing meaningful dialogue and precluding grassroots civil society participation in policy development.

Niger, a former French colony located in West Africa on the fringes of the Sahara, is one of the poorest countries on earth – it is ranked bottom of the United Nations' Human Development Index. Niger scores near the low end of every indicator including life expectancy and per capita purchasing power, but what brings it to the lowest extremity of the development scale is its education performance. In 2001, its adult literacy rate of 16.5 per cent was half that of any other country. Only 30 per cent of primary school age children and only one in twenty secondary school age children were in school, the latter a decline from ten years previously. In 2001, Niger spent 2.7 per cent of its meagre GDP on education – about $7 per capita – again a decline from ten years earlier.

It is no surprise, therefore, that education is a high priority in both the country's poverty reduction strategy (Government of Niger, 2002) and the World Bank's country assistance strategy (2003a). The Bank has provided several low-interest loans during the past decade to support expanding basic education, which has undoubtedly helped to improve primary school enrolment since 1990. But, despite higher enrolment, Niger lags even further behind other countries than it did in 1990 (UNDP, 2004: 273), and the resource transfer away from secondary education has significantly worsened that sector's performance.

The Bank assumes poor educational outcomes are the result of weak national education policies, rather than simple shortage of resources or the lingering effects of colonisation. For example, at independence in 1960, Niger's primary school enrolment rate was 2 per cent and that year only four students in the country graduated from secondary school (Murphy, 2003a: 11). For the Bank's global managers, "attainment of universal primary completion depends even more crucially on education system reform than on incremental financing" (Bruns *et al.*, 2003: 9). In Francophone West Africa, "the main problem is the high unit cost for education", a problem whose only solution is "a reduction in the average salary levels" of teachers (Mingat, 2002: 7–9). The Bank's strategy is to pressure West African governments into recruiting large numbers of young graduates at one-third the salary levels of permanent teachers, with neither benefits nor job security. In October 2000, the Bank took the unusual step of convening six Sahelian region heads of state to pressure them to introduce a contingent teacher scheme. Mingat and Tan took as proof that teacher salaries were too high that when Burkina Faso hired "assistant teachers" at lower salaries than fully qualified teachers, it received 18,000 applications for 800 positions, including many "with much more education than was required", while Senegal received twenty-eight applications for each available position in a new category of "volunteer" teacher at one-third the salary of a regular teacher (Mingat and Tan, 1998: 41).[7] They ignored in their equations that – in large measure due to World Bank-mandated structural adjustment measures – there were no jobs even for highly qualified youth, who thus had no choice but to work at near-starvation wages.

Even some Bank staff dismissed the policy of drastically reducing teacher salaries as a "simplistic" solution to an institutionally embedded problem that should be addressed on a country-by-country basis (Zymelman and DeStefano, 1989: 49). UNICEF researchers warned that: "expansion of access has involved strategies which could pose a threat to quality. Where the quality of educational provision has deteriorated seriously, enrolment levels have tended to decline, demonstrating the inextricable relationship between quality and access" (Mehrotra and Buckland, 1998: 18).

Idi Abdou has never heard of Education International or of the Global Campaign for Education, although as the secretary general of UNAVES, the association of Nigerien secondary school "volunteer" teachers, he represents one of the key civil society stakeholders in the country's education sector. His association's head-quarters are in a bare one-room cement structure on a dirt side street of a down-scale neighbourhood in Niamey, Niger's capital. Despite the inauspicious surroundings, the interview is regularly punctuated by visitors from across Niger, who come to report on the situation in their region. At the time of the interview, UNAVES was leading an industrial action in which teachers refused to report students' grades, an action the government later thwarted by giving all the students pass marks (Adamu, 2004).

Abdou has worked as a contract teacher in secondary schools for the past ten years, and apart from a short hiatus has been secretary general of UNAVES since its formation in 1996. The association has 2,288 members, accounting for 60 per cent of all the secondary teachers in the country. The secondary school *volontaires* earn $100 a month, while their counterparts in primary schools only make $70. In comparison, the starting monthly salary for a secondary school teacher with regular status is $250 per month and the average teacher would earn between $300 and $400. Abdou says it is impossible to live on $100 a month:

> In Niamey the rent is a minimum $30 a month. It will cost you $30 to get to and from the school you are working at. That only leaves you $40. You have to spend at least $10 for water and electricity. Only $30 remains. But food costs at least $40. And then you have to dress, and as a teacher you are expected to wash.
>
> (Abdou, 2003)

UNAVES is registered as an NGO because the government refuses to grant it the status of a labour union. While, as seen in Chapter 4 above, participation is the Bank's watchword, and the Bank officially encourages its staff to develop links with trade unions because they "add value" to participatory processes, this does not seem to have trickled down to Niger. Abdou holds a letter he wrote to the Bank several months previously asking for a meeting, to which he never received a reply:

> The World Bank won't talk with us, we don't know why. We would like to meet with the World Bank because the government always hides behind them, says that it is because of the Bank that we cannot be recruited into the regular public service.

UNAVES's primary goal is to integrate the *volontaires* into the regular teach-ing fraternity. Abdou has participated in two government committees set up to find a solution. Both came up with similar proposals that would permit *volon-taires* to join the civil service after four years, with a one-year internship after-wards at a reduced salary, before full integration. The last committee, set up under the prime minister's aegis, had reported four months previously, but

UNAVES still had not heard back from the government, so the association launched its industrial action. Abdou had little doubt the World Bank was behind the problem:

> [w]herever this World Bank programme of *volontaires* is introduced there are social problems. It isn't just the system of *volontaires*, either. A peasant can't go to the hospital any more because he can't afford to pay the charges the Bank made the government introduce.
>
> (Abdou, 2003)

Abdou dismisses the Bank's emphasis on basic education:

> They only want to teach people the twenty-six letters of the alphabet, but can you develop a country like that? It is a kind of colonisation so that the real education, science, that is reserved to the developed world. That way the World Bank will always have to bring experts to Africa to tell us how to do things because there will be no one trained here.
>
> (Abdou, 2003)

In February 2003, Niger's National Assembly sent a mission, in which this author participated, to monitor and evaluate the execution of PRSP-funded projects in the country's north-central region. Fourteen sites were visited, including four newly opened primary schools. In one school, the *volontaire* teacher of a class of approximately sixty seven-year old children was off sick, and the children were being loosely supervised by the other teacher, a regular employee. In a second school, the *volontaire*'s classroom was empty as the teacher had apparently departed on a multi-day trip to the regional centre to collect her pay cheque. In a third school, the *volontaire*, from the capital city, had disappeared some time previously to return home, a problem that the regional director of education said occurred regularly. In the fourth school, both the volunteer and regular-status teacher were present and the school was functioning normally.

A sample of four schools is insufficient to draw definitive conclusions, but suggests that *volontaires* may not yield good-quality or consistent education. As noted by Mehrotra and Buckland (1998), poor-quality education inevitably leads to parental resistance to sending their children to school, especially where the potential for upward social mobility provided by education is severely restricted, as in Niger.

Surprisingly, given Niger's weak educational outcomes and the Bank's emphasis on the basic education MDG, the nearest full-time Bank education specialist is based in Senegal, 2,110 kilometres away. Djibrilla Karamoko, a Bank health economist in Niamey, looks after the education files part time. In an interview, he acknowledged that the rapid expansion of volunteer teachers in Niger – around 10,700 in August 2003 – presented "a difficult question". He agreed with Abdou that living on $100 or less per month "would be difficult, especially in Niamey".

However, Karamoko insists that the government has promised the inter-national financial institutions that it will not increase the size of the civil service and it will "have to honour that commitment". With attrition, at most 200 new teachers could be integrated into the civil service annually, whereas the Bank estimates at least 2,500 new teachers a year will be needed to achieve universal primary education. The Bank's Niger project documentation talks of increasing the number of $70 per month contractual teachers from 7,774 in 2002 to 23,000 by 2007. Karamoko suggests the need for long-term thinking: "I know women, personally, who love teaching, who teach out in the villages as *volontaires*, but they don't know if they have a future … it is a problem" (Karamoko, 2003). The Bank's only written proposals for satisfying contractuals' long-term needs are: "health insurance, a slight increase of salaries upon contract renewal (every two years) and the opportunity to become civil service teachers if selected competi-tively for school head positions" (World Bank, 2003b: 18). The Bank acknowl-edges that "[c]ontractual teacher arrangements could lead to unrest", and that it will be necessary to maintain close collaboration with teachers' unions and ensure that the government maintains "sustained political commitment".

Niger's IMF representative Simon N'Guiamba was asked about the apparent problems with implementation of Niger's PRSP, and particularly its education components. He argued that the PRSP is not an IMF or Bank programme, but belongs to Niger. It is not up to the IMF to interfere in how a sovereign nation goes about its business:

> [W]e went to Agadez with the government and we saw some schools they have built, some health centres and water projects, as far as we could see they were running well but it isn't our job to do an evaluation, that is for the government.
>
> (N'Guiamba, 2002)

N'Guiamba's comments about Niger's sovereignty are true only in the strictest legal sense. The government is insolvent without external resources pro-vided through donor grants and concessional loans. Because of the Bank's success in using its convening power to enlist most donors in the coordinated PRSP strategy, receipt of external resources requires the Bank and Fund's support. They have made education sector restructuring through early retire-ments and the hiring of *volontaires* a key conditionality (Government of Niger, 1998), and provided several concessional loans to cover the recruitment of *volontaires*. The government has no choice but to accept the money with its attendant conditions, because it could not finance the expenditure itself and thus could not fulfil its commitment to move towards universal primary education. If it did not promise to honour this commitment, it would be subjected to punitive measures by the Bretton Woods institutions and bilateral donors. The Bank and Fund are able, therefore, both to dictate the exact content of government policy, and simultaneously evade responsibility for problems resulting from those policies.

India, the World Bank and para-teachers

The universal basic education policy is, by definition, being implemented across the world. In most African countries, as in Niger, global social policies are more or less directly imposed on governments by the international financial institutions. In other parts of the world, where governments' needs to comply with financial conditionalities are less pressing, the process through which global priorities become national policies is more subtle, and in some ways more revealing about the spread of global managerialism as an organic disposition of contemporary elite governance. This section examines how universal basic education has been implemented in India.

India has long been a crucial operating terrain for the World Bank, as noted in Chapter 2 above. Not only does the country account for a substantial proportion of Bank loans and credits, impressive economic growth since the 1990s is rapidly turning the country into a global superpower. Nevertheless development has been uneven, and the country continues to face enormous quality of life challenges. Almost half of India's children suffer from malnutrition, the child mortality rate of 74/1,000 remains very high even in comparison with other developing countries, while 40 per cent of the population are illiterate. Huge disparities between rich and poor, and India's large population, mean that despite improvements in overall economic statistics, the country still accounts for a large proportion of the world's most disadvantaged and excluded people.

The Bank does not treat India in the same disciplinary manner as sub-Saharan Africa. As a nascent superpower, the country is an important partner in emerging global governance. The global managerial agenda is transmitted more through a collegial, iterative process. The ties between India's top political leadership, the World Bank, and other transnational institutions are extremely close. India's prime minister since 2004, Manmohan Singh, worked for the United Nations Conference on Trade and Development (UNCTAD) early in his career, was governor and deputy governor of the World Bank and IMF for over ten years while Reserve Bank of India director and finance minister between the 1970s and 1990s, and has sat on numerous bank and IMF special committees throughout his career. Montek Singh Ahluwahlia, who heads India's Planning Commission, and is seen as the strategic mastermind of the country's post-2004 government, spent twelve years working for the World Bank in Washington, and three years in a senior position with the IMF between 2001 and 2004. The country's third key policy leader, Finance Minister P. Chidambaram, is a lawyer and has not been employed by the Bank or IMF. Apart from his legal qualifications he holds an MBA from Harvard Business School and was senior advocate in India for several major western companies including GE, Bechtel and Enron.

India's education system inherited gross discrepancies between elite and popular education from the colonial period. In recent years, the bulk of the middle classes and elites in both urban and rural areas have abandoned the state system entirely in favour of private schools (Pandey, 2006a), leaving government schools as the domain of the urban and semi-rural working classes and poor. Beneath this social stratum, about 20 per cent of the population in more remote rural areas have not been served at all by the state school system.

In 1990 India committed itself to ensure universal basic education at the UNESCO-organised Jomtien conference at which the global universal education goal was first adopted. The first major initiative to operationalise the Jomtien commitment was the District Primary Education Programme (DPEP), launched by the Indian central government in 1994. DPEP involved the decentralisation of education administration to the district level, with an emphasis on local community input. Kumar *et al.* (2001) note "... the marked Indianisation of the planning process". In contrast to Africa, Indian scholars and educational planners were involved from the beginning in the formulation and preparation of the projects. The fact that DPEP was entirely funded by outside donors, mainly the World Bank, was carefully avoided in the initial project document: "there is not even a cursory mention" (Kumar *et al.*, 2001). Government of India documents claim that DPEP is a "homegrown idea" and "national project", although the national education planning agency that helped coordinate the baseline study acknowledged that "the four-stage planning strategy of the World Bank has been strictly adhered to" (NCERT, 1994: 3). The initial DPEP programme did not mention the use of contract teachers; the emphasis in Bank documents of the time is on the need for "professional management".

Prior to DPEP, a project to reach out to isolated rural areas had been sponsored by the Swedish International Development Agency in the large northern state of Rajasthan. The Shiksha Karmi Project (SKP) involved the recruitment of local educated but unemployed youth to become "para-teachers" in communities too small and too isolated to merit a normal state primary school (Govinda and Josephine, 2004). The use of local young people to work in the schools was a means to address the resistance of regular teachers to working in these locations with few amenities, and also to increase community ownership and acceptance of education (Pandey, 2006). The initial results from the Rajasthan experiment were positive, and various similar schemes were sponsored by other donors in other Indian states.

As the 1990s progressed, DPEP and SKP concepts became intertwined. The idea of using para-teachers extended beyond their generally accepted employment in remote areas, to the broader state school system. By the end of the 1990s, the rationale for using para-teachers shifted from addressing the particular needs of isolated regions to saving money through replacement of regular teachers and thus enabling the government to achieve universal elementary education at affordable cost. At the same time, an anti-teacher discourse became prevalent, with a variety of studies undertaken designed to show the high absenteeism and poor quality of the regular teaching workforce, and the high quality and joyful learning being provided by the para-teachers (Kumar *et al.*, 2001a; Govinda and Josephine, 2004). The empirical findings of these studies have been widely challenged, but they received the World Bank's imprimatur, and were included in the Bank's global Millennium Development Goals report that listed a variety of reasons why, in different countries of the developing world, professional teachers were a roadblock to implementation of universal education (World Bank, 2004b: 115–116). By 2001, the national Planning Commission drawing up the country's 10th Five-year Plan was emphasising the need to "remove legal impediments in the recruitment of para-teachers", as well as the importance of transferring responsibility for teacher hiring to the local level (Planning Commission, 2001: 38), effectively dismantling the existing state-wide professional teaching corps. Many larger Indian states have enthusiastically adopted the policy. Madhya Pradesh, with a population of sixty million, has completely abolished central hiring of teachers, and others have followed to a greater or lesser extent (Govinda and Josephine, 2004). The World Bank presents Madhya Pradesh as a globally meritorious example of a "pragmatic strategy" that enabled the state "to eliminate its backlog of children out of school in just 18 months, at one-third the usual cost" (World Bank, 2005: 83). Overall figures for the number of para-teachers and their proportion to the overall teaching corps are difficult to assess because of the disappearance of central teaching registries as part of the reforms, but Pandey (2006) estimates that already about one-third of all teachers in Madhya Pradesh, for example, are para-teachers.

The conditions under which para-teachers are hired and work vary greatly between the Indian states, but generally bear remarkable similarities with their African counterparts, despite India's vastly superior resources. In Andhra Pradesh, their salary is less than $25 per month (much less than is provided even in Niger), compared with an entry-level salary of over $100 for regular teachers, and they receive only ten months' salary per year as they are not paid during school holidays. Other states are somewhat more generous, and a few even have a system for the eventual recruitment of para-teachers into the regular teaching profession (Govinda and Josephine, 2004). As in Africa, the starvation wages are often justified because the teachers are presented as "community volunteers", although both internal and external reviews show that para-teachers view their work as a normal but badly underpaid job. Again as in African cases, most para-teachers receive no benefits such as sick pay or maternity leave, work full time in schools alongside properly paid and qualified teachers and have the same responsibilities, but enjoy no job security. They are usually hired by the local municipal or village council, and in the event of any discord with local elites are frequently denied salary and/or dismissed at short notice.

Because the para-teacher concept began in India in isolated communities, and para-teachers are usually, though not always, from the community where they teach, there is often an assumption that they are underqualified in comparison with the regular professional teachers, thus justifying their inferior employment conditions. In fact, Mehta (2003) found that on average, para-teachers were better educated than their professional teacher peers, a finding confirmed by Pandey and Raj (2003) in a study in Uttar Pradesh. Where para-teachers are undereducated, however, is in the profession of teaching. In many states, pre-service teacher training is minimal: seven days in Andhra Pradesh, twelve days in Madhya Pradesh, fifteen days in West Bengal and seventeen days in Kerala.

The World Bank, bilateral donors and the Indian government all emphasise the importance of "community leadership" in driving the universal education programme. Typically, a Village Education Committee (VEC) is established that is responsible for hiring and firing para-teachers. Parent teacher associations and women's groups are also expected to participate in the life of the local school. Kumar *et al.* (2001) sharply criticise the concept of community leadership in the para-teacher programme as a manipulation of participation, in terms redolent of the critiques of World Bank participation programmes in Cooke and Kothari (2001), discussed in Chapter 4 above. They argue that the Indian state has used community participation approaches regularly since independence, in order to legitimise and implement state programmes. However, in the context of India's hierarchically structured rural society, benefits were typically "cornered by the already better-off and dominant sections of society", and thus "community empowerment" actually retrenched dominant local elites. In the contemporary era of globalisation and its attendant radical restructuring of society:

> the idea of an empowered community, actively involved in the running of the village primary school, makes a reassuring, warm reading. It gives the so-called human face to structural development programmes. The face hides the massive cultural dissonance and economic pauperisation of the weaker sections of society.
>
> (Kumar *et al.*, 2001)

Bank-sponsored analyses of the operation of the village education committees tend to confirm Kumar *et al.*'s scepticism. A survey of the DPEP programme in Uttar Pradesh found that:

> parents do not know that a VEC exists, sometimes even when they are supposed to be members of it; VEC members are unaware of even key roles they are empowered to play in education services; public participation in improving education is negligible, and correspondingly, people's ranking of education on a list of village priorities is low.
>
> (Banerjee *et al.*, 2006: 2)

Conclusion

This chapter began by outlining the framework through which the theorists of transnational elite governance envisage the operation of a global managerial system. Civil society or, more accurately, large international NGO executives are a key part of the global governance agenda. Transnational institutions and specifically the World Bank have chosen to engage – and co-opt – civil society as a tool in increasing their democratic legitimacy, expanding support for managerialist endeavours, and undercutting potential opposition. This coincides with the way in which the global elite governance theorists Reinicke and Rischard conceive of organised civil society leaders as part of a governance network that short-circuits traditional democratic institutions. Partnership with civil society leadership is particularly crucial in permitting the extension of the global governance agenda beyond the domain of economic policy, already achieved through structural adjustment, and into the broad social policy arena, including education programming (which is the subject of the two case studies later in the chapter).

The second section examined the responses of international civil society organisations and theorists to the Bank's entreaties. There is broad support for engagement with the Bank across mainstream and more radical international civil society voices, including joint transnational initiatives designed to discipline national state elites into pursuing Bank/NGO policy agendas. This engagement is justified as a response to globalisation and the decreasing relevance and legitimacy of state-based elites, while civil society-led "participation" is posited as a higher form of democracy than the representative version involving universal suffrage.

The character of the elite alliance between the Bank's global bureaucrats and international NGO executives can be understood through Bourdieu's (1994) class theory, which rejects economic essentialism in favour of a multiplicity of capitals that combine in individuals and social groups as symbolic capital. While the Bank's managers bring economic capital to the policy-making table, they need the social capital of organised civil society to constitute sufficient overall symbolic capital to assure policy hegemony. Cox's (1983) Gramscian approach is also useful in explaining the Bank–international INGO collaboration as the construction of a nascent international hegemonic social bloc. Another lens through which to view the Bank's efforts to impose its will on the global social terrain is provided by institutional theory, explored in Chapter 1 above. As revealed through the tracing of the Bank's birth and development (Chapter 3 above), the organisation's transnational managerial identity was institutionalised from its inception, adapting to and profiting from the changing external environment through the vicissitudes of Cold War and neo-liberalism, while retaining throughout its globalist genetic code. Thus, the Bank's continuing efforts to expand its managerial horizons represent at the same time its institutionalisation in the global social terrain and the expansion and entrenchment of a global managerial elite order.

The third section of the chapter examined two cases of the manifestation of the global managerialist impulse in the field of education. The cases, in Niger and India, highlight the inauthenticity of the participatory discourse in which Bank and international NGO leaders engage at headquarters. While the universal basic education goal is undoubtedly a laudable one in principle, it is a fallacy to suggest that it is being driven from the grassroots. In Niger, the concerns of a key civil society organisation representing the teachers who are being enlisted to carry out the programme are completely ignored. In India, the Bank's own evaluation shows that the village education committees that supposedly animate the universal education programmes are largely non-functional, with many members even unaware that they are part of the committee.

The Niger case in particular highlights the problematic relationship between Education International, the international teachers' union, and the universal education initiative. EI's progress reports on the Education For All programme and the FTI reflect ambivalence about the projects' direction. While EI argues that expanding access to education should be in teachers' interests, it notes that in practice they carry the burden of expansion through low wages and the contingent labour schemes that Mingat and other Bank experts promote (Education International, 2003). Yet, despite complaining that using contingent labour to replace properly trained and paid teachers is a breach of International Labour Organisation conventions (Education International, 2002), the organisation continues to partner the Bank in the Education For All initiatives. The union may calculate that expanding the teaching profession even through contingent labour will eventually result in integration of these *volontaires* into the regular profession, but the UNAVES case and the Bank's long-range planning suggest most will be retired before they become regular teachers. Further, the Bank's Fast Track Initiative edict that half the education budget must be allocated to primary education would have to be broken if universal access to secondary education and broader access to tertiary education are conceivably to be achieved. And, since the framework insists that government spending must account for no more than 18 per cent of GDP, and education budgets are to be restricted to 20 per cent of government spending, all these goals would have to be met from 3.5 per cent of Niger's meagre GDP.

EI's partnership with the Bank, Oxfam and other international INGOs continues despite its reservations. The EFA coalition legitimises the enforcement of education policies which are both of questionable merit and imposed with minimal consultation either with governments or with grassroots NGOs, particularly those whose perspectives differ from the Bank's. This is consistent with Rischard's prescription for solving the world's problems through committees including "big NGOs and networks of NGOs that have a lot of knowledge". The cases illustrate the disciplinary practices that lurk in the shadows of Bank–international INGO collaboration. At the global level, the Bank is happy to co-write a social policy script with the self-appointed representatives of civil society, but at the hard, implementation end, grassroots participation is meaningless or non-existent because the universal global script has already been written.

Some critical analysts present the Bank's education policy as a primarily ideological script reflecting an underlying neo-liberal economic agenda. Cammack (2002, 2003) argues that the Bank's focus on basic education at the expense of secondary and tertiary education is designed to create a functional workforce for global capitalism without the intellectual training to ask too many questions. This argument is plausible in the case of India, which is rapidly engaging with the global economy and which, if current trends continue, will require many more skilled workers for transnational production and service activities. Basic education is considered a useful investment in most neo-liberal economic models. However, Niger's almost total disengagement from the global economy suggests that, if purely economic interests were driving policy, the country's education system would be entirely abandoned. It is unlikely that Nigerien peasants will be needed as a workforce for global capitalism in the foreseeable future. The Bank's determination to impose comprehensive social policies even where they make little economic sense is more satisfactorily explained by post-developmentalism which, as was discussed in Chapter 1 above, characterises the developmentalist compulsion as constitutive of the ubiquity of power and the drive to construct and impose hegemonic discourse; what might be called the managerial imperative.

Globalisation represents, beyond its ideological manifestations, a realignment of social stratification on an international basis, as has been discussed in Chapters 1 and 4 above. An important and largely unexplored feature of contemporary international social policy is the sociological impact and meaning of the imposition of global programmes such as EFA. One reason for the zeal with which both the World Bank and national elites have pursued restructuring of the education sector is that it is a key step in the dismantlement of the nationalist class alliances that formed the basis of the struggles for colonial independence in the post-Second World War period. These alliances brought together intellectuals and local business elites who felt constrained and discriminated against by the imperial presence. After independence, most countries followed variants of a social contract in which intellectuals (of whom teachers made up a prominent group) were integrated within a burgeoning state bureaucracy, while the business community was protected from international competition by various trade barriers. Globalisation results in the business community abandoning the protectionist model (often under substantial pressure from transnational institutions like the Bank), detaching itself from its national roots, and adopting an international perspective, along with top echelons of the state elites. The lower-level nationalist cadre, including the organised teaching profession, now represents a cost burden in global competition, and an undesirable source of resistance to the global managerial project. Professional teachers are a large, relatively well-organised group, structurally committed to a discarded and now-undesirable development model. They have relatively high social status and a strategic location in the community. Their replacement by a lower-status contractual corps, subject to control by local elites, removes a potential destabilising factor in the transnational reorientation of the social order. Figure 5.2 shows three notional stages in hegemonic order in a developing country, from the imperial period, to post-independence, to the emergence of a transnational order.

This chapter adopts a critical approach to organised civil society and to the Millennium Development Goals, two subjects of which criticism is largely taboo. Civil society organisations are, in fact, notoriously sensitive to criticism of their motives. In 2005 Oxfam, for example, responded bitterly to an article in the British left-of-centre magazine *New Statesman* suggesting that it was too close to New Labour. Its director was "shocked at the injustice", a "punch in the stomach" to those campaigning against poverty, implied the article would endanger "700,000 people who rely on Oxfam to survive" in Darfur, and stated that the magazine had discredited itself by daring to criticise Oxfam (Quarmby, 2005; Stocking, 2005). This overreaction to relatively mild criticism (much less strident than Oxfam metes out to its selected enemies) underscores the extent to

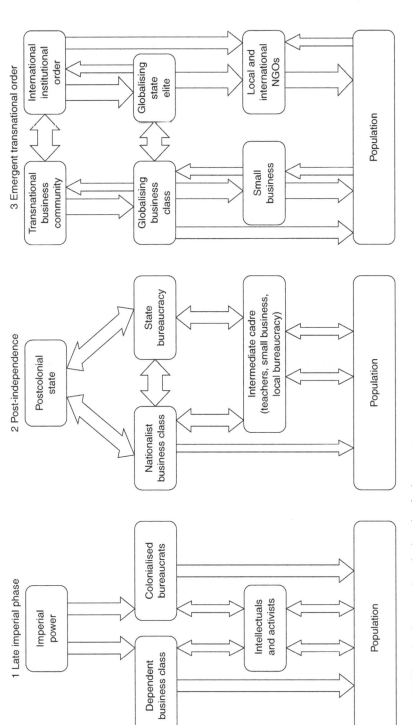

Figure 5.2 Changing hegemonic order in a developing country.

which international development NGOs have been able to capture a moral high ground from which their claims to represent the inherent interests of the world's poor go unchallenged. This makes them an extremely valuable partner for the World Bank (and New Labour) in extending concertive managerialist hegemony into the social policy arena.

As noted in Chapter 4 above, the Millennium Development Goals have also assumed a status beyond criticism, and again represent a highly appealing flag in which the World Bank can wrap itself. The main Goals[8] are indeed, by themselves, beyond reproach. However, their promotion outside the social contexts in which the conditions they are aiming to treat are caused inevitably leads to a charity approach that ultimately blames the victims for their misfortunes. Most Africans are poor because the continent was ruthlessly colonised, their states were granted independence in a state of penury, and their leaders corrupted as pawns in a chess game of great power rivalry. Poverty in India is rooted in subjugation to a contemporary elite wearing the mantles of both caste domination and succession to the colonial rulers of the British Raj. Poverty, hunger, sickness, malnutrition and illiteracy are everywhere the interconnected outcomes of entrenched social inequality. The contradiction of the Bank's approach to meeting the Millennium Development Goal of universal basic education is that many of the contractual labourers recruited to "affordably" educate the poor are themselves paid a salary below the absolute poverty threshold of $1 per day, parsimoniously adopted as the first Millennium Development Goal's indicator of unacceptable poverty. Peter is robbed to pay Paul.

6   The Bank and the private sector

This chapter explores the forging of another global alliance, this time between international financial institutions and globalising private business. The analysis, which focuses on the privatisation of the global steel industry, and specifically the giant Karmet steel mill in Kazakhstan, illustrates the international financial institutions' proactive role in the world economy, their practice of "picking winners", and their agnosticism as to the ethnic origins and geographic roots of those winners.

As noted in Chapter 1 above, critical theories of the global system tend to emphasise the inequality between the developed and developing worlds as an inherent feature of the global order. Decisive power rests with the bourgeoisie of the developed capitalist countries, although a subordinate local "comprador" bourgeoisie helps to exploit the developing countries, receiving in its turn a share in the resulting profits. This case study challenges that model. A globalising corporation with roots in the developing world becomes the favoured partner of the World Bank in its pursuit of the interconnected goals of definitively incorporating the former Communist states into a single global economic order, and restructuring state-owned steel companies around the world into part of a globalised, privately held industry. The case study also shows the international financial institutions as leaders in global restructuring, rather than handmaidens of large western corporations.

The chapter is divided into three sections. The first traces the rise of Lakshmi Mittal's steel empire from its modest beginnings as an offshoot of his father's company. The second section explores the international financial institutions' activities in post-Communist Kazakhstan as they sought to mould the country's economic and social systems into the global order. The third section examines the intersection between Mittal, the international financial institutions, and Kazakhstan through Mittal's purchase of the Karmet steel plant.

The meteoric rise of Lakshmi Mittal

Origins

Lakshmi Mittal's steel empire has its roots in Ispat Industries, a medium-sized Indian steel producer founded by his father, who came from a prominent

Marwari trader family (Hardgrove, 2004). Ispat Industries saw moderate prosperity in the highly regulated "licence raj" era of early post-independence India, where the steel industry was – and still remains – dominated by state-owned plants. In 2004, it had a market capitalisation of approximately $135 million, making it the 158th most valuable Indian private company and the country's seventh largest private steelmaker (*Business Today*, 2004).

Lakshmi Mittal went to Indonesia in his early twenties to supervise Ispat's first foreign venture, a steel plant which opened in 1976 (Bist, 2004). He has never since lived in India. In 1989 he leased a state-owned steel plant in Trinidad. He purchased a Mexican state-owned plant in 1992, and exercised his option to purchase the Trinidad plant in 1994. In 1995, he and his father split their business, with Lakshmi retaining all of the international operations under the LNM (Lakshmi N. Mittal) Group umbrella. This comprised LNM Holdings (a privately held company) and Ispat International (a publicly traded company), registered in the Caribbean tax haven of Netherlands Antilles and in the Netherlands respectively.[1] The group expanded quickly through a series of acquisitions of mainly state-owned steel mills, beginning with the Karmet purchase in 1995 which I examine more closely below. In late 2004 Ispat simultaneously purchased a large private American steel plant and restructured, creating Mittal Steel, the world's largest steel producer (Bream, 2004: 1), a remarkable achievement given that the company had only begun its international expansion fifteen years previously. In 2006, Mittal succeeded in a bitter takeover battle for Arcelor, Europe's largest and the world's second largest steel company. Lakshmi Mittal became the CEO of the new entity, Arcelor Mittal, with his son Aditya the Chief Financial Officer. The two companies are in the process of formally merging in 2007.

Mittal Steel's corporate offices are in London, where Mittal now resides. At the time of the 2004 restructuring, he paid himself a $2 billion dividend. A British newspaper claimed in 2004 that Mittal was easily the richest individual living in Britain, with total wealth of around £12 billion (he still travels on an Indian passport) (Milmo, 2004: 12. In March 2005, *Forbes* ranked him the world's third richest person, with personal worth of $25 billion, an increase of $18.8 billion in one year (*Forbes*, 2005: 166). In 2005 and 2007 Mittal gave two donations to the British Labour Party of £2 million each, making him easily the largest single donor to the governing party.

Ispat, the World Bank and the allure of state property

Mittal's relationship with the World Bank dates back to his first acquisition of a formerly state-owned steel plant, built by the Trinidadian government in 1980 at a cost of US$460 million, and bought outright by Mittal for US$70 million under a secret clause in the terms of the lease agreement he had signed with the government in 1989 (Parliament of Trinidad and Tobago, 1990, 1992). Six months after purchase, Mittal, through the holding company Seolak Investment Ltd, registered in the British Virgin Islands, was granted a $27.3 million loan by the International Finance Corporation (IFC), a World Bank subsidiary. The loan covered about 20 per cent of the costs of upgrading the plant to increase its capacity and improve environmental standards.

The Trinidad government was required to privatise state industry as a condition for receiving IMF and World Bank financing beginning in 1988 (ILO, 2000). A senior official from the IMF negotiating team resigned, claiming the IMF had deliberately exaggerated the parlousness of Trinidad's economic situation, making it impossible for the country to secure private financing, thus forcing it to rely on IMF financial support and follow its dictates (Budhoo, 1990). The structural adjustment programme led to social unrest and an attempted coup d'état in 1990 (Meighoo, 2003). The Trinidadian case highlights the crucial and controversial role of the international institutions in forcing developing countries to abandon state-led development in favour of the global integration of the structural adjustment period, as discussed in Chapter 2 above.

Mittal's second, and much larger, acquisition in Mexico followed a similar pattern. Like Trinidad, the Mexican government had followed a state-led economic development strategy until the early 1980s. The country's industrial development during the 1970s was largely financed by private bank loans, but a spike in oil prices reaching its peak in 1981 led to global recession and sudden credit tightening. Mexico threatened to default on its international debt obligations, but under pressure from American banks that held Mexican debt, a bail-out package was organised by the IMF and World Bank, involving the central banks of the major developed countries. This episode marked the beginning of a trend towards the public assumption of debt through international financial institutions and the adoption of an international disciplinary regime through loan conditionalities (Vazquez, 2002).

In 1988, the Bank extended a US$400 million loan to Mexico to restructure its nationalised steel industry and "expose the industry to international competition",[2] but by 1991 the industry was being broken up and privatised, and in November of that year Ispat International acquired the Lazaro Cardenas HYL III plant, which had only been brought into production in late 1988 (*HYL Report*, 1997: 3). The sale price was $220 million, although Ispat only put down $25 million, with the remainder financed by Mexican government bonds. The Mexican government had invested $2.2 billion into building the plant (Sull, 1999: 372).

Between 1991 and 1997 Mittal purchased steel plants from state owners in Mexico, Canada, Germany, Kazakhstan and Ireland, as well as smaller private plants in Germany and France. Ispat's first foray into the former Soviet bloc, the 1995 acquisition of Kazakhstan's Ispat Karmet, was by far the largest of this early round of acquisitions. This case is examined more closely below. Ispat later bought two further plants in Germany from the private industrial group Thyssen (Mehta, 1999) and a third in France from private French interests (European Commission, 1999).

The Canadian plant was opened by the Quebec government in 1964 as part of a nationalist strategy to decrease dependence on the Anglophone-dominated

Canadian federal government. It was privatised to Ispat in 1994, three weeks before elections in which the governing pro-business Quebec Liberal Party lost power to the social democratic Parti Québecois which had threatened to cancel the privatisation (*Financial Post*, 1994). The government was left with a C$693.6 million (about US$500 million) deficit on its books (*Montreal Gazette*, 2004: B5). The plant was profit-making at the time of the privatisation. Opponents of the Quebec privatisation programme claimed that:

> The privatisation of Sidbec-Dosco is another good example of a fire sale. After having invested $1.5 billion in Sidbec, the government has sold it to a Mexican enterprise[3] for as little as $45 million; the new owner made profits of $60.5 million in the first year alone, which was more than the purchase price for the whole facility.
>
> (Lauzon *et al.*, 1998: 145)[4]

The Irish plant was purchased in 1996 for £1, with Ispat receiving £38.2 million in various subsidies, in return for promising to invest £30 million. The plant never turned a profit and Ispat closed it in 2001 (Pallister, 2002).

In 1998, Ispat bought the giant private sector Inland Steel operation in Chicago, for $1.43 billion. After Inland, Ispat reverted to purchasing ailing publicly owned steel plants in developing and transitional countries, with the policy support and/or financial underpinning of international financial institutions. In 2001, it bought the Romanian state-owned steel producer Sidex, which alone accounted for 4 per cent of Romania's GDP. That deal provoked substantial controversy in the United Kingdom when it was revealed that Prime Minister Blair had urged the Romanian government to accept Ispat's bid, a few months after Mittal had made a £125,000 donation to Blair's Labour Party. Britain also supported an EBRD loan of $100 million to help LNM Holdings purchase the plant, against American opposition (Grice, 2002).

The scandal led to media inquiries into a mutual support network involving senior Labour politicians and Indian expatriate businessmen including Mittal. In 2001, Labour's then Minister for Europe, Keith Vaz, had launched an Anglo-Romanian Action Group geared to promote privatisation of Romania's state assets. Vaz, who has described himself as "a leading member, if not the leading member, of the Asian community in this country" (Vasagar, 2001), had received £5,000 in contributions to his 1997 election campaign from Usha Mittal, co-owner of LNM Holdings and wife of Lakshmi Mittal (Murphy, 2003: 22). Mittal attended as Vaz's guest of honour a 2002 British government dinner for Kazakh President Nursultan Nazarbayev, shortly before the World Bank extended another loan to Ispat Karmet (Murphy, 2002). Nazarbayev attempted to have Mittal named Kazakhstan's honorary consul to Britain, but the idea was dropped after the controversy regarding Mittal's relationship with New Labour. In 2002, Vaz was suspended from the House of Commons for misleading MPs about his financial dealings with other expatriate Indian businessmen (House of Commons, 2002). Mittal let it be known that he felt much of the criticism levelled at him was "tinged with racism" (*Economist*, 2002: 62), a perspective repeated widely in the Indian press (Gupta, 2002; Kanavi, 2004: 50).

Also in 2001, LNM Holdings bought an Algerian publicly owned steel plant and related assets (*Metal Bulletin*, 2001). Post-independence, the Algerian government, along with others in North Africa and the Arab world, had pursued a state-led economic development strategy. Since the 1980s, the World Bank and IMF had been pressuring Algeria to reverse this course. In 1994, it agreed, and support for a privatisation process was included in the Bank's 1997 structural adjustment loan (World Bank, 1997). Privatisation proceeded slowly, leading the Bank to extend a further loan to hasten the process (World Bank, 2000). The government's Alfasid steel plant was subsequently privatised to LNM Holdings, with a reported tax holiday. In 2003, the World Bank subsidiary IFC provided the Ispat's newly acquired plant with a $25 million loan. The IFC(2003) explained its loan as "supporting the government's ongoing privatization program by participating in a highly visible and successful privatization". The cycle is similar to that in Trinidad: the IFIs play a triple role, as a country's "external auditors" providing a pessimistic accounting of the nation's finances, as "management consultants" offering advice on necessary policy changes, and as bankers both providing capital and leveraging other public and private funds.

In 2002/2003, LNM Holdings acquired the formerly state-owned steel plant in Nova Hut, Czech Republic. Although the country has been following a privatisation programme since the end of Communism in 1989, large industrial plants were difficult to privatise; they were outdated, had large and organised workforces that could not easily be displaced, and were major polluters. In short, they were unattractive to most potential investors. However, closing Nova Hut was politically dangerous due to the large number of jobs at stake, and its iconic status. As part of the negotiations for entry into the European Union, the Czech government was pressured to end subsidies (European Commission, 2002: 37–48). Given the central place that accession played in the development strategies of the Central European states, this pressure was essentially irresistible.

As in other former Communist states, the World Bank invested in the Czech transition programme, providing a $450 million structural adjustment loan in 1991. In 1997, Nova Hut received a $250 million IFC loan for upgrading of facilities and restructuring in preparation for privatisation; the loan was syndicated to various other financial institutions including the EBRD. The loan made the World Bank the Nova Hut plant's largest creditor (Bulkacz, 2004).

Mittal paid the government $6 million for 52 per cent of the plant and promised to invest $242.8 million over the next ten years. LNM announced that its total investment in the plant in purchase price, share acquisitions, debt assumption and investments would be over $900 million. The deal was conditional on the Czech government assuming various of the plant's debts, the transfer of tax credits to Ispat, and continued operational subsidies of an undisclosed amount (Ispat Nova Hut, 2003: 49–60).[5]

The privatisation to LNM Holdings had been proposed by the World Bank's IFC as early as 1999 (Cattell, 1999). However, the government had already extended a part-purchase option to a company controlled by Nova Hut managers. The government cancelled the option in 2000. Subsequently the managers' company successfully sued the Czech government for unlawfully cancelling the deal. Court documents reveal the World Bank had pressured the government to make the cancellation (CTK Business News, 2004).

In its first year of Ispat ownership, the Nova Hut plant reported a $170 million profit. By August 2003, when the new owners announced plans to make the company private, its shares had appreciated more than threefold in the six months since privatisation (Reuters, 2003). In an unusual twist, the Czech government's counter-espionage Security Information Service (BIS) warned of the rise of non-transparent business interests registered in offshore tax havens in the privatisation process, specifically naming the Nova Hut privatisation as problematic (BIS, 2003).

Poland's steel industry presented similar challenges. Southern Poland's large plants employed thousands but depended on state subsidies and caused environmental problems; both issues became part of EU accession negotiations. The World Bank provided Poland a ten-year, $280 million loan in 1991 to help design, finance and implement an overall privatisation programme, along with several other more general structural adjustment loans. In 1997, the EBRD provided a $25 million loan for more privatisation preparations.

The Polish privatisation deal was concluded on October 2003 with Ispat emerging successful over US Steel. It was reported LNM Holdings would repay $406.9 million in the company's accumulated debt, "possibly on a discounted basis", and the operation would receive another €670 million in state subsidies in return for reducing output by 15 per cent, as agreed by the European Union. The Ispat deal contravened the Polish government's own privatisation law requiring privatisations to include an agreement with trade unions (Koza, 2003). After completing the Polish purchase, Mittal obtained a $100 million loan from IFC for environmental and general upgrading of all the plants in the privately held LNM Holdings arm of the Ispat empire (IFC, 2004).[6]

The Ispat group's corporate structure drew attention from within and outside the steel industry (see Figure 6.1).[7] Although Mittal's companies had a single website, www.ispat.com, and he and the multilateral banks invariably described the steel operations as a single entity, the overall group was nowhere legally incorporated, but rather was divided into two nominally independent holding companies, LNM Holdings and Ispat International. LNM was privately held by Mittal and his wife, and registered in the Netherlands Antilles tax haven. Ispat International, while majority owned by Mittal, traded on the New York stock market and was subject to the accounting requirements of both the Netherlands and the New York Stock Exchange. Until the restructuring, all Mittal's acquisitions in the former Communist states, as well as Ispat Annaba in Algeria, were part of LNM Holdings, while the western country plants as well as Trinidad and Mexico were part of the publicly traded Ispat International.

The role of offshore tax havens in international economic affairs has received attention from critical management scholars (Mitchell *et al.*, 1998; Hampton and

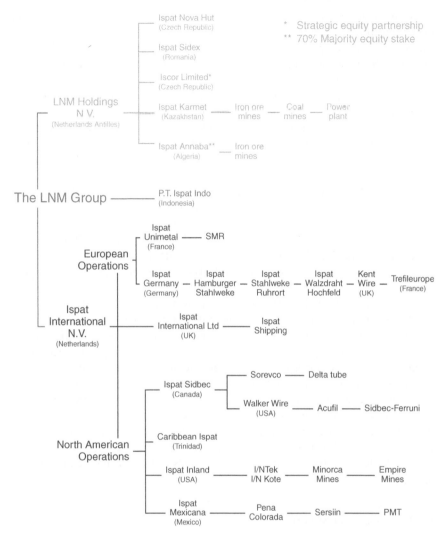

Figure 6.1 Ispat's corporate structure before Polish acquisitions and restructuring, 2004 (source: www.ispat.com).

Christensen, 2002; Sikka, 2003). While corporations and wealthy individuals have long used tax havens to avoid taxes and shield their activities from scrutiny, the importance of offshore tax havens has increased exponentially in recent years in line with rising transnational economic activity. The Mittal case illustrates the contradictory response of international institutions putatively charged with eradicating tax havens.

In 2000, the OECD named thirty-five countries operating as tax havens, improperly permitting large companies to avoid taxation, because of "a lack of transparency", "laws or administrative practices that prevent the effective exchange of information for tax purposes with other governments on taxpayers benefiting from no or nominal taxation", and "absence of a requirement that the activity [by the company in the jurisdiction] be substantial". The World Bank and the EBRD were asked to collaborate in eliminating these "harmful tax practices" (G7 Finance Ministry, 2001).

As noted earlier, Mittal has made extensive use of tax havens. The British Virgin Islands (BVI) – on the original OECD tax haven list – provided the corporate base for his first foray into purchasing steel plants being privatised under international institution pressure. The World Bank provided Mittal's BVI subsidiary with a loan in 1994 to upgrade his Trinidad plant. BVI belatedly agreed to comply with OECD transparency guidelines in 2002. Mittal's larger purchases of formerly state-owned steel plants, mainly in transitional and developing countries, were grouped under LNM Holdings, registered in the Netherlands Antilles, another tax haven listed by the OECD in 2000 as non-compliant with international tax standards (Weschler, 2001). Netherlands Antilles promised to reform its practices by 2005, and was taken off the tax haven list in 2001. However, in the meantime, both the World Bank's IFC and the EBRD had provided LNM Holdings companies with additional loans.

The Mittal steel empire's rise was fuelled by acquisitions of privatising steel plants, mainly in developing and transitional countries. These acquisitions were marked by several consistent features. Countries were pressured to privatise by international financial institutions as a condition for receiving loans needed to repay foreign institutional investors. International financial institutions helped restructure countries' steel industries to make them more attractive for purchase. Subsequent to purchase, several Ispat plants received loans from the World Bank and other international financial institutions. In at least one case, the Bank successfully intervened against a domestic consortium to pressure the government to sell to Ispat. Loans to Ispat's LNM Holdings arm by the Bank and the EBRD ignored undertakings by both institutions to help eliminate tax havens.

Cultivating Kazakhstan

The World Bank has been involved in Kazakhstan since shortly after the collapse of the Soviet Union. The EBRD, a regional transnational bank that operates exclusively in the former Communist countries, has been present in the country since late 1993.

The World Bank and the EBRD have similar mandates in the former Communist countries. Their primary stated goals are to dismantle the former state-owned economic system and to integrate the new privatised economies into a global economy. Shortly after Kazakhstan's independence, the World Bank argued that: "The Government will need to manage a program that entails the progressive privatization of virtually the entire productive economy" and carry out full "price liberalization and the implementation of a trade framework where there are no quantitative restrictions on exports nor imports" (World Bank, 1993a: iii–v). The privatisation and global integration mission is also inscribed in the EBRD's raison d'être: "the Bank shall assist the recipient member countries to implement structural and sectoral economic reforms, including demonopolization, decentralization and privatization, to help their economies become fully integrated into the international economy" (EBRD, 1990: Article 2.1).

The Bank envisaged three main vectors for intervention in Kazakhstan: balance of payments support during early transition shocks, "project financing" and "technical assistance", a significant element of which "will need to take the form of training".

It urged Kazakhstan to establish its own currency, emphasised that the right to employment would "have to go", implicitly endorsed discrimination against ethnic non-Kazakhs, urged the government to cut public sector employment, proposed a reduction in both wages and unemployment benefits and the implementation of wage controls, complained about the "elaborate network of social protection" for "pensioners, the disabled, families with many children, single mothers, and the unemployed" which "the country cannot afford to maintain", called for user-pay health care and elimination of household energy subsidies, recommended Kazakhstan's integration into international accounting systems, emphasised regulatory changes to attract foreign investment, opposed the initial programme of privatisation of state enterprises to worker collectives, and proposed in conjunction with USAID and the EBRD an alternative "detailed program of privatization" open to foreign investors (World Bank, 2003a: 25, 54, 137, 58, 59, 60, 92, 103, 71, 72, 78–80, 74).

Key prescriptions included rapid privatisation of almost all enterprises, although it did acknowledge the absence of a consistent and impartial legal framework for conducting business, and the "strong bias" towards privatisation to "unaccountable nomenclatura-led group structures", which "might affect the population's attitude to economic reform" (2003: 78, 70–71, 81, 85). However, corruption is only mentioned once, referring to the dangers of retaining a state planning economic model (2003a: iv). The main risk facing Kazakhstan would be "[f]ailure to speed the reform process" (2003a: 38).

As a middle-income country, Kazakhstan can only borrow from the World Bank at near-market rates. Although the Bank has extended about $2 billion in sovereign loans since independence in 1992, the current portfolio is a relatively insignificant $250 million. Since 1993, the Bank's IFC private sector loans subsidiary has extended $350 million in twenty-one loans and private-sector equity positions in Kazakhstan-based projects,[8] with the Ispat Karmet $76 million loan and $5 million equity the largest single investment (Decker, 2004).

In 2002, the EBRD claimed to be "the largest foreign investor in Kazakhstan outside the oil industry". By 2004 its loans to several dozen private ventures in the country exceeded $1 billion. The largest borrower is Ispat Karmet; the EBRD originally approved €182 million in loans, but the company drew down only €52.6 million.

Kazakhstan secured substantial IMF balance of payments support in the early transition years, and again in 1998 to deal with the Asian and Russian economic crises, but repaid all its IMF loans in 2000. It is unlikely to require further support (IMF, 2003).

A crucial attraction of ending state socialist rule was the opportunity for elites to derive direct financial benefit from their social dominance (Kagarlitsky, 1994) and participate freely in global elite networking (Lane, 1996). Networking opportunities occurred in a variety of ways including participation in formal transnational governance structures, integration into the global corporate system, and through structured socialisation opportunities. The IFIs play an important role in each of these three elite globalisation channels.

The demise of the state socialist bloc resulted in the dismantlement of the parallel international institutions that had been sponsored by Moscow, including Comecon[9] and the Warsaw Pact. All the former Communist countries joined the World Bank, the IMF and the EBRD shortly before or after the collapse of the socialist bloc. Kazakhstan and the other ex-Soviet Central Asian republics are members of the Asian Development Bank. In 2004, eight countries formerly in the socialist bloc joined the European Union, and Bulgaria and Romania joined in 2007. Former socialist bloc countries also participate in wider networks including the Organisation for Security and Cooperation in Europe and the Council of Europe, though the latter refused to admit Kazakhstan due to its poor democratic record. Several former republics of the Soviet Union are part of the World Trade Organisation, and others, including Kazakhstan,[10] are negotiating admission.

Beyond the formal institutional framework of global managerialism, integration occurs through absorption into commercial networks, which also provide financial opportunities for the transforming elites. Multinational corporations are active throughout the economies of Kazakhstan and most other former Soviet republics and hold a dominant market position in a number of areas, including consumer goods and industrial machinery. Direct foreign investment has been substantial, though concentrated in the natural resources and metals sectors, and often enjoying a troubled relationship with state actors mainly due to endemic corruption (Peck, 2004).

Kazakhstan's financial sector has been proactive in reaching out for foreign backing, permitting finance-based groups to capture increasing shares of a rapidly growing economy (Pirani, 2004), even though the IMF has adjudged the country to be in material non-compliance with international standards because of the absence of separation between the state and the Kazakh banking sector.

Numerous members of the former Communist elite have resurfaced as private business players, though only rarely have they entirely broken their ties with the state (Olcott, 2002: 162–167; Murphy, 2006). One of Kazakh President Nursultan Nazarbayev's sons-in-law is thought to own a controlling interest in both the country's largest bank, Kazkommertsbank (Peck, 2004: 243) and Halyk Bank, the third largest (Pala, 2005), while the chief executive of Turan-Alem, the second largest, was found dead in a suspicious "hunting accident" in December 2004 after publicly associating with the political opposition (Bekenov and Karajanov, 2004). Nonetheless foreign private banks (Pala, 2005a) and the transnational development banks have been lining up to provide capital to assist the development and growth of integrated financial-industrial conglomerates. The IFC provided loans of $10 million and $25 million to the largest Kazakh bank, Kazkommertsbank, in 1996 and 1999, and $12 million in loans and equity to Turan-Alem Bank, the country's third largest bank. The EBRD provided €20 million in loans and equity to Turan-Alem in 2001 and €30 million in equity to Kazkommertsbank in 2003. In addition, both the EBRD and the IFC provided over €230 million between 1998 and 2003 to Almaty Merchant Bank, Halyk Savings Bank, Turan-Alem and Kazkommertsbank, among others, to guarantee loans to support trade, small and medium-size businesses, and agribusiness. In 2004 and 2005, EBRD staff proposed three further loan and equity infusions in Kazakh banks, including a €27.5 million equity infusion to Kazkommerts-bank and an increase in the EBRD's equity stake in Turan-Alem.[11]

The IFIs proved lenient in their attitude towards clear evidence of corruption in the privatisation process. Western support to Kazakhstan's privatisation programme was jointly coordinated by the World Bank, USAID and the EBRD. The head of USAID's privatisation programme in Kazakhstan defined the partnership's criterion of success:

> The success was defined in that a large number of assets were sold off. We weren't defining success in terms of transparency. There was some kind of transparency of the process. .... Of course in Kazakhstan it wasn't the same as say Britain ... it did allow for a fair amount of kleptocratic operation.
>
> (Linden, 2000)

Corruption was often on a large scale, directly touching leading figures in the state administration:

> According to the [US] Justice Department, payments totaling $115 million flowed from the accounts of numerous U.S.-based oil companies to a private account in New York held by a Swiss bank by way of several offshore locations. From this account, investigators believe Giffen[12] transferred at least $60 million to Swiss accounts overseen by [President] Nazarbayev, former prime minister Akezhan Kazhegeldin, and his successor, Nurlan Balgimbayev, who currently heads the state-owned energy company Kazakhoil.
>
> (McKeeby, 2000: 1)

In 2002, Kazakh Prime Minister Imangali Tasmagambetov admitted that a secret personal bank account had been held in Switzerland since 1996 by President Nazarbayev, containing state funds valued at around $1 billion; however, he said it had been established purely to prevent a financial crisis from destabilising Kazakhstan, and was used to save the country from bankruptcy, but he did not provide any more specific account details (Reuters, 2002). Tasmagambetov's revelation came after a Swiss prosecutor revealed he was pursuing a criminal investigation against Nazarbayev.

The transnational banks also draw post-Soviet elites into appropriate ways of thinking through training, international exchanges and provision of international consultants. In this vein, the World Bank is "refocusing" its work in Kazakhstan towards "policy dialogue and knowledge transfer".[13] Despite its favourable economic situation, the Kazakh government continues to solicit funding for training its public and private sector managers, and to bring in international consultants from the multilateral banks and other international institutions:

> Kazakhstan has received considerable technical assistance and training by the Fund in virtually every area of economic policy, including through about 75 technical assistance missions provided during 1993–2002 ... In addition to short-term missions, the Fund has provided advisors .... Other international agencies and governments, including the World Bank, EU TACIS, EBRD, UNDP, OECD also are providing a wide range of technical assistance.
>
> (IMF, 2003: 30)

The Bank's training arm, the World Bank Institute, operates a centre located in Almaty, geared to "providing learning programs and policy advice in economic management and poverty reduction, environmentally and socially sustainable development, financial and private sector development, human development, infrastructure, and knowledge for development"[14] The World Bank and the EBRD, together with four other multinational institutions and the Government of Austria, run the Joint Vienna Institute (JVI), which "provides training for officials of Central and Eastern European countries, the former Soviet Union, and former centrally planned economies in Asia".[15] Since 1992 approximately 15,000 officials have attended JVI's courses. Courses on "economic and financial management and administration" are provided free of charge by each sponsoring organisation, subject to participants' nomination by their government and invitation by the sponsor.

In this section, I have detailed the objectives and practices of the international financial institutions in post-Communist Kazakhstan. The IFIs pressed Kazakhstan to remodel its economic and social structure in their image of a liberal free market. In return, the country's integration into global and regional networks would be facilitated, and Kazakh corporations' efforts to raise capital internationally directly and indirectly supported. Leading Kazakh private and public sector officials would benefit from international training and networking opportunities. The IFIs overlooked the kleptocratic nature of the privatisation process and the intertwining of state and private interests. It is within this context that I turn to Lakshmi Mittal's acquisition of the Karmet steel plant.

Saving Karmet

Ispat's purchase and renovation of the Karmet plant, supported by the IFIs, is a point of intersection with the macro process of Kazakhstan's integration into the

Figure 6.2 Karmet gates, Temirtau, 2004 (photograph, Jonathan Murphy).

global capitalist economy (see Figure 6.2). This section explores how Karmet was transformed from a symbol of the victory of state socialism into a poster child for Kazakhstan's integration into a new IFI-shaped privatised global steel industry. After outlining the chronology of Karmet's development and privatisation, I examine the different perspectives of key actors in the privatisation, including Ispat managers, the international financial institutions, and representatives of the political opposition. Finally, I look at what the privatisation has meant for the people who depend directly and indirectly on Karmet for their livelihoods.

The Karmet chronology

The Karaganda Metallurgical (Karmet) plant was established during the Second World War in the central region of the Kazakh Republic of the Soviet Union, about thirty-five kilometres northwest of the coal-mining and gulag centre of Karaganda. As early as 1929–1930, the area had been proposed for steel production because of its abundant supplies of coal and water, although large iron ore deposits were further afield in northern Kazakhstan (Herrington *et al.*, 2002). Beginning in 1934, a large water reservoir and hydroelectric plant was built to prepare for construction of a steel plant using concentration camp labour. With the onset of war, the Soviet leadership decided to relocate heavy industry far away from the risk of capture or damage by German forces, and ordered rush completion of the Karaganda plant. By December 1944, the first open hearth furnace was operational; the speedy effort led the newly named town of Temirtau (Kazakh for Iron Mountain) to be awarded the Red Banner of Labour (Nazarbayev, 1985: 13–16). Although the war ended shortly afterwards, the plant's favourable location and Soviet reliance on heavy industrial development fuelled continual expansion (Temirtau, 2004: 6). By 1991, the plant was one of the five largest in the Soviet Union with an annual capacity of 6 million tonnes of liquid steel (IFC, 1997).

The Soviet Union's collapse quickly led to crisis at Karmet. The Soviet Union's integrated markets disappeared overnight. Production declined by more than half between 1992 and 1994, and was often offloaded on credit or in barter arrangements. A management contract with US Steel failed to halt losses (Levine, 1995). In 1995 the government cancelled that contract (*Moskovskie Novosti*, 1995) and sold the plant for about $310 million to Ispat,[16] in the country's largest privatisation to date. Ispat also purchased nineteen coal mines that supply the steel facility, iron ore mines that in 2003 supplied 55 per cent of the plant's needs, and two large hydroelectric generating facilities that provide the substantial amounts of electricity required for production (IFC, 1997).

The details of Ispat's purchase are controversial. The leading western scholar on Kazakhstan categorises the Karmet privatisation as suspect (Olcott, 2002: 140), but the World Bank claims that it was the result of a "competitive" process (IFC, 1998).

An analysis of the purchase chronology shows it is indeed virtually impossible that a competitive bidding process could have taken place. The US Steel-led management team took over the plant in July 1995 (Gotova, 1995: 9). The Kazakh government stripped it of the management contract on 1 November (*Moskovskie Novosti*, 1995: B9), awarded management of the plant to Mittal's group eight days later (*American Metal Market*, 1995: 3), proclaimed a decree authorising privatisation of the plant another eight days after that on 17 November and agreed to sell it to Mittal after another week (*Izvestiia*, 1995: F1). One legal analysis concluded:

> creditors had no opportunity to satisfy themselves as to the terms and conditions of sale, the notice arrangements, or to participate themselves. These circumstances, coupled with a comparison of Karmet's replacement cost (usually estimated far in excess of $1 billion) to the bid obtained ($50 million), create substantial concern as to whether the auction actually realized the best available value for Karmet's assets.
>
> Analysis of the third Karmet decree shows a disregard for the structure and substance of Kazakh bankruptcy law and a subversion of a basic purpose of that law and the Foreign Investment Law, namely the protection of the rights of creditors generally and of foreign investors in particular.
>
> (Pentsov *et al.*, 1996)

In 2002, the BBC investigated various aspects of LNM Holdings' operations, concluding in part that,

> Mr. Mittal gave $100m to the controversial Chodiev group for its help in the purchase of a steel plant in the former Soviet republic of Kazakhstan. Key members of the Chodiev group are said to have had business links with organized crime in the former Soviet Union.
>
> (BBC, 2002a)

Ispat's Karmet operation was initially financed through loans from a consortium led by the Netherlands-headquartered ABN-AMRO Bank, secured against contracts and purchasers' letters of credit. However, shortly after consolidating its acquisitions, Ispat approached the World Bank's IFC arm and the EBRD for a substantial capital injection to pay for restructuring and upgrading the operations. The parties agreed in 1997 on an overall investment programme valued at $856 million, with $365 million to be provided by multilateral bank financing (Decker, 2004). However, after the 1998–1999 Asian and Russian financial crisis, Ispat scaled back investment, drawing down less than half the loan.

Subsequently, Ispat Karmet benefited from three more IFI investments. In 1999 and 2001, IFC advanced $6 million to support two loan funds, one controlled by Ispat and the other by Kazkommertsbank, to be used to provide loans to small and medium-sized Ispat Karmet suppliers, especially those created through Ispat restructuring and outsourcing. As noted above, in 2004, IFC extended a $100 million loan to Ispat to upgrade its facilities worldwide, including the Karaganda plant.

Explaining Ispat Karmet

Ispat managers state that the primary advantage of IFI involvement is reputational. The company is owned and managed mainly by Indian-born people, which "has advantages as we all come from similar backgrounds and can understand each other", but at the same time "we have to prove that we can follow international practices":

> We are satisfied with our relationship with EBRD/IFC, it is not just the financing but it also gives us credibility, that we are not a fly by night operation. Once people see there is a tie up with them, that creates an integrity bonus for us.
>
> (Choudhary, 2003)

The EBRD and IFC are similarly satisfied with their relationships with Lakshmi Mittal and the Karmet plant. For both institutions, Kazakhstan has been a difficult country in which to do business, and the Ispat-owned plant, a stable money-maker from the beginning, is a rare success story.

Michael Davey, an Australian national, is the EBRD's resident representative in Kazakhstan. His Almaty offices are in the same plush new office building as the World Bank and Citibank. The European Commission's delegation to Kazakhstan is across the street. Like many EBRD staff, Davey is bullish on Ispat:

> Ispat is an excellent example of what a well-disciplined and well-run enterprise can achieve. Really IFIs should not take any credit at all, but we do use Ispat as an example of our work here in Kazakhstan. Before we lent to Ispat in 1997, we did not have a large impact in Kazakhstan.
>
> (Davey, 2003)

Both the World Bank and EBRD have indeed extensively marketed their relationships with Ispat Karmet as examples of their effectiveness in promoting economic transition in the former Soviet Union, presenting the details of their activities in numerous international conferences and development donor fora.[17] As detailed earlier in the chapter, the Ispat/IFI relationship blossomed as the company acquired large steel plants in several formerly Communist countries in East-Central Europe, often receiving financing support from EBRD and/or the World Bank.

While EBRD steel analyst Chris Beauman has characterised steel industry criticism of the Karmet deal as "a hint of sour grapes" (cited in Marsh, 2003: 10), Davey is careful not to endorse the Karmet privatisation process: "that was during the Kazhegeldin[18] era privatisations and so there was not a great deal of transparency for privatisations in general in that period". However, "[i]llicit trading in the period 1989 to 1995 is not a big concern for us", as long as the potential financial partner is not implicated in activities such as extortion, drugs and prostitution, which would make them "untouchable". Davey says that the EBRD conducts extensive "due diligence" before investing in any projects, which includes carrying out background checks; "you can get a lot of good background information, there are so many out-of-work KGB people around, people who are really good".

The first article of the EBRD's Articles of Agreement restricts the Bank to working only in countries "committed to and applying the principles of multiparty democracy, pluralism and market economics" (EBRD, 1990). Davey claims the Bank regularly assesses Kazakhstan's compliance, working closely with its member governments, "especially the United States", and also with the Organisation for Security and Cooperation in Europe (OSCE).[19] He also says the Bank has consulted with Kazakh civil society on this issue. While countries like Turkmenistan and Belarus are "beyond the pale", "Kazakhstan is not that close to the line".

Davey's perspective is largely shared by Scott Clark, the Canadian director of the EBRD. In an interview in London, Clark (2003) criticised the bank's lax enforcement of its "democracy Article", citing Uzbekistan in particular, where the EBRD was still doing business:

Uzbekistan is clearly not a democratic country, not by any definition … I mean how low do you set the bar. Torturing people, there aren't degrees of torturing people, if they are torturing people they are torturing people. Boiling people, that is torture.

Nevertheless, Clark felt that the situation in Kazakhstan, while not perfect, was, "the least of our worries in the 'Stans. They supply ninety percent of the fuel for the Americans in Afghanistan".

Despite Davey's and Clark's sanguine view of Kazakhstan's democracy record and assertion of close collaboration with OSCE, Beata Romuliwocz (2003), the OSCE's political officer in the country, painted a generally negative picture of the state of democracy in Kazakhstan. She noted that the two most prominent members of the opposition were "political prisoners" who had been imprisoned "because they became dangerous to the government"; unlike other ethnic Russian opposition leaders, they had support in the dominant Kazakh ethnic population. The government "is trying to stack the electoral commission" and the political party law "excludes most parties". The mass media, while nominally free, are effectively "80 per cent controlled by the administration or associated with the administration". The government is in the process of developing a law on NGOs, which "as far as we can see has no purpose other than to cut down on political activity by NGOs".

Corruption allegations implicating the President, which are in the US courts, present a problem and there is speculation that he and his family "may not survive this". Speaking personally, Romuliwocz felt that, "the situation here is slightly dangerous; you could end up with a Saudi scenario. You [the West] support one family and end up with a problem. Not supporting a democratic alternative, the cost could be high".

Dissident leaders harshly criticised EBRD's role in Kazakhstan. Nurbulat Masanov, the country's best-known political scientist, stripped of his professorship at the Kazakh State University and his membership of the Kazakhstan Academy of Science because of his opposition to the regime, accused the EBRD of whitewashing Kazakhstan's democracy and human rights record: "As for the EBRD I don't take these guys seriously at all. The people representing the European Bank here are in the pocket of Nazarbayev" (Masanov, 2003).

Masanov believes that in Kazakhstan, where political control remains tight while economic controls are loosened, "the only people who benefit are those around the President". He claims there is an unwritten rule that certain sectors are reserved for Nazarbayev and his family; first, it was oil, and then metals production, and then energy consumption. The list just keeps growing.

While reserving his harshest criticism for the EBRD, Masanov expresses general frustration with representatives of multilateral and bilateral organisations in Kazakhstan. He says trying to influence international bureaucracies is ineffective, because, "[b]ureaucracy supports itself all over the world". He has met with both the World Bank and IMF, but they say they are interested only in economic reforms and are not responsible for promoting political reforms. He believes the indulgence with which western interests treat Kazakhstan's democratic deficits comes down to a cash nexus:

> the West has worse than double standards. Do you think that the reason they don't make sanctions is because of the weather? It is because there's lots of money to be made here … Nazarbayev gets away with things ultimately because he offers a price to the West, economic liberalization but political dictatorship, and the allure of money is enough that they accept it.

Rozlana Taukina is a veteran journalist who ran a successful television station in Almaty shortly after the collapse of the Soviet Union, but ran foul of the tightening restrictions on free speech and the ruling elite's monopolisation of the media in the mid- and late 1990s. She became a human rights advocate. She heads the national NGO Zhurnalisty *v* bedye (Journalists in Trouble) as well as a CIS-wide association of independent electronic media, and participates in Bankwatch, an international NGO alliance that keeps track of multilateral Bank activities in the former Communist countries:[20]

> [w]e are concerned that all these Central Asian countries get lots of aid from the international banks like the World Bank and EBRD, but the people remain poor. Why should people be so poor in an oil rich country like Kazakhstan?
>
> (Taukina, 2003)

The people of Karmet

Karmet is an eighteen-hour train journey from Almaty, across the dry steppes of southern and central Kazakhstan to Karaganda, the country's second largest city with about 500,000 inhabitants. Karaganda was a showcase for Soviet heavy industrial development. While many provincial towns in Kazakhstan look frayed and neglected ten years after the collapse of the Soviet Union, Karaganda's central spaces are clean and bright, and there are a handful of garish new buildings housing the offices of a private bank headquartered in the city. As in most cities outside the commercial capital of Almaty and the national capital Astana, Lenin's statue still graces the square in front of City Hall, though Ispat's logo is fixed prominently to the top of the building (see Figure 6.3).

Temirtau is an hour's drive from Karaganda, through ragged suburbs and past abandoned industrial plants, then out onto the plains. About 5 kilometres from Temirtau, a haze is evident in the sky ahead, which soon develops into a noxious fog enveloping the road and slowing traffic. On the approach to Temirtau, Karmet is visible on the east of the main road, its chimneys and buildings extending for several kilometres. On our first journey to Temirtau from our base in Karaganda, the taxi driver is inquisitive about our visit.[21] When we tell him that we have meetings at Karmet, he launches into a diatribe about Ispat, blaming the company for the death of his father, a veteran miner:

Figures 6.3 Lenin and Ispat Karmet, 2004 (photograph, Jonathan Murphy).

Do you want to know what I really think of the changes since the end of the USSR? About my father, he was a miner. It was a different story under the Soviet Union, a miner was a respected person, a person was very proud to be a miner, now miners are nothing, and they are treated like criminals. Ispat, they are bastards. My Dad wasn't young but they made him work two shifts in a row. He had a heart attack at the end of one of those double shifts and he died.

Although Ispat Karmet's offices are located at the end of a long, tree-lined boulevard, the buildings themselves are painted a shabby brown, with only the Ispat Karmet nameplate indicating a change from the Soviet past. Inside, there have been few, if any, renovations since the end of the Soviet era.

At the plant, we have separate meetings with four senior managers at Karmet, three Indian-origin expatriates and one Kazakhstani, Anatoly Kim, who is the head of the plant's technical department. A. Regie Paul is the head of strategy and organisational development, M. Rajendran the general manager of Ispat's non-steel operations, and V.V. Vaideeswaran general manager for finance. Earlier, between plane connections, I had met with Nawal Choudhary, general director and CEO of the Karmet facility, at the company's office/guest house in Almaty.

The expatriate managers had varied experiences; although all had been born in India, they come from different parts of the country, and all but Choudhary had spent much of their working lives in the West, mainly working for non-Indian-owned companies. The interviews revealed a remarkable consistency in issue identification and management approach, and with the partial exception of Kim, who was somewhat more critical of Soviet-era management paradigms, the men's viewpoints appeared essentially interchangeable.

The bottom line is that Ispat came to Karmet with the intention of building on strengths: "We took the view that we should work with the existing situation and carry out reforms as necessary rather than turning everything upside down".

The plant made money from the first day of Ispat's acquisition, and has made money each year subsequently, even during the Asian and Russian financial crises. It continues to return a significant dividend to LNM Holdings.

The expatriate managers had a notably non-ideological view of the Soviet system, emphasising that the Soviet Union "was a developed country": "[e]verything was not wrong in the Soviet Union, it is wrong to think that the way forward is to throw away everything that was done there". Nevertheless, when Ispat arrived, the plant was in serious trouble. A series of management contracts had been signed with western companies but the outside managers had no real financial commitment, and thus little will to turn the plant around. With the collapse of the Soviet planned system, sales arrangements often involved barter, which was highly susceptible to corruption and undermined any sense of market price for goods. The town of Temirtau was in a catastrophic situation; workers had not been paid for several months, the electric power system had been partially shut down, and "it was difficult even to get toothpaste and toothbrushes". The economy had become demonetised, and the plant even issued promissory tokens which were used in the local market as an alternative to real money.

The first thing Ispat did was to pay the back wages, creating some liquidity in the community. It was a difficult operation because people who had been hurt by the transition period's currency and banking instabilities were not interested in receiving cheques. The amounts of money were too large for the fledgling domestic banking system to handle, but fortunately, one western Bank, ABN-Amro, had just opened in Kazakhstan. The company flew cash into Temirtau in a private aircraft with the army as security: "it was like the Wild West then".

The Karmet purchase involved "only the plant assets, as well as the clearly defined wage liabilities". Most of the plant's social assets, such as sports complexes, hospitals and schools, were taken on by the city of Temirtau. However, Ispat ended up retaining quite a few ancillary businesses, ranging from the tram line ("the only reliable way to get to the plant in winter") to the plant's canteens, summer camps, a dental clinic, a hotel and even a textile mill originally set up to make Karmet workers' uniforms.

While many of these services "probably ought to be outsourced", this needs to be done carefully so as not to cause social dislocation and a breakdown in supplies to the plant; the company is collaborating with the World Bank's IFC on a special loan programme to help expand the network of small and medium-size suppliers in Temirtau and Karaganda (IFC, 2000).

Some outside businesses were brought into the company's fold to assure production inputs. The electrical generating system and the central heating plant belonged to the city when Ispat arrived, but the municipal government was insolvent and the plant's supply irregular, so Ispat bought the electricity company, guaranteeing power and heat for itself and the city's residents. The company also purchased a number of coal mines in the Karaganda coal basin, ensuring the plant's supplies.

The Ispat managers praise the workforce: "Human resources are a big asset here; all the people are qualified, trained. Generally throughout the population there is a highly trained workforce, though skills in management and finance were lacking and we had to bring people in".

Although by western standards the plant is overmanned, Ispat has not substantially reduced the number of employees; a few managers involved in activities considered undesirable were let go, but most of the technical managers were retained. In all, Ispat brought in thirty to thirty-five expatriates to work in general management, marketing and finance.

Kim was more explicit than the expatriate managers in criticising Soviet management, which he categorised as excessively hierarchical. The absence of feedback loops led to poor decisions, with numerous projects being started and then abandoned when the management team changed. Kim claimed that by 1994, there were at least thirty incomplete abandoned projects at the plant. Paul, who had been brought into Ispat to implement a strategic plan, emphasised the need for a balance between the advantages of the old management system – effective in executing core production activities – and newer management models where different parts of the operation work together to create a dynamic and flexible operation geared towards identifying and responding to market opportunities:

Of course there are benefits to the command and control system, there is discipline, and people are very committed to their jobs. There is a fairly solid fabric here. We are just trying to look more into the outside world.

Ispat's main challenges were marketing, ensuring necessary investments in the plant, and introducing a modern system of financial accounting. Under the Soviet system materials and investment were centrally allocated and thus there was no need to worry about marketing or investment. With the collapse of the Soviet distribution network, new markets were needed. The domestic Kazakhstan market is far too small to sustain a plant of Karmet's size: "usually steel plants have a domestic market for at least a quarter or a third of the product, but not here, so everything is dependent on marketing". Northwest China, which is developing rapidly, is the biggest market now for Karmet products, along with Iran and Russia.

The expatriate managers emphasise the synergy between the ex-Soviet steel industry and an Indian-managed company. Indian plants were built or modernised during the 1960s and 1970s using Soviet technology, and as a result, not only are Indian steel sector managers familiar with Soviet plants, many also speak Russian and can communicate with the workforce. Choudhary takes the connection further: "having a different [Indian] background we understood the problems a little better [than western managers]. There are many sentimental issues, like the social protections; these shouldn't just be abandoned".

Ispat Karmet, like other operations in the Ispat family, has prioritised compliance with international standards; the plant was the first in Kazakhstan to achieve ISO9001 certification, and as part of its agreement with the EBRD, it implemented international accounting standards in 1997, seven years ahead of the rest of Kazakhstan. The Karmet managers believe Ispat's global presence gives advantages, from access to high-quality research and development at the Ispat Inland unit in Chicago to the ability to run a "multicultural operation" and learn from the company's experience elsewhere in turnarounds of formerly government-owned plants.

Although Ispat approached the IFIs with a genuine desire to access capital for upgrading the facility, the managers stress that this was not essential to the success of the operation. Indeed, in the initial agreement signed with the EBRD and IFC, the overall investment programme was valued at $856 million, with $365 million to be provided by multilateral bank financing. However, in the wake of the 1998–1999 Asian and Russian financial crisis, Ispat scaled back the investment programme and drew down on less than half the available EBRD/IFC financing. Vaideeswaran says that the EBRD would like to lend Ispat Karmet more money, but the LNM Group has "a policy to lower debts as much as possible and manage things with our own cash".

The managers emphasise the frugality of the operation in several respects. Most obviously, the company has contained labour costs. Although wages have doubled in real terms since the takeover, and are above the Kazakh average, they remain about 30 per cent below comparable salaries at the large Russian plants. Union representatives, who "have been to the US and Canada and know what workers there make", are constantly asking for higher salaries. The expatriate managers note that the cost of living is higher in Russia and much higher in North America, and highlight the Kazakhstan operation's very high delivery costs because of the distance to ports and to its main markets.[22]

Perhaps unsurprisingly, the managers seemed more cautious in describing relationships with the Kazakh government than they had been in discussing Karmet's internal challenges. One of the managers noted that there was sometimes a disconnect between the country's top leaders and local officials: "Nazarbayev may know what is a market economy but the local tax people didn't necessarily". Not long after the privatisation, the company was subjected to an extensive audit, and presented with a large tax bill. They went to the minister of revenue and eventually worked out an understanding.[23] Generally, the managers laud the government for its commitment to the plant's success, several mentioning President Nazarbayev's long tenure at Karmet[24] as a possible explanation. They viewed the government's overall orientation towards the market as very positive, and several managers dismissed suggestions that corruption was a major concern.

Ispat would not provide access to shopfloor workers at the plant, so instead we interviewed residents of Temirtau at random in the town centre, as well as local NGO representatives and the director of an independent television channel in the city. In total fifteen people were interviewed using a semi-structured method. All but two interviewees had a close attachment to the plant. Three worked at the plant, six had close relatives working at the plant, and four had previously worked at the plant.

The three plant employees seemed quite open about the situation at Ispat, and their perspectives were consistent with one other. All said things were better during the Soviet period but had become catastrophic after the collapse and before "the Indians" took over. They credited the new owners with stabilising the situation at the plant but said that they had to work quite a bit harder than during the Soviet era: "[m]orale was better then. Now the managers are extremely strict". They all said that they are paid regularly, but complained that wages are lower in real terms than before:

As far as our standard of living goes, well it depends on how you look at things. We used to be able to travel a lot. Now we can't afford to. But we do have enough money to live, for the essentials, but we cannot travel.

As a group, the interviewees emphasised that living conditions were much better during the Soviet era, but that the past few years had seen a small improvement:

Life generally in Temirtau, it was terrible about four years ago. The power was off all the time, lots of people were leaving. It is not so bad now. But during the USSR, all the utilities worked all the time.

The attitude towards Ispat seemed neutral or slightly positive. The firm was definitely seen as "Indian", though this was not necessarily a negative assessment:

I have heard that in order to get a job at Karmet you have to pay bribes. I am not saying it was the Indians who thought that up, that existed before, too.

The Indians didn't pay us all the money that we were owed from before.

Respondents' attitudes towards the Kazakh government were, however, consistently negative. All but the youngest interviewees and an immigrant couple from Mongolia compared contemporary life unfavourably with that in the Soviet era. Several interviewees commented negatively on the privatisations:

I don't know what everyone thinks but a number of people think foreign companies that took over our big plants are just using them for their own benefit and don't care about the people. They are just pumping out the resources from Kazakhstan and when these resources are used up they will abandon the country and go somewhere else.

Conclusion

The close relationship between the multilateral banks and Ispat/Mittal is mutually beneficial. Mittal is an aggressive international operator, and the banks facilitated its access to opportunities by making financial resources available, but more critically by legitimising the company in the eyes of the government and private finance sources. For the banks, Ispat is a vehicle to achieve marketisation of difficult parts of transitional countries' economic structure, thus demonstrating the validity and viability of their ideological commitment to "capitalism". While there is no evidence that the World Bank or the EBRD pushed the Kazakh government to select Ispat, there has undoubtedly been such pressure on other privatising governments, extending in the case of the Czech Republic to forcing the national government to illegally breach a contract in order to make a steel plant available to Ispat. The banks have also been remarkably willing to extend financing to Ispat's private arm, LNM Holdings, despite the company's private status and registration in a tax haven, and consequently hazy finances.

The multilateral banks, and particularly the World Bank and its sister IMF, play a larger role in directing the restructuring of the transnational economy than is evidenced by examining Bank and IFC private sector financing alone. In the Kazakh and other cases examined in this chapter, the Bank and the IMF placed substantial pressure – often with the assistance of major state powers – on developing and transitional country administrations to "restructure" their economies by shifting state enterprises to the (transnational) private sector. Typically, this pressure is irresistible; in the case of Trinidad because the country desperately needed the multilateral institutions' cash, in Poland and Czechoslovakia because pursuing the "free market" strategy was part of the price of entry to the European Union, and in Kazakhstan because the governing elite needed to be able to demonstrate its genuine commitment to leave a recent Communist heritage behind. After the multilateral institutions had prised privatisation commitments from governments, in several cases they then "helped" Ispat to pick up the plants.

As noted earlier, (post)Marxist globalisation theorists and even CMS and development scholars influenced by post-developmentalism almost universally describe the banks' activities in the global economy as "neo-liberalism". Such a conclusion relies on a definition of neo-liberalism so broad as to be meaningless. The Ispat/Mittal case demonstrates mutually reinforcing global networks involving transnational entrepreneurs, state actors and multilateral institution bureaucracies. If anything, the banks' bureaucrats appear to be the key decision-makers, with the transnational corporation and the state actors profiting within the rules established by the banks.

Chapters 4 and 5 above addressed the Bank's use of managed participation and co-optation of civil society. This chapter has provided a further sobering indication of the nature of the emergent global order. Neither the Bank nor the EBRD has much interest in transparency, human rights or democracy in

Kazakhstan. This was notable particularly in the case of the EBRD, whose articles of agreement expressly forbid it to operate in countries that do not respect democratic rights. Elsewhere (Murphy, 2006), I have documented how the "new" "capitalist" elite in Kazakhstan is predominantly a recycling of the old Communist nomenklatura, a pattern that prevails elsewhere in the former Communist bloc (Hanley *et al.*, 1995). The questionable capitalist pedigrees and current governance and business practices of the post-Soviet elites have not deterred the international financial institutions from embracing them as part of the new global managerial elite.

The fact that Ispat Karmet's managers produced an operating profit from the first day of private ownership suggests that the Banks' rhetoric about the "failure" of the Soviet economy is exaggerated. Many other plants across Kazakhstan and the former Soviet Union fell victim to asset-stripping and cannibalisation in the transition. The multilateral financial institutions and their advisers actively promoted this "shock therapy" that entailed the total dislocation of the economy, as discussed earlier in this chapter, and in regard to the Soviet bloc more generally by Wedel (1998) and others. The human cost of the unnecessary collapse of the state socialist economies has been enormous, with life expectancy declining dramatically in many countries, including Kazakhstan and Russia (McKee, 2001). The benefits of the new global order have accrued to a selected few.

As for Ispat/Mittal, it has undoubtedly brought benefits to the population of the Karaganda region. The company has stabilised the local and regional economy and has breathed life into a city which was on the verge of collapse. Temirtau residents interviewed were more interested in work conditions and standard of living than the plant managers' nationality, suggesting that the popular appeal of nationalist opposition to globalisation may be limited.

Ispat/Mittal is a remarkable example of a globalised organisation. Ispat Karmet managers emphasised their common Indian heritage, although none of Lakshmi Mittal's steel companies have been registered in India, Mittal has not lived in India for thirty years, and most of his top managers have substantial international experience. Ispat fits neither the globalisation deniers' minimisation of transnationalisation (Callinicos, 1989; Hirst and Thompson, 1996), nor the in rootless globalisation thesis (Giddens, 2000; Hardt and Negri, 2000: 237). While the company is not geographically rooted – the LNM Group was not legally registered anywhere (Speed, 2002) – it is certainly "culturally" rooted. This rooting extends beyond the key personnel in the plant and includes networking with politicians in the Indian diaspora,[25] although Mittal's relationship with both Blair and Nazarbayev shows that the political network extends well beyond a single ethnic group.

When Mittal started his extraordinary rise to global business baron in the mid-1990s, his example could have been considered the exception that proved the rule of western domination of the globalising world. Even in 2002, when I first started charting Ispat's successes, outbound investments from developing world corporations were targeted and relatively small scale (Boston Consulting Group, 2006). From 2004 onwards, both Indian and Chinese companies' foreign investments have increased exponentially, although from a very small initial base (Lane and Schmukler, 2006: 7). In 2004, the Chinese computer manufacturer Lenovo purchased IBM's global personal computer business, bringing Chinese outbound investment to $5.5 billion, a 93 per cent increase over 2003. In 2005, it rose to $12.3 billion, before jumping another 31 per cent to $16.1 billion in 2006 (*People's Daily*, 2007). Indian companies, which are still theoretically subject to capital controls, notched $4.3 billion in 2004, rising to $4.5 billion, before jumping to $7.3 billion in only six months of 2006 (Srinivas, 2007). In early 2007, the Indian conglomerate Tata purchased European steelmaker Corus for $6.2 billion, the single biggest Indian outbound investment, while the Birla family conglomerate Hindalco purchased the world's largest rolled aluminium producer Novelis for $6 billion. Total developing country corporate investment overseas increased tenfold between 1990 and 2005, from $148 billion to $1.4 trillion (UNCTAD, 2006). While the total flow of inbound investment to developing countries remains about three times larger than outbound investment, the trend is rapidly reversing, with Indian outbound investment exceeding inbound investment to India in 2006. China's outbound investment is almost certain to continue to grow exponentially simply because of the overhang of dollars held in China. In 2005, China's and India's shares of world output reached 15.4 per cent and 5.9 per cent respectively. Goldman Sachs project that if current trends continue, China's GDP will be higher than that of the United States by about 2035, and India will overtake the US in about 2042 (Poddar and Yi, 2007: 5). This would restore China and India to roughly their position in the world economy in 1700, before the industrial revolution and the onset of rapacious western colonialism (Maddison, 2003: 261).

This rapid shift towards a multi-polar world economy is occurring at the same time as the delocalisation of transnational companies, of which the Mittal case in this chapter is one example. Mathews (2006) has conceptualised Mittal Steel along with other companies with roots in developing and peripheral countries as examples of a new type of "dragon multinational". These companies thrive because of their ability to operate transnationally, rather than through financial muscle accumulated through initial growth in a domestic market, as was the case with the classic giant American multinational corporations of the twentieth century such as Ford. In addition, the spatial reordering of the global economy has expanded the utility of tax havens and offshore business hubs, including British Virgin Islands and Netherlands Antilles used by Mittal, and other centres such as Hong Kong, Mauritius and Singapore.

There is, in summary, overwhelming evidence that the imperialist, postcolonial model of globalisation is becoming rapidly outdated. The success of elites from developing countries does not signify, however, that the world is becoming more equal. In general, the GINI coefficient of inter-national (between countries) income inequality has increased at greater or lesser rates throughout the period between 1820 and the present day, with the exception of the interwar period that ended in the Holocaust and Hiroshima. Inter-national inequality increased moderately during the developmentalist phase between 1950 and 1980, and faster during the neo-liberal period from 1980 to 2000. Superficially, inter-national inequality has moderated since the last years of the twentieth century, when countries are population-weighted, because of the economic success of India, China and other high-population Asian countries. However, it is more useful in an era of globalisation to measure inequality between *households* rather than countries. This reveals that income inequality remains at historically high levels and is probably increasing (Milanovic, 2005). The income of the top 5 per cent of the world's population accounts for about 45 per cent of total global US$ income. The bottom 5 per cent accounts for 0.1 per cent, or 1/300th of the top 5 per cent. The sociological significance of globalisation is that the winners are to an increasing extent distributed internationally and active transnationally: a global managerial elite.

Conclusion

This book argues that a new type of hierarchical social order is developing on a world scale. It is an order that I describe as global managerialism (see Figure C.1). The proposition of the global managerial order rests upon four theoretical pillars. The first is that the apparent trend towards globalisation is real, and of wide-ranging economic, political and social impact. The second is that the architecture of the new global order is based on formal and informal transnational organisational networks, rather than on the traditional hierarchical structure epitomised in the nation state. Third, power is concentrated in a definable global elite, comprised of transnationally oriented economic, political and social leaders. Fourth, the global elite's power is exercised through managerialism, characterised by the de-ideologisation and technisation of decision making. This depoliticisation is inauthentic, however, as global managerialism entrenches human inequality and the concentration of power in the hands of a largely self-appointed elite. I will use the following few pages to summarise the arguments underlying each of the four propositions, to counter possible objections to the explanatory framework presented in this book, and to underline why this book represents a significant addition to a critical understanding of globalisation.

Globalisation

The perspective presented in this book depends fundamentally, of course, on the reality of globalisation and its central relevance to understanding our world. It is true that globalisation has been the cause of a remarkable outpouring of "hype", much of which has had political motives, in particular to justify the necessity of dismantling the welfare states that provided Europeans with a degree of security during the first decades after the end of the Second World War. It is not necessary to draw such political conclusions to acknowledge that the world is far more closely integrated than it was in the past, notwithstanding some of the assertions of globalisation doubters such as Hirst and Thompson. Even if, as they claim, some indicators of global integration such as international trade have previously been as large as a proportion of overall economic activity as they are now, the overall breadth and depth of current globalising factors far exceeds previous periods.

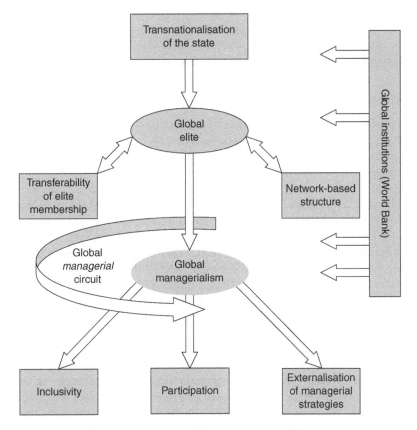

Figure C.1 A model of global managerialism.

In the business field, globalisation is characterised not merely by elevated levels of international trade, but much more significantly by the transnationalisation of business processes in both production and services, by the broad reduction and often elimination of national barriers to international economic activities, and the emergence of authentically transnational corporations, such as Mittal's steel empire discussed in Chapter 6 above. In the political sphere, globalisation is reflected in the establishment and subsequent strengthening of a transnational architecture including the Bretton Woods organisations in the economic sphere, as well as the perhaps less effective but nonetheless omnipresent United Nations system. At a sub-global level the success of the European Union and to a less comprehensive extent other regional blocs provides further indication that the nation state's relatively short period as the unchallenged organisational kingpin of the global order is coming to a close. On the level of political organisation and discourse, the predominance of post-ideological political movements epitomised by the Third Way, discussed in Chapter 4 above, speaks to a worldwide homogenisation of political approaches and the domination of a managerialist orientation to politics. The globalisation of social policy has received much less critical attention, but is nonetheless proceeding apace with initiatives such as the Millennium Development Goals and the World Bank's poverty reduction and comprehensive development frameworks, discussed in Chapter 3 above.

Institutions and governance

The relative diminution of the power of the nation state is inherent in an expansive view of globalisation as is presented here. Nevertheless, the character of the emerging global framework is substantially different from its nation state antecedents. This is not unexpected, as the organising principles and symbols of forms of social order have historically differed as society developed through family, clan, imperial and nation state guises. The emerging global order is characterised by a network structure that is based on interrelating organisations and less formal networks. There is significant diversity in organisations. The Bretton Woods institutions enjoy a relatively high level of transnationalisation, with the emergence of a specifically transnational "voice" that cannot be reduced to the interests of a single nation state, as is discussed in the section of Chapter 2 (pp. 31–52) that explores the World Bank's relationship with the United States. The United Nations and its constituent agencies are kept more closely under the tutelage of nation states, which probably accounts for its relative lack of success in expanding its role beyond that of crisis mediator of last resort. Despite the apparent conflict of interest between nation states and a global governance order, there is considerable personnel and philosophical overlap between the senior levels of national bureaucracies and the transnational organisations. Global elites from business and national governments also meet together in informal networks and loose-knit elite organisations such as the Davos and Bilderburg conferences. The transnational institutional networking process is self-described as "convening power": the ability of an organisation to pull together like-minded organisations to tackle a policy issue, as discussed in Chapter 4 above.

The mode through which global governance extends its domain differs from the traditional system of formal legal authority of the nation state. Global governance is generally characterised by the application of policy norms that are developed through informal and semi-formal convened processes, as discussed above. These processes are invariably dominated by technical expertise but frequently incorporate forms of managed participation. In the absence of authentically democratic decision making, civil society organisations play an important role in legitimising policy norms, and the World Bank has gone to considerable lengths to enlist civil society executives, particularly in international social policy governance initiatives. The tri-cornered governance network approach, led by transnational officials and including national government bureaucrats, business leaders, and civil society executives, is theorised by transnationalist policy experts Rischard and Reinicke, and discussed in Chapter 5 of this book.

Norms-based governance may appear to lack the formal authority of legislated state power, but actually tends to be extremely effective because of its inclusiveness, adaptability and popular legitimacy. At their most effective, global policy norms can assume a status "beyond criticism". In the developing world, centralising institutions such as the World Bank and IMF link global governance norms together into comprehensive development frameworks, which are imbued with disciplinary authority through funding conditionalities. These conditionalities are further reinforced by interlocking networks of bilateral and multilateral funders whose resources are mobilised in return for overall policy compliance. The process through which universal basic education has become a global policy norm is discussed in the case studies in Chapter 5 above. Chapter 6 addresses the role of the World Bank and other transnational institutions in shaping a homogenised global economy, both at national and global industry levels. A norms-based approach is dependent on the marginalisation of alternatives, and the Bank and its sister organisations devoted considerable effort to destroying the state socialist structure of industry in the former Soviet bloc, even at tremendous human cost and through the wanton destruction of economic capacity. Similarly, at the global industry level, the transnational institutions both pressurised governments to divest of their heavy industries, often at fire sale prices, and subsidised new entrants.

Elite domination

The global order is elite-driven. Elites from different segments of society and organisational networks cooperate together in establishing and maintaining a managed order that benefits them both materially and through preserving elite status. Elite status is conferred through the possession of power, which is secured and manifested in a number of different ways. Power refers to the ability to achieve some end; in the context of social stratification it entails a group's ability to exercise authority over other groups and to reproduce itself. In contrast to a Marxist perspective, critical elite theory argues that economic power or capital is only one tool through which power is manifested and exercised. Political and institutional power, as well as the power of social legitimation, are also important means through which power is exercised in contemporary society. In a complex society, a power elite, therefore, must possess substantial control over key nodal power points in society, including economic, political, institutional and social. A stable hegemonic elite will encompass key possessors within each of these nodes.

The broader the representativity of a power elite, the more stable its hegemony. Hegemony in contemporary society is achieved primarily through discursive domination. Nevertheless, material power is essential because it underpins this discursive production of legitimacy, as well as providing a vehicle for the transfer of elite status to future generations. Political power defined broadly includes government and ancillary institutions such as the judiciary, as well as norm-producing institutions which are of particular importance in the global, "post-government" order. Legitimacy is a particular challenge to an elite order which is by definition founded upon inequality. This is partly achieved by the possession and projection of technical expertise; this explains the lengths to which the World Bank goes to market itself as the "Knowledge Bank", as discussed in Chapter 4 above. In the democratic era, technical expertise alone does not guarantee authority, however, and popular legitimacy must be established. This can be generated through the success of managerialist political movements. The philosophical commonalities between the World Bank and the Third Way political movements are also discussed in Chapter 4. Global managerialism relies primarily for its day-to-day legitimacy on managed participation through which popular consent for managerialist programmes and projects is manufactured. Organised civil society plays an important part in conferring such participatory legitimacy. Global managerialism's entry into the social policy domain is founded largely on an alliance between international NGO leadership, the World Bank, other transnational agencies, and globalising bilateral development agencies such as the DFID, the British international development ministry. Chapter 5 explores the development of such an alliance, focusing particularly on the universal basic education Millennium Development Goal. The authoritarian manner in which global social policies are implemented on the ground refutes claims that they are driven from the grassroots.

The proposition of an emergent global managerial elite contrasts with the international class analysis of imperialist, dependency, world-system and post-colonial theories. These post-Marxist approaches claim that in a global economy the elites of developing or peripheral countries are definitively subordinate to the elites of the developed countries; their role is primarily to act as the agents of developed country imperialism, according to the theory of the "comprador bourgeoisie". Their perspective is disproved by the emergence of a number of developing countries as major economic powers. It is simply not plausible to propose that the Chinese, Indian, Korean and Malaysian elites, for example, are agents of the European and North American ruling classes. Neither do developing and transitional country elites have an enduring commonality of interest with their citizenry. Developing country elites' global success is based upon their capacity to deliver cheap goods and services through the exploitation of pools of low-wage labour. This requires an open world economy. Major developing country elites participate assiduously in formal and informal transnational elite networking, and support the transnational rule-setting process, while naturally seeking to secure the best possible operating conditions to serve their interests.

Managerialism

Managerialism is the (non)ideology of the contemporary global elite. Managerialism aims to depoliticise collective decision making through the deconstruction of issues in social life and organisation into a series of discrete problems that can be resolved through the application of technical expertise. Managerialism seeks to obscure the presence of fundamental differences of interest; accepting the managerial solution is always presented as a win–win scenario. Contemporary managerialism retains the traditional managerial emphasis on technocratic expertise, but blends this with the consistent use of managed participation, in which citizens are engaged in the managerial process and guided towards appropriate solutions. The World Bank's poverty reduction approach, discussed in Chapter 3 above, is built on this formula. The case study of universal basic education in India, in Chapter 5 above, demonstrates this approach at the micro level. Opposing viewpoints are either incorporated into the managerial participatory process, or, if this is impossible, marginalised as extremist.

Managerialism's dismantling of issues of power relationships into a series of discrete technical decisions is complemented by the reintegration of these technical decisions into overall policy frameworks whose complexity requires a management systems approach, once again placing the manager at the organisational apex of the policy process. Policy comprehensiveness also assures broad engagement in the management process; the World Bank's poverty reduction process engages both economic and social managers; these managerialist projects also involve political leaders, although the managerialist antipathy towards authentic democracy is manifested in the World Bank and IMF's almost allergic reaction to dealing with directly elected parliaments.

Managerialism maintains an instrumental relationship with traditional ideologies. Managerialism offers a vehicle through which powerful ideological movements can realise their ambitions; as discussed in Chapter 2 above, Fascism, Communism and the New Deal all emphasised a technocratic approach to implementation of their programmes. Neo-liberal ideology was paradoxically implemented at the global level through the managerialist approach of structural adjustment, in which national elites were required to accept and implement comprehensive economic reforms in order to access international assistance. Nevertheless, managerialism's natural political perspective is post-ideological, epitomised by the Third Way political movement discussed in Chapter 4 above.

Comparative theoretical approach

The book's theoretical approach is described in Chapter 1 and developed in contrast with other critical approaches to globalisation. Essentially, global managerial theory argues in contrast to poststructuralism that society is *stratified* between those who hold power – the economic, political and social managers – and those who do not. The relationship is not static, nor is domination absolute. Indeed, in contemporary society, power is exercised primarily through consent; this is, however, a managed consent. Stratification is generationally reproduced, although as in all class systems there is a membership circulation that renews and reinvigorates the managerial elite.

In contrast to Marxist-inspired theories, the global managerial elite theory rejects the existence of an overarching deep structural economic motor, and instead presents the managerial elite as a pragmatically generated social stratum motivated by the desire to capture, exercise and maintain power. There are no inherently necessary components of a managerial elite, but as has been noted above, the more firmly and broadly the elite controls the commanding heights of the key nodal points of social power, the more secure will be its hegemonic position. Bourdieu's theory of multiple capitals, discussed in Chapter 1 above, provides a useful perspective to understanding managerial elite formation. In complex societies, elites bring together different capitals (or in my formulation, different types of power) to construct a dominant symbolic capital, or in my terms, a system of social domination. The importance of the differentiation between elite theory and Marxist-inspired economic determinism is shown through the example of diverse power systems which are comprehensible in elite theory but not in traditional Marxist class theory. In Communism, for example, managerial elite power rests on political authority, with economic and civic power fused into the political domain in a subordinate position. Similarly, in societies under military rule, physical authority plays a larger and more overt role than in western capitalist societies, with other nodal points, in this case the polity and civic power, playing a consequently subordinate role.

Managerial elite theory builds by presenting data rather than attempting to fit those data into a preconceived generating motor. It thus does not claim any predictive powers, other than the empirical observation of the ubiquity of systems of social domination and thus the likelihood that *no matter the presenting ideology or discourse, social stratification and elite domination are probable outcomes*. Social movements should be viewed in terms of their presenting ideas, but also as potential vehicles for elite renewal or replacement.

Objections to the theory of global managerialism

Some of the main challenges to global managerial theory have already been addressed in the text and the preceding summary of its main propositions. I have shown how the qualitative importance of contemporary globalisation, the emergence of a global governance framework, the existence of a cross-sectoral transnational elite, and the centrality of managerialism to elite domination, together form the foundation of a robust critical model of global social organisation.

In a short text with a broad approach, empirical justifications are necessarily indicative rather than comprehensive. Further empirical work is needed in particular to more thoroughly document transnational elite membership, and especially the interconnections between different sectors of the elite. Additional theoretical and empirical development of the concept of managerialism would also strengthen global managerial theory. I have outlined the commonalities between the managerialist concepts employed by the World Bank, and critical management studies accounts of micro-, company-level control techniques. Further analysis and documentation are needed of the interlocking processes through which these common perspectives are developed, including the role of institutions such as business schools and management consultancies.

Global managerial elite theory does not claim any particular predictive capacity. It is possible, therefore, that while a global managerial system appears to be emerging, this represents only a passing phase towards a different structure of international system. In particular, the rapid rise of India and China, among other

Asian powers, may be indicative of the emergence not of a global system, but rather of a spatial reorganisation of the global structure in which power is shifting away from Europe and North America and towards Asia. A country such as China could thus be poised to replace the United States as a hegemonic power in the type of nationally anchored international system theorised by Robert Cox and discussed in the first chapter above (p. 13). Such a development cannot *a priori* be ruled out, but even with continuing rapid growth, China is many years away from achieving global economic weight comparable to America of the post-war generation, and the British empire at its peak, and has nothing like the latter's political influence. A considerably greater proportion of the world's population is engaged in the global system, with many more key economic nodes, than has previously been the case. Further, the global economic system is considerably more integrated than ever before. It is thus not apparent that any single power will in the foreseeable future be in a position to dominate the global system, barring a catastrophic breakdown of international order. Such a breakdown is obviously possible, and even the present expansive transnational managerialist system has its dissidents among national elites, most notably at present Hugo Chavez and his Bolivarian Movement in Venezuela, which has secured some government allies and achieved popular support outside the country. Chavez's approach is an important challenge to global managerialism because it has demonstrated the possibility of alternative governance and development strategies, but his movement has the characteristics of a counter-elite rather than post-elite formation, much as the Bolshevik Revolution installed a political leadership that accrued power to itself and managed "in the interests of the people".

At the beginning of the book, I suggested that global managerialism develops both spontaneously and through conscious action. This should not be interpreted to suggest that there is any kind of conspiracy to establish a global managerial order. By and large, managerialist strategies are pursued because they represent what their initiators believe to be the best strategy to follow in very particular circumstances, without any thought being given to wider ramifications. Each such decision is part of complex chains of decisions, rationalisations and non-decisions that continue, and occasionally divert, a managerialist trajectory, as argued by historical institutionalist theory discussed in Chapter 1. It would be inaccurate, however, to suppose that elite policy directions are always tangential and never conceptualised more broadly. Chapter 2 related, for example, how a small group of intellectuals organised assiduously over many years to challenge Keynesianism, eventually succeeding in installing a neo-liberal paradigm in its place. Chapter 5 documented the very explicit global managerialist manifesto that has been developed by managerialist thinkers associated with the World Bank and other transnational institutions. Policy norm-setting, which lies at the core of transnational managerial governance, is carried out consciously. Often its domain is narrow, such as the quality standards for a particular internationally traded product. Other policy norms are far more comprehensive and strategic, such as the OECD's propagation of New Public Management as a managerialist alternative to traditional public sector bureaucracy.

It could be argued that managers do not represent a specific managerial perspective, but are rather instruments of particular interests, and thus could equally represent the common good. This would be the position of traditional Marxists, for example, who argue that managers are simply doing the bidding of a largely separate capitalist class. This issue dates back to James Burnham's early iteration of managerial theory, where he argued that managers were *replacing* capitalists as the barons of industrial society. Although the debate about the separation of ownership and control is still being ongoing in some quarters, the version of managerialism presented in this book is based on a pragmatic identification of interests between different dominant groups. There is no reason why managers and owners, groups which in any case significantly overlap, should have a fundamental difference of interest, although to the extent that they can be separated sociologically, they may contribute different forms of capital, or power, to an overall hegemonic elite.

Conversely, from the managers' own perspective, it might be argued that this book paints far too negative a picture of their role, which is after all merely to act rationally and to apply technical skills to resolve objectively existent problems. I have demonstrated, particularly in Chapter 5, how global managerialism in practice reinforces and even deepens an inegalitarian order, including when it claims to be addressing social ills such as poverty and exclusion. There is, of course, a voluminous literature covering different examples where managerial approaches have been used to nefarious ends. This risk of managerialism can be somewhat exaggerated; in the most egregious cases, such as Zygmunt Bauman's identification of managerialism with Nazi atrocities (Bauman, 1989), managerial techniques were clearly subservient to totalising ideologies. Unlike some critical management thinkers such as Grey and Parker, I do not believe that management *per se* is inherently negative. The capacity to manage lies at the foundation of much, if not all, collective human achievement. However, this should be distinguished from the pseudo-ideology and practice of managerialism, which is based on the assumption by a discrete social elite of the right to manipulate the rest of the population into pursuing particular courses of action. No matter how laudable these endeavours might seem, they are founded on a denial of fundamental human equality, and inherently generate further unequal power relationships which themselves call for further managerialist intervention, in a self-perpetuating cycle of disempowerment.

Finally, the reader may well find a generally pessimistic worldview in this book. Certainly, it is argued that there is no simple way out of inequality. Inequality and domination are enduring features of human society, and efforts to will them away have usually ended in alternative forms of domination, though the human objects of domination may change. It is naïve to believe that complex human society can be organised without a division of labour, and the management function and its consequent hierarchy is thus probably inevitable. However, levels of inequality vary substantially between societies, and there is a correlation between democratic systems and relatively lower inequality. This has often been advanced as a reason to oppose globalisation, but that is a regressive and dangerous perspective. The history of human development is one of gradual expansion of horizons beyond the family and clan to the nation state, and the logical conclusion of this process is the global level, in which artificial distinctions between humans, who share far more than they are separated by, can be erased. The path to follow is one of gradual democratisation of the global system, the replacement of managed participation with genuinely inclusive decision making, and ultimately an authentic global democracy.

Notes

1 Towards a theory of global managerialism

1 Indeed it is only through an acknowledgement of the presence of unequal power relationships in all the structures of human organisation that a thoroughgoing project for relative emancipation could be conceived.

2 Without retreating from his theoretical framework, Amin now rejects autarky and identifies with deepened democracy and the global social movement as the way out of the dependency system.

3 This awkward formulation is used because the unbracketed term post-Marxist has become associated with a wide range of social theories including those of poststructuralist authors such as Laclau and Mouffe who reject the quasi-totality of Marxist theory, retaining only a vague identification with political progressivism. (Post)Marxism denotes theories that are recognisably in the tradition of Marxism.

4 From an unpublished book, C. Chase-Dunn and B. Lerro, "Social Change", www.irows.ucr.edu/cd/courses/261/b10ch2/b10ch2.htm.

5 See www.hrw.org/wr2k5/pdf/eu.pdf, accessed on 11 April 2005.

6 See, for example, official reports on the 7 July 2005 London tube bombings and the backgrounds and motivations of the bombers. The House of Commons Intelligence Security Committee report is at http://image.guardian.co.uk/sys-files/Politics/documents/2006/05/11/isc_7july_report.pdf (particularly pages 11–13, 30). The Home Office Official report is reproduced at http://news.bbc.co.uk/1/shared/bsp/hi/pdfs/11_05_06_narrative.pdf.

7 "The US and Thailand are planning a free trade agreement, in the latest US move towards bilateral deals with favoured partners" ("Bangkok plans free trade talks with Washington", *Financial Times*, 18 October 2003, 6).

8 China's steel production grew 300 per cent between 2001 and 2005, while India's is expected to grow 262 per cent between 2006 and 2020. Refereed publications by Chinese academics have increased forty-fold in the past twenty-five years, while Indian research publications, from a much larger base, have increased 2.5 times in the same period (*Business Standard*, Mumbai, July 31 2006, 8).

9 In a highly unscientific survey based on conversations with Bank employees, reaction to concertive approaches appeared trifurcated according to organisational status. Senior and very junior employees seemed equally cynical, while middle-ranking employees tended to identify overtly with the organisation. Several hypotheses for this result are possible. It could be that senior management observe at first hand the autocratic nature of the organisation and, in particular, the sycophancy surrounding the Bank's president, while junior employees, almost all engaged as contingent employees on short-term contracts, are daily reminded of their underprivileged status and the falsehood of claims of inclusivity and teamwork. Middle-ranking employees, on the other hand, may find concertive myths plausible, sustaining and comforting.

Alternatively, the junior and senior ranks, for different reasons, have much less to lose than the middle ranks in criticising the Bank.

10 In its contemporary iterations, institutional theory has become decontextualised, privileging internal institutional dynamics to the exclusion of cross-cutting structuring factors such as hierarchical systems of social and economic power (Hinings and Greenwood, 2002). In a sense, the institutionalist critique of taken-for-granted instrumental purposiveness of organisations has been taken to its furthest frontier, voiding organisations of objective function and thus situatedness in a broader structure of social meaning (Selznick, 1996).

2 The genetic code of global managerialism

1 The Bretton Woods system is used in this thesis to describe the institutions established at the Bretton Woods conference of 1944: the World Bank, the IMF and, to a lesser extent, the semi-abortive international trade organisation, which was first implemented in partial form as the General Agreement on Tariffs and Trade, and only in 1995 finally launched as the World Trade Organisation. The same term is sometimes used in popular discussions of economics to describe the gold-backed US currency system designed by White and the US Treasury, which underpinned the original Bretton Woods system, and which collapsed in 1973. This latter usage is not applicable here, and neither is the collapse of the gold-backed currency system discussed.

2 From January 1942, the term "United Nations" was used to describe the Allied coalition of countries fighting the Axis coalition. The term was also intended to describe the foundation of a post-war order. At the autumn 1944 Dumbarton Oaks conference, an agreement was signed between the United States, Russia, Britain and China to establish a formal United Nations organisation, although it was not until the San Francisco conference in April 1945 that fifty countries met to agree upon the articles of association for the new organisation. White was a senior member of the United States delegation to both the Dumbarton Oaks and San Francisco conferences.

3 Keynes has this to say about the attitude of White House economist Laughlin Currie during the 1943 negotiations:

> Currie is an old friend of mine and I know him well, but there is no-one more difficult to handle. He is extremely suspicious and jealous, very anti-British on issues such as India – and always inclined to assume the worst.
> (Letter to Sir Wilfrid Eady, 3 October 1943, in Keynes, 1980: XXV)

4 Morgenthau's phrase, "Prosperity, like peace, is indivisible", is an exact repetition of White's 1943 presentation to the American Economic Association.

5 McCloy was active in senior Republican circles for over fifty years. John Kenneth Galbraith described him as the "Chairman of the Establishment", a depiction Bird (1992) uses as the title and theme of his biography. In summarising McCloy and the establishment, Bird makes the following relevant observation:

> The ideas that the American establishment stood for are still the driving ideas of the republic. Liberal internationalism abroad and a moderate social compact based on a free market economy at home still define what is considered as legitimate political thought.
> (1992: 663)

6 Between 1973 and 1988, the Bank disbursed $283 million in twenty-five separate project loans to Bénin.

7 The Washington Consensus has been summarised by its main author (Williamson, 2000: 251–264) as including the following ten points:

- • fiscal discipline
- • a redirection of public expenditure priorities toward fields offering both high economic returns and the potential to improve income distribution, such as primary health care, primary education and infrastructure
- • tax reform (to lower marginal rates and broaden the tax base)
- • interest rate liberalisation
- • a competitive exchange rate
- • trade liberalisation
- • liberalisation of inflows of foreign direct investment
- • privatisation
- • deregulation (to abolish barriers to entry and exit)
- • secure property rights.

3 The Poverty Bank

1 International Bank for Reconstruction and Development. This is the original – and still official – name for the Bank. It is used to differentiate the organisation's market-rate lending activities from the low-interest loans provided through its IDA arm.

2 Author's interview with Kazuko Motomura, country director, Asian Development Bank, Dushanbe, Tajikistan, 19 May 2004.

3 Kyrgyzstan, long a World Bank and bilateral donor poster child, faced increasing civil unrest from 2002, and was hastily dropped as a Bank "priority". Unrest culminated in a largely peaceful revolution in April 2005.

4 Some NGOs and multilateral institutions have attempted to resolve the language problem through translation into the vernacular (typically of social marketing billboards). This would not be an effective strategy for lengthy written texts such as the PRSPs and other World Bank-sponsored documents, as the vernacular languages are either not taught in schools or are taught to only a very basic level, whereas comprehension of Bank documents would require advanced levels of literacy. Meanwhile, the Bank has pressured developing country governments to reduce the proportion of expenditures they make on secondary and tertiary education, in favour of basic education:

> Dans la plupart des pays cibles de cette étude, l'enseignement supérieur est à la fois sur-dimensionné en quantité et mal ciblé en termes de qualité et de pertinence des formations pour les besoins du marché du travail.

> (In the majority of countries selected for this study, higher education is at the same time over-provisioned and badly targeted in terms of quality and the pertinence of training to labour market needs.)

> (Mingat, 2002: 16–17)

5 Briefly, the goals are to: eradicate extreme poverty and hunger; achieve universal primary education; promote gender equality and empower women; reduce child mortality; improve maternal health; combat HIV/AIDS, malaria and other diseases; ensure environmental sustainability; and develop a global partnership for development.

6 Figures drawn from United Nations, *Millennium Development Goals Report, 2006*, New York, United Nations Statistics Division.

7 The study is based on the perspectives of local NGOs with links to the Sweden-based People Participating in Poverty Reduction Project.

8 "IFIs accepted the continued protection of cashew nuts in Mozambique and the abolition of school fees in Tanzania and health fees in Uganda" (Sanchez and Cash, 2003: 25).

9 Bolivia, Mozambique, Nicaragua, Tanzania, Uganda, Vietnam and Zambia.

10 The "totalitarian" and "clash of civilisations" theses, which reflect the Manifest Destiny perspective in US intellectual thought and underpin American unilateralism, are both identified with Democratic Party intellectuals (Brzezinski and Huntington, 1964; Huntington, 1993).

11 In the USAID lexicon, sustainable development refers to development through economic growth rather than having a specifically environment-focused meaning.

12 The GINI coefficient is a measure of inequality in a population, often used to measure income inequality (Damgaard and Weiner, 2000).

4 The Managerial Bank

1 Krueger (1998: 1990) estimates that about 2 per cent of investment in developing countries is financed by the Bank, though the proportion is considerably higher in sub-Saharan Africa.

2 Shifting the Bank's natural internal policy direction would involve a combination of: reduction in the numerical and strategic "weight" of economists in the Bank; reorientation of major economics faculties towards heterodox thinking; and recruitment of economists from other regions, where alternative perspectives are more easily tolerated.

3 Williams (1992: 165) offers a devastating critique of the Bank's regular claims that the results of research or consultative exercises illuminate its policy directions, whereas the opposite seems to be closer to the truth.

4 To give two examples: in Bakau, The Gambia, in December 2003, the author visited the offices of the Pro-Poor Action Group (Pro-PAG), an NGO established in January 2003 through UK DFID funding, to "animate" poor people's participation in the country's PRSP, the Strategy for Poverty Alleviation II. The organisation, headed by a former senior official in the country's Education Ministry, appeared to be an entirely external creation with limited, if any, roots in the local population. In Tajikistan, in May 2004, a leader of a relatively longstanding NGO complained that the government had set up a number of "fake" NGOs in order to access western funds; this complaint was backed up by a number of other NGO representatives (author's interview with Mavzhuda Rakhmanova, Dushanbe, Tajikistan, 19 May 2004).

5 From the World Bank website www.worldbank.org, at "About Us: Organisation", on 5 May 2004.

6 Author's interview with a World Bank consultant, name withheld, 7 May 2004.

7 Author's interview, Delhi, 28 May 2004.

8 When low- interest loans are taken into account, as they are in the standard OECD global data on development aid.

9 Source: www.fec.gov, accessed on 14 March 2007.

5 The Bank, global social policy and civil society

1 International development research centre, IDRC. See www.idrc.ca/index_en.html, accessed on 15 June 2006.

2 See www.globalpublicpolicy.net/index.php?id=168, accessed on 15 June 2006.

3 Accessed at www.richard.net on 14 August 2004.

4 Though many, if not most, would be dividing their time between civil society responsibilities and other duties.

5 Policy note GP 14.70.

6 The methodology used by the Bank in drawing up the measures was to average the fiscal characteristics of the education system in developing countries with relatively successful education systems and use those averages as targets for all developing countries (Bruns *et al.*, 2003: 61–70). This method, which is a simplified version of approaches used previously by one of the report's co-authors, Mingat, commits an

elementary statistical error in assuming that correlation is equal to causation. The Bruns *et al.* method is further flawed by the exclusion of the former Soviet bloc countries from the equation on the grounds that they are "unique" (Bruns *et al.*, 2003: 62fn.). This is, of course, the same argument that the Bank always uses to exclude Cuba as a potential model, even though it is an obvious example for any developing country but must for ideological reasons be omitted from consideration.

7 Mingat and Tan's other key contributions to education research are that pupil–teacher ratios make little difference to student attainment and, therefore, it does not make sense to improve those ratios (Mingat and Tan, 1998), and that developing country public investment in higher education is a poor use of resources (Mingat and Tan, 1985). These perspectives are equally controversial but equally assiduously pursued by the World Bank.

8 The "eighth" and final MDG, "develop a global partnership for development", includes several sub-goals that enshrine free trade and a key role for the private sector in development, to which legitimate objections could be raised.

6 The Bank and the private sector

1 Corporate information accessed at www.ispat.com on 5 August 2004.

2 World Bank project ID P007660, 3 March 1988–31 December 1996.

3 Ispat Mexicana. The Sidbec plant is integrated into Ispat International.

4 Published records state that Ispat also assumed Sidbec's C$280 million in debts (*Mergers & Acquisitions in Canada* 6, 9, September 1 1994). The relationship between the $280 million in debt Ispat assumed and the $693.6 million which remained on the Quebec government's books is unclear.

5 The European Union eventually permitted $222 million in subsidies to Nova Hut for the years 1997–2003. It is not clear how much of these resources flowed through to Ispat and in what form.

6 LNM Holdings also owns the South African steelmaker, ISCOR, not discussed in this chapter.

7 As noted above, the Mittal empire was restructured in late 2004, and in 2006, the company agreed a merger with Arcelor in which Mittal would predominate.

8 www.ifc.org/ifcext/eca.nsf/Content/Kazakhstan_InvestmentProjects, accessed on 3 August 2004.

9 The Council for Mutual Economic Assistance (CMEA).

10 See www.wto.org/english/thewto_e/acc_e/a1_kazakhstan_e.htm, accessed on 10 May 2005.

11 www.ebrd.org/projects/psd/index.htm, accessed on 10 May 2005.

12 Giffen, an American former consultant to the Kazakh government, was indicted in 2003 for channelling kickbacks to President Nazarbayev and his close associates on deals that Kazakhstan signed with US oil companies. Giffen's trial was still continuing in July 2007. Earlier a Mobil executive was sentenced to a three-year prison term by a US court for a related offence.

13 Information posted on the World Bank's Kazakhstan website www.worldbank.org.kz/, accessed on 4 August 2004.

14 "About WBI", accessed on the World Bank Institute's website at www.worldbank.org/wbi/ on 4 August 2004.

15 Information accessed at www.imf.org/external/np/ins/english/JVI.htm on 4 August 2004.

16 Varying figures ranging from $50 million to $420 million have been cited in different documents.

17 For example, www.undp.org/business/docs/ifc.ppt, http://www.ifc.org/ifcext/tatf.nsf/AttachmentsByTitle/DonorReport.pdf/$FILE/DonorReport.pdf, and http://unece.org/ie/industry/documents/gabor.pdf, all accessed on 31 July 2006.

18 Akezhan Kazhegeldin was prime minister of Kazakhstan from 1994 to 1997. After declaring his intention to contest presidential elections he was accused of corruption and went into exile, from where he has returned the favour by spearheading a markedly successful and well-documented campaign to tar President Nursultan Nazarbayev as corrupt. See, for example, *New York Times*, 28 July 2000, p. A5.

19 The OSCE was founded as the Conference on Security and Cooperation in Europe (CSCE) as an outcome of the international Helsinki meetings, which established ten principles for international cooperation in Europe. These included respect for international law as well as for human rights. Until the Communist bloc collapsed, the OSCE mainly acted as an East–West forum for resolving human rights and security issues between the two blocs. After 1990, the CSCE gradually assumed a broader disciplinary role in monitoring and enforcing human rights, democracy and the market system in the transitional countries. The organisation was renamed OSCE in 1995 (OSCE, 2000).

20 www.bankwatch.org.

21 The author travelled to central Kazakhstan with Timur Tulushuev, who assisted in translation.

22 Subsequent to our field research, tough negotiations between the company and the union – hampered because strikes are outlawed in Kazakhstan – resulted in significant wage increases, apparently to an average of about $300 per month (Economist Intelligence Unit, 2004: 1).

23 In the former Soviet Union, including Kazakhstan, the operation of the tax system is highly politicised and often corrupt. Foreign companies, in particular, are often targeted for special and unreasonable attention in tax investigations. Thus, while Ispat's recourse to the minister might appear unusual by western standards, it would be considered normal practice in Kazakhstan.

24 In 1960, Kazakhstan's current president, Nursultan Nazarbayev, began work at Karmet, where in 1969 he joined the local branch of the Komsomol, the Communist Party's youth wing. Nazarbayev moved rapidly upwards through the Komsomol and later the full Party hierarchy, eventually becoming the last leader of the KSSR Communist Party and then first leader of independent Kazakhstan.

25 This does not imply that such networking is improper.

Bibliography

Abdou, I. (2003), President, UNAVES. Interview, 29 August. Niamey, Niger.

Acsay, P. (2000), "Planning for postwar economic cooperation: The United States Treasury, the Soviet Union, and Bretton Woods, 1933–1946", PhD Dissertation, Saint Louis University, Missouri, USA.

Adams, R. and Clark, C. (2007), "White House turns to veteran diplomat to head World Bank", *Guardian*, 30 May, 1.

Adamu, M. (2004), "Niger: Ajustement structurel ou 'réduction de la pauvreté?'", 13 February, Liège, Belgium, Comité pour l'Annulation de la Dette du Tiers Monde (CADTM). Accessed at www.cadtm.org/article.php3?id_article=456 on 4 July 2004.

Aglietta, M. (1997), *Régulation et crises du capitalisme*, Paris, Odile Jacob.

American Metal Market (1995), "Ispat, Karmet ink agreement", 9 November, 3.

Amin, S. (1972), "Underdevelopment and dependence in Black Africa: Origins and contemporary forms", *Journal of Modern African Studies*, 10, 503–524.

—— (1974), *Accumulation on a World Scale: A Critique of the Theory of Underdevelopment*, 2 vols, London, Monthly Review Press.

ANGOC (Asian NGO Coalition for the East Asia-Pacific Regional NGO Working Group on the World Bank) (2001), "Rapid assessment of the PRSP process in Cambodia: two banks, two processes, two documents". Accessed at www.bigpond.com.kh/users/ngoforum/Woking_Group_Issues/Developmentassistance/PRSP/ on 19 April 2004.

Annisette, M. (2004), "The true nature of the World Bank", *Critical Perspectives on Accounting*, 15, 303–323.

Arnold, M. (2006), "Royal the favourite to reign over left in French politics", *Financial Times*, 2 February, 9.

Arnold, P. and Sikka, P. (2001), "Globalisation and the state–profession relationship: the case the Bank of Credit and Commerce International", *Accounting, Organizations, and Society*, 26, 475–499.

Babbitt, H. (2000), "Poverty reduction and partnership frameworks – implications for donors". Statement at the OECD Development Assistance Committee High Level Meeting, May. Accessed at www.worldbank.org/participation/CASusaid.htm on 26 April 2004.

Banerjee, A., Banerji, R., Duflo, E., Glennerster, R. and Khemani, S. (2006), "Can information campaigns spark local participation and improve outcomes? A study of primary education in Uttar Pradesh, India", World Bank Policy Research Working Paper 3967, Washington, World Bank.

Banerjee, S. and Linstead, S. (2001), "Globalisation, multiculturalism, and other fictions", *Organization*, 8, 683–722.

Barton, C. (2004), "Are the MDGs a new form of conditionality?", in Women's International Coalition for Economic Justice, *Seeking Accountability on Women's Human Rights: Women Debate the UN Millennium Development Goals*, New York, WICEJ, 20.

Bauman, Z. (1989), *Modernity and the Holocaust*, Cambridge, Polity Press.

BBC (2002), "Argentina warned over loan threat", 26 September. Accessed at http://news.bbc.co.uk/1/hi/business/2283802.stm on 3 June 2004.

—— (2002a), "The steel maharajah", 24 July. Accessed at http://news.bbc.co.uk/1/hi/business/2146757.stm on 2 August 2004.

Bekenov, A. and Karajanov, Z. (2004), "Kazak banker accident under scrutiny", *Reporting Central Asia*, 337, 27 December.

Berger, P. and Luckmann T. (1972), *The Social Construction of Reality*, London, Cox & Wyman.

Berle, A. and Means, G. (1932), *The Modern Corporation and Private Property*, New York, The Commerce Cleaning House.

Bevir, M. (2005), *New Labour, a Critique*, London, Routledge.

Bird, K. (1992), *The Chairman: John J. McCloy, The Making of the American Establishment*, New York, Simon & Schuster.

BIS (2003), *Annual Report: 2002*. Accessed at www.bis.cz/_english/info_.html on 10 August 2004.

Bist, R. (2004), "The making of an Indian steel king", *Asia Times*, 19 March.

Blair, T. (1998), *The Third Way: New Politics for the New Century*, London, Fabian Society.

Blum, J. (1959), *From the Morgenthau Diaries, Volume One: Years of Crisis*, Boston, Houghton Mifflin.

Bobbio, N. (1972) *On Mosca and Pareto*, Geneva, Librairie Droz.

Booth, D. (2001), "PRSP processes in eight African countries: initial impacts and potential for institutionalisation". Paper presented to the WIDER Development Conference on Debt Relief, Helsinki, 17–18 August.

Boston Consulting Group (2006), "China's Global Challengers". Accessed at www.bcg.com/publications/files/Chinas_Global_Challengers_May06.pdf on 17 April 2007.

Boughton, J. (2000), *The Case Against Harry Dexter White: Still Not Proven*, IMF Working Paper 00/149, Washington, DC, IMF.

—— (2002), *Why White, Not Keynes: Inventing the Postwar International Monetary System*, IMF Working Paper 02/52, Washington, DC, IMF.

—— (2003), "New Light on Harry White", working paper provided to the author, dated 17 November 2003.

Boughton, J. and Sandilands, R. (2003?), "Politics and the attack on FDR's economists: from grand alliance to the Cold War", *Intelligence and National Security*, 18, 73–99.

Bourdieu, P. (1994), *Raisons pratiques: Sur la théorie de l'action*, Paris, Seuil.

Bream, R. (2004), "Mittal plan for global steel group", *Financial Times*, 26 October, 1.

Bretton Woods Project (2001), "Anti-corruption claim filed on World Bank internet gateway", 17 July. Accessed at www.brettonwoodsproject.org on 5 May 2004.

—— (2005), "Wolfowitz era begins: Realpolitik 1, Democracy 0". Accessed at www.brettonwoodsproject.org/article.shtml?cmd[126]=x-126-174508 on 5 April 2005.

Bruns, B., Mingat, A. and Rakotomalala, R. (2003), *Achieving Universal Primary Education by 2015: A Chance for Every Child*, Washington, World Bank.

Brunsson, N. and Jacobsson, B., eds (2002), *A World of Standards*, Oxford, Oxford University Press.

Brzezinski, Z. and Huntington, S. (1964), *Political Power: USA/USSR*, New York, Viking.

Buckles, P. (2002), "The United States Agency for International Development and poverty reduction", in Asian Development Bank, eds, *Defining an Agenda for Poverty Reduction*, Manila, ADB, 85–88.

Budhoo, D. (1990), *Enough Is Enough*, New York, Apex Press.

Bulkacz, V. (2004), "A central base for World Bank financing", *Prague Club Magazine*, 2.

Burnham, J. (1941), *The Managerial Revolution*, New York, John Day.

Business Today (2004), *BT 500: India's Most Valuable Companies*, 7 November.

Caiden, G. (1991), *Administrative Reform Comes of Age*, New York, De Gruyter.

Callinicos, A. (1989), *Against Postmodernism: A Marxist Critique*, Cambridge, Polity.

—— (2000), "World capitalism at the abyss", *International Socialism Journal*, 81, 3–43.

Cammack, P. (2001), "Making the poor work for globalisation?", *New Political Economy*, 6, 397–408.

—— (2002), "The mother of all governments: the World Bank's matrix for global governance", in R. Wilkinson and S. Hughes, eds, *Global Governance: Critical Perspectives*, London, Routledge, 36–54.

—— (2003), "The governance of global capitalism", *Historical Materialism*, 11, 2, 37–59.

—— (2003a), "What the World Bank means by poverty reduction". Paper presented to the conference "Staying Poor: Chronic Poverty and Development Policy", Chronic Poverty Research Centre, University of Manchester, 7–9 July.

—— (2003b), "Giddens' way with words". Unpublished article.

Campbell, J. and Lindberg, L. (1990), "Property rights and the organization of economic activity by the state", *American Sociological Review*, 55, 5, 634–647.

Carty, L. (1993), "Imperialism: historical periodization or present-day phenomenon?", *Radical History Review*, 57, 38–47.

Castells, M. (1996–1998), *The Information Age: Economy, Society and Culture*, 3 vols, Oxford, Blackwell.

Cattell, B. (1999), "IFC suggests Indian partner for Nova Hut", Prague Post, 1 September.

Chakrabarty, D. (2000), *Provincializing Europe*, New Delhi, Oxford University Press.

Cheru, F. (1999), *Effects of Structural Adjustment Policies on the Full Enjoyment of Human Rights*, Report E/CN.4/1999/50 presented to the United Nations Commission on Human Rights, New York, United Nations.

—— (2001), *The Highly Indebted Poor Countries (HIPC) Initiative: A Human Rights Assessment of the Poverty Reduction Strategy Papers (PRSP)*, Report E/CN.4/2001/56 presented to the United Nations Commission on Human Rights, New York, United Nations.

Choudhary, N. (2003), General Director, Ispat Karmet, Interview, 30 June, Almaty, Kazakhstan.

Chrisafis, A (2007), "Sarkozy's London mission", *Guardian*, 30 January, 14.

Civicus (2003), *Annual Report, 2002*, Johannesburg. Accessed at www.civicus.org/new/media/ENGannualreport.pdf on 25 June 2004.

Clark, J. (1998), *The Bank's Relations with NGOs: Issues and Directions*, Social Development Paper 28, Washington, DC, World Bank.

—— (2003a), *Worlds Apart: Civil Society and the Battle for Ethical Globalisation*, Bloomfield, Conn., Kumarian Press.

Clark, S. (2003), Executive Director (Canada), EBRD, Interview, 20 November, London.

Cockett, R. (1994), *Thinking the Unthinkable: Think-tanks and the Economic Counter-revolution, 1931–1983*, London, Fontana.

Commission for Africa (2005), *Our Common Interest: Report of the Commission for Africa*, London, Commission for Africa.

Cooke, B. (2002), "Managing the neo-liberalization of the Third World: the case of development administration and management", Manchester, Institute for Development Policy and Management.

Cooke, B. and Kothari, U., eds (2001), *Participation: The New Tyranny?*, London, Zed.

Cooley, A. and Ron, J. (2002), "The NGO scramble: organizational insecurity and the political economy of transnational action", *International Security*, 27, 5–39.

Cooper, D., Ezzamel, M. and Willmott, H. (2007), "How to study 'institutionalization': a critical theoretic perspective". Paper presented at the Cardiff Organizational Studies Group, 14 February.

Cox, R. (1981), "Social forces, states, and world orders: beyond international relations theory", *Millennium: Journal of International Studies*, 10, 126–155.

—— (1983), "Gramsci, hegemony and international relations: an essay in method", *Millennium: Journal of International Studies*, 12, 162–175.

—— (1987), *State, World Orders, and Production*, New York, Columbia University Press.

—— (2002), *The Political Economy of a Plural World*, London, Routledge. (With M. Schechter).

Craig, B. (1999), "Treasonable Doubt: The Harry Dexter White Case", PhD Thesis, American University, Washington, DC.

Craig, D. (2006), *Plundering the Public Sector*, London, Constable and Robinson.

Craig, D. and Porter, D. (2003), "Poverty reduction papers: a new convergence", *World Development*, 31, 53–69.

Crosswell, M. (2000), *USAID and Poverty*, Washington, USAID.

—— (2003), "Development and poverty reduction – issues and lessons from country experience", unpublished USAID discussion document, 12 August.

CTK Business News (2004), "FNM lawyer helps Petrcile win arbitration vs. FNM", 20 May.

Culpeper, R. (1997), *Titans or Behemoths*, London, Intermediate Technology Publications.

Currie, L., Ellsworth, P. and White, H. (2002 [1932]), "Memorandum prepared by L.B. Currie, P.T. Ellsworth, and H.D. White (Cambridge, Mass., January 1932)", *History of Political Economy*, 34, 3 (Fall), 533–552.

Czarniawska, B. (2004), "Of time, space, and action nets", *Organization*, 11, 773–791.

Damgaard, C. and Weiner, J. (2000), "Describing inequality in plant size or fecundity", *Ecology* 81, 1139–1142.

Danish Ministry of Foreign Affairs (2003), "Review of Nordic monitoring of the World Bank and IMF support to the Poverty Reduction Strategy Papers (PRSP) process". Accessed at www.nord-syd.dk/dokumenter/1061979820.doc on 24 April 2004.

Davey, M. (2003), Resident Representative, European Bank for Reconstruction and Development, Interview, 27 June, Almaty, Kazakhstan.

De Beus, J. and Koelble, T. (2001), "The Third Way diffusion of social democracy: Western Europe and South Africa compared", *Politikon: South African Journal of Political Studies*, 28, 181–194.

Dean, J. (2005), "Communicative capitalism: circulation and the foreclosure of politics", *Cultural Politics* 1, 51–74.

Decker, K. (2004), *Multilateral Development Bank Investment in Kazakhstan*, Washington, Bank Information Center. Accessed at www.bicusa.org/bicusa/issues/KZ_MDB_summary.pdf on 3 August 2004.

DeLong, B. (2000), "Review of Robert Skidelsky, *John Maynard Keynes: Fighting for Britain 1937–1946*" (December). Accessed at www.j-bradford-delong.net/Econ_Articles/Reviews/skidelsky3.html, on 14 November 2003.

Derrida, J. (1994), *Spectres of Marx*, London, Routledge.

Development Committee (2004), *Education For All (EFA) – Fast Track Initiative Progress Report*, 25 April, Washington, World Bank/IMF.

DFID (2001), "DFID views on the PRSP process", in IMF/World Bank PRSP Comprehensive Review (2002), *External Comments and Contributions on the Joint Bank/Fund Staff Review of the PRSP Approach, Volume I: Bilateral Agencies and Multilateral Institutions*, Washington, International Monetary Fund and World Bank, 117–129.

Dimaggio, P. and Powell, W. (1983), "The iron cage revisited: institutional isomorphism and collective rationality in organizational fields", *American Sociological Review*, 48, 147–160.

Djelic, M.-L. (2001), *Exporting the American Model: The Post-War Transformation of European Business*, Oxford, Oxford University Press.

Domhoff, W. (2003), *Changing the Powers that Be*, Lanham Md., Rowman and Littlefield.

Eberlei, W. and Henn, H. (2003), *Parliaments in Sub-Saharan Africa: Actors in Poverty Reduction?*, Eschborn, GTZ.

EBRD (1990), Agreement Establishing the European Bank for Reconstruction and Development, Paris. Accessed at www.ebrd.org/about/basics/index.htm on 4 August 2004.

Economist (2002), "The Mittal Way", 23 February, 61–62.

Economist Intelligence Unit (2002), *Country Report, Kazakhstan*, London.

Education International (2002), "Education pour tous, qualité pour aucun?". Declaration at the 8th meeting of African education ministers under the auspices of UNESCO, 2–6 December.

—— (2003), *Education for All: Is Commitment Enough?*, Brussels, Education International.

Einzig, H. (1941), *Hitler's "New Order" in Europe*, London, Macmillan.

Elliot, J. (2007), "Passage from India: India's billion dollar buyouts", *Fortune Europe*, 155, 3, 13.

Emmanuel, A. (1972), *Unequal Exchange: A Study of the Imperialism of Trade*, London, New Left Books.

Escobar, A. (1995), *Encountering Development: The Making and Unmaking of the Third World*, Princeton, NJ, Princeton University Press.

European Commission (1999), "Regulation (EEC) No. 4064/89 Merger Procedure". Accessed at http://europa.eu.int/comm/competition/mergers/cases/decisions/m1509_en.pdf on 9 August 2004.

—— (2001), "PRSP Review: Key Issues", in IMF/World Bank PRSP Comprehensive Review (2002), *External Comments and Contributions on the Joint Bank/Fund Staff Review of the PRSP Approach*, Volume I: *Bilateral Agencies and Multilateral Institutions*, Washington, International Monetary Fund and The World Bank, 71–86.

—— (2002), *Progress Towards Meeting Economic Criteria for Accession: The Assessment from the 2002 Regular Report (October)*, Enlargement Papers 10, Brussels.

Fairclough, N. (2000), *New Labour, New Language*, London, Routledge.

—— (2001), *Language and Power*, London, Longman.

Ferguson, J. (1988), "Cultural exchange: new developments in the anthropology of commodities", *Cultural Anthropology*, 3, 4, 488–513.

—— (1990), *The Anti-politics Machine: "Development" and Bureaucratic Power in Lesotho*, Cambridge, Cambridge University Press.

Financial Post (1994), "Sidbec-Dosco sale wrapped up", 20 August, 10.

Fine, B. (2001), "The Post-Washington Consensus" in B. Fine, C. Lapavitsas and J. Pincus, eds, *Development Policy in the Twenty-first Century: Beyond The Post-Washington Consensus*, London, Routledge, 1–28.

—— (2002), *Social Capital versus Social Theory*, London, Routledge.

Forbes (2005), "The world's top ten billionaires", No. 175, 6, 28 March, 166–167.

Foster, J. (2002), "Monopoly capital and the new globalisation", *Monthly Review*, 53, 8.

Fukuyama, F. (1989), "The end of history", *National Interest*, 16, 3–18.

—— (2006), "After neoconservatism", *New York Times Magazine*, 5 March, 8–10.

G7 Finance Ministers (2001), "Fighting the abuses of the global financial system", Joint statement, 7 July.

Gavin, F. (1996), "The legends of Bretton Woods", *Orbis*, 40, 2, 183–198.

Gbado, B. (1998), *En marche vers la liberté. Tome 1: Bénin: passage d'un régime autoritaire à un Etat de droit*, Cotonou, Ruisseaux d'Afrique.

General Council for Islamic Banking and Financial Institutions (2003), "Interview between HE Dr Mohammed Khalfan Bin Kharbash, UAE Minister of State for Finance and Industry, and Riz Khan, 28 June, 2003, Dubai, UAE". Accessed at www.islamic financeonline.com/interview.htm on 4 June 2004.

Gereffi, G. (1996), "Global commodity chains: new forms of coordination and control among nations and firms in international industries", *Competition & Change*, 1, 427–439.

Gereffi, G. and Korzeniewicz, M., eds (1994), *Commodity Chains and Global Capitalism*, Westport, Conn.: Praeger Publishers.

Gervais, M. (1992), "Les enjeux politiques des ajustements structurels au Niger", *Revue Canadienne des Etudes Africaines*, 26, 226–249.

Giddens, A. (1999, 2000), *Runaway World: How Globalisation Is Reshaping our Lives*, London, Profile.

Goldfinch, S. (1998), "Remaking New Zealand's economic policy: institutional elites as radical innovators 1984–1993", *Governance*, 11, 177–207.

Gordon, H. (1992), *The Shadow of Death: The Holocaust in Lithuania*, Lexington, Ky., University of Kentucky Press.

Gotova, N. (1995), "Management company replaced for Karmet", *Segodnya*, 4 July, 9. Translated.

Government of Niger (1998), *Enhanced Structural Adjustment Facility Policy Framework Paper, 1998–2001*, prepared in conjunction with the staffs of the World Bank and the IMF. Accessed at www.imf.org/external/np/pfp/niger/index.htm on 4 July 2004.

—— (2002), *Poverty Reduction Strategy*, Niamey.

Government of Tajikistan (2002), *Poverty Reduction Strategy Paper*, Dushanbe, Tajikistan.

Govinda, R. and Josephine, Y. (2004), *Para Teachers in India: A Review*, New Delhi, National Institute of Educational Planning and Administration.

Graham, C. and Neu, D. (2003), "Accounting for globalization", *Accounting Forum*, 27, 449–471.

Gramsci, A. (1992), *Prison Notebooks*, New York, Columbia University Press.

Grey, C. (1999), "'We are all managers now'; 'We always were': on the development and demise of management", *Journal of Management Studies*, 36 (September), 561–585.

Grice, A. (2002), "Suspicions grow as Downing St changes its story. PM denies he knew of donations before he signed", *Independent*, 14 February, 4.

Gupta, S. (2002), "Free & Fair Inc.", *Indian Express*, 23 February. Accessed at www.indianexpress.com/columnists/shek/20020223.html on 26 October 2004.

Gwin, C. (1997), "US relations with the World Bank", in D. Kapur, J. Lewis and R. Webb, eds (1997b), *The World Bank: Its First Half Century, Volume Two: Perspectives*, Washington, DC, Brookings Institution Press, 195–274.

Hailey, J. (2001), "Beyond the formulaic: process and practice in South Asian NGOs", in B. Cooke and U. Kothari, eds, *Participation: The New Tyranny?*, London, Zed, 88–101.

Halimi, S. (1997), "New Zealand: from welfare state to market economy", *Le Monde Diplomatique*, April. Accessed at www.casi.org.nz/politicaleconomy/wstoms.html on 23 January 2004.

Hall, S. (2003), "New Labour's double shuffle", *Soundings*, 24, 11–24.

Hampton, M. and Christensen, J. (2002), "Offshore pariahs? Small island economies, tax havens and the re-configuration of global finance", *World Development*, 30, 1657–1673.

Hanley, E., Yershova, N. and Anderson, R. (1995), "New wine in old bottles: the circulation and reproduction of Russian elites: 1983–1993", *Theory and Society*, 24, 639–668.

Hanley, J. (2002), "Edwin Chadwick and the poverty of statistics", *Medical History*, 46, 21–40.

Hannan, M. and Freeman, J. (1977), "The population ecology of organizations", *American Journal of Sociology*, 82, 929–964.

Harberger, A. (1999), "Interview with Arnold Harberger", *Revista Acta Académica*, Universidad Autónoma de Centro América (November). Accessed at www.uaca.ac.cr/acta/1999nov/dlevy.htm on 4 June 2004.

Hardgrove, A. (2004), *Community and Public Culture: The Marwaris In Calcutta, c.1897–1997*, New York, Columbia University Press.

Hardt, M. and Negri, A. (2000), *Empire*, London, Harvard University Press.

Hardy, C. (2003), "Refugee determination: power and resistance in systems of Foucauldian power", *Administration and Society* 35, 4, 462–488.

Harrod, R. (1951), *The Life of John Maynard Keynes*, London, Macmillan.

Head, I. (2001), "On a hinge of history". An Address to the Academy for Educational Development 40th Anniversary Celebrations, Washington, DC, 6 December.

Henkel, H. and Stirrat, R. (2001), "Participation as spiritual duty; empowerment as secular subjection", in B. Cooke and U., Kothari eds (2001), *Participation: The New Tyranny?*, London, Zed, 168–184.

Herrington, R., Smith, M., Maslennikov, V., Belogub, E. and Armstrong, R. (2002), "A short review of Palaeozoic hydrothermal magnetite iron-oxide deposits of the south and central Urals and their geological setting", in T. Porter, ed., *Hydrothermal Iron Oxide Copper-Gold & Related Deposits: A Global Perspective*, vol. 2, Adelaide, PGC Publishing, 343–353.

Higley, J. and Burton, M. (2006), *The Elite Foundations of Liberal Democracy*, Lanham, Md., Rowman and Littlefield.

Hildyard, N., Hegde, P., Wolvekamp, P. and Reddy, S. (2001), "Pluralism, participation, and power: joint forest management in India", in B. Cooke and U. Kothari, eds, *Participation: The New Tyranny?*, London, Zed, 56–71.

Hinings, R. and Greenwood, R. (2002), "Disconnects and consequences in organization theory?" *Administrative Science Quarterly*, 47, 411–421.

Hirst, P. and Thompson, G. (1996), *Globalisation in Question*, Cambridge, Polity.

Hobsbawm, E. (2002), *Interesting Times: A Twentieth Century Life*, London, Allen Lane.

Hobson, J. (1961 [1902]), *Imperialism. A Study*, London, George Allen & Unwin.

Hoogvelt, A. (2001), *Globalization and the Postcolonial World. The New Political Economy of Development*, London, Palgrave.

Horton, R. (2002), "WHO's mandate: a damaging reinterpretation is taking place", *Lancet*, 360, 960–961.

House of Commons Standards and Privileges Committee (2002), *Fifth Report: Complaints Against Mr. Keith Vaz*, London, House of Commons, 8 February.

Hozumi, T. (1996), "The economic thought of German Social Democracy in the Weimar Republic, focussing on the theory of Organized Capitalism". Paper presented to the European Social Science History Conference, Noordwijkerhout, Netherlands, 9–11 May. Accessed at: http://web.archive.org/web/19970804022252/www.iisg.nl/esshc/paper/toshipap.html.

HUAC (US Congress House Committee on Un-American Activities) (1948), *Hearings Regarding Communist Espionage in the United States Government*, 80th Congress, 2nd Session, 1948–1950, Washington, DC, US Government Printing Office.

Hudock, A. (1999), *NGOs and Civil Society: Democracy by Proxy*, London, Polity.

Huntington, S. (1993), "The clash of civilizations", *Foreign Affairs*, 72, 22–49.

HYL Report (1997), "The Imexsa HYL III plant: best of the biggest", IX, 3, 3. Accessed at www.hylsamex.com.mx/hyl/reportes/1997/fall.pdf on 6 August 2004.

IFC (1997), "Kazakhstan: Ispat Karmet. Summary of Project Information (SPI)", Project 007837, Washington, DC.

—— (1998), "Summary of Project Information 7837: Ispat-Karmet Limited". Accessed at www.ifc.org on 8 August 2007.

—— (2000), "Kazakhstan: Ispat Karmet SME resource. Summary of project information (SPI)", Project 10448, Washington, DC.

—— (2003), "Algeria: Ispat Annaba. Summary of project information (SPI)", Project 11165, Washington, DC.

—— (2004), "World region: LNM Holdings NV. Summary of project information (SPI)", Project 22639.

ILO (2000), *The Employment Impact of Restructuring and Privatization in Trinidad and Tobago*, ILO Caribbean studies and working papers, no. 2, ILO, Port of Spain.

IMF (2003), *Republic of Kazakhstan: 2003 Article IV Consultation*, Washington, IMF.

IMF/IDA (2002), "Niger Poverty Reduction Strategy Paper Joint Staff Assessment", Report 23483-NIR, Washington, World Bank.

IMF/World Bank PRSP Comprehensive Review (2002), *External Comments and Contributions on the Joint Bank/Fund Staff Review of the PRSP Approach, Volume 1: Bilateral Agencies and Multilateral Institutions*, Washington, DC, International Monetary Fund and World Bank.

Ispat Nova Hut (2003), *Annual Report: 2003*. Accessed at www.novahut.cz/VZ_2003_EN.pdf on 10 August 2004.

Izvestiia (1995), "Kazakhstan: government has decided to sell the KarMet metallurgical enterprise to Ispat International (UK)", 24 November, F1. Translated.

Jenkins, R. (1994), "Capitalist development in the NIC's", in L. Sklair, ed. (1984), *Capitalism and Development*, London, Routledge, 72–86.

Kagarlitsky, B. (1994), *Square Wheels: How Russian Democracy Got Derailed*, New York, Monthly Review Press.

Kanavi, S. (2004), "Sultan of steel", *Business India*, 10–23 May, 46–53.

Kapur, D. (2000), "Who gets to run the world?", *Foreign Policy*, 121 (November/ December), 44–50.

—— (2002), "The changing anatomy of governance of the World Bank", in J. Pincus and J. Winters, eds (2002), *Reinventing the World Bank*, Ithaca, NY, Cornell University Press, 54–75.

Kapur, D., Lewis, J. and Webb, R. (1997a), *The World Bank: Its First Half Century, Volume 1: History*, Washington, DC, Brookings Institution Press.

—— (1997b), *The World Bank: Its First Half Century, Volume 2, Perspectives*, Washington, DC, Brookings Institution Press.

Karamoko, D. (2003), Interview with author, 2 September, Niamey, Niger.

Karlsson, M. (2000), "Is the World Bank still needed in today's global economy?", *Insight on the News*, Washington, DC, 22 May.

Kaufmann, D., Kraay, A. and Mastruzzi, M. (2006), *Governance Matters V: Governance Indicators for 1996–2005*, Washington, World Bank. Accessed at www.worldbank.org/ wbi/governance/govdata/ on 15 March 2007.

Kelsey, J. (2000), *Reclaiming the Future: New Zealand and the Global Economy*, Toronto, University of Toronto Press.

Keynes, J. (1980), *The Collected Writings of John Maynard Keynes*, 30 volumes, London, Macmillan.

Khor, M. (2003), "Mainstreaming development in trade and finance: a key to global partnership", *NGLS Round-up*, 105, 2–4.

—— (2003a), "Developing a global partnership for development: critical issues and proposals for trade and finance", Singapore, Third World Network.

Kim, A. (2003), Chief of Technical Department, Ispat Karmet, Interview, 2 July, Temirtau, Kazakhstan.

Klein, N. (2000), *No Logo: No Space, No Choice, No Jobs: Taking Aim at the Brand Bullies*, London, Flamingo.

Kothari, U. and Minogue, M., eds (2002), *Development Theory and Practice*, London, Palgrave.

Koza, P. (2003), "Poland approves steelmaker sale", *Daily Deal*, 22 October.

Krueger, A. (1998), "Whither the World Bank and the IMF?", *Journal of Economic Literature*, XXXVI (December), 1983–2020.

—— (2003), "Address on Globalisation", Seventh St Petersburg International Economic Forum, 18 July. Accessed at www.imf.org/external/np/speeches/2003/061803.htm on 3 June 2004.

Kumar, K., Manisha P. and Sadhna, S. (2001), "The trouble with 'Para teachers'", *Frontline*, 18, 22, 93–94.

Kumar, K., Priyam, M. and Saxena, S. (2001a), "Looking beyond the smokescreen: DPEP and primary education in India", *Economic and Political Weekly*, 36, 560–568.

Kunda, G. (1992), *Engineering Culture: Control and Commitment in a High-Tech Corporation*, Philadelphia, Pa., Temple University Press.

Laclau, E. (1971), "Feudalism and capitalism in Latin America", *New Left Review*, 67 (May–June), 166–190.

Laclau, E. and Mouffe, C. (1985), *Hegemony and Socialist Strategy*, London, Verso.

Laughlin, J. (2004), "The 'transformation' of governance: new directions in policy and politics", *Australian Journal of Politics and History*, 50, 8–22.

Lane, D. (1996), *The Rise and Fall of State Socialism: Industrial Society and the Socialist State*, Cambridge, Polity.

Lane, P. and Schmukler, S. (2006), *The International Financial Integration of China and India*, Washington, DC, World Bank.

Lauzon, P., Bernard, M., Patenaude, F. and Poirier, M. (1998), *Privatisations – L'autre point de vue*, Montreal, Les Editions du Renouveau québécois.

Leblanc, M. (2000), "Kyrgyzstan technical note – appreciation of PRSP initiative and definition of FSP involvement in poverty reduction", Brussels, Réseau Européen de Sécurité Alimentaire. Accessed at http://europa.eu.int/comm/europeaid/projects/resal/Download/report/mission/nei/1000stkyrprsp.pdf on 20 April 2004.

Lee, Y. (2005), "New government, new language? The Third Way discourse in Taiwan", *Modern Asian Studies*, 39, 631–660.

Lenin, V. (1964 [1916]), *Imperialism, the Highest Stage of Capitalism*, in V. Lenin (1964) *Collected Works, Vol 22*. Accessed at www.marxists.org/archive/lenin/works/1916/imp-hsc/index.htm on 25 October 2004.

Levine, R. (1995), *The Mineral Industry of Kazakhstan*, Washington, DC, United States Geological Survey.

Leys, C. (1985), "Thatcherism and British manufacturing", *New Left Review*, 151, 1–25.

Linden, G. (2000), Head of Markets in Transition, USAID Kazakhstan, Interview, 29 June, Almaty, Kazakhstan.

Lindsey, H. (1996), *Planet Earth-2000*, Palos Verde, California, Western Front.

Lok, J. and Willmott, H. (2006), "institutional theory, language and discourse analysis: a comment on Phillips, Lawrence and Hardy", *Academy of Management Review*, 31, 477–480.

Ma, S. (2007), "Political science at the edge of chaos? The paradigmatic implications of historical institutionalism", *International Political Science Review*, 28, 57–78.

McKee, M. (2001), "The health consequences of the collapse of the Soviet Union", in D. Leon and G. Walt, eds, *Poverty, Inequality and Health*, Oxford, Oxford University Press, 17–25.

McKeeby, D. (2000), "'Crude business': corruption and Caspian Oil, *Caspian Energy Update*, 31 August.

McLennan, G. (2004), "Travelling with vehicular ideas: the case of the Third Way", *Economy and Society*, 33, 484–499.

Maddison, A. (2003), *The World Economy: Historical Statistics*, Paris, OECD.

Maile, S. and Hoggett, P. (2001), "Best value and the politics of pragmatism", *Policy and Politics*, 29, 509–519.

Manning, N. (2001), "The legacy of the New Public Management in developing countries", *International Review of Administrative Sciences*, 67, 297–312.

Marsh, P. (2003), "Steel baron sharpens turnaround routine", *Financial Times*, 16 July, 10.

Marshall, A. and Woodroffe, J. (2001), *Policies to Roll Back the State and Privatise: Poverty Reduction Strategy Papers Investigated*, London, World Development Movement. Accessed at www.wdm.org.uk/cambriefs/debt/rollback.pdf on 14 April 2004.

Marx, K. and Engels, F. (1999), *The Communist Manifesto: With Related Documents*, Boston, Bedford/St Martin's.

Masanov, N. (2003), Political scientist and opposition spokesperson, Interview, 25 June, Almaty, Kazakhstan.

Mathews, J. (2006), "Dragon multinationals: new players in 21st century globalisation", *Asia Pacific Journal of Management*, 23, 5–27.

Mason, E. and Asher, R. (1973), *The World Bank Since Bretton Woods*, Washington, DC, Brookings Institution.

Mehrotra, S. and Buckland, P. (1998), *Managing Teacher Costs for Access and Quality*, UNICEF Staff Working Paper, New York, UNICEF.

Mehta, A. (2003), *Elementary Education in India: Where Do We Stand?*, New Delhi|: NIEPA.

Mehta, M. (1999), "Steel's still-growing giant", *Industry Week*, 18 January.

Meighoo, K. (2003), *Politics in a Half-Made Society: Trinidad and Tobago 1925–2001*, Kingston, Randle.

Metal Bulletin (2001), "Algiers sweetens pill for Ispat in Alfasid takeover", 1 November.

Michael, B. (2002), "Book Review of *High Noon: Twenty Global Problems, Twenty Years to Solve Them*", *International Journal of Organizational Analysis*, 10, 386–389.

Mikesell, R. (1994), *The Bretton Woods Debates: A Memoir*, Princeton, NJ, Department of Economics.

Milanovic, B. (2005), *Worlds Apart: Measuring International and Global Inequality*, Princeton, NJ, Princeton University Press.

Milmo, C. (2004), "Tycoon with steel in his soul is now Britain's richest man", *The Independent*, 26 October, 12–13.

Mingat, A. (2002), *Deux études pour la scolarisation primaire universelle dans les pays du Sahel en 2015*, Dakar, World Bank. Accessed at www.worldbank.org/afr/hd/wps/sahel.pdf on 3 July 2004.

Mingat, A. and Tan, J. (1985), "On equity in education again: an international comparison", *The Journal of Human Resources*, XX, 298–308.

—— (1998), *The Mechanics of Progress in Education: Evidence from Cross-Country Data*, World Bank Policy Research Paper 2015, Washington, DC, World Bank.

Mitchell, A., Sikka, P. and Willmott, P. (1998), "Sweeping it under the carpet: the role of accountancy firms in moneylaundering", *Accounting, Organizations and Society*, 23, 589–607.

Monbiot, G. (2005), "I'm with Wolfowitz", *The Guardian*, 5 April, 19.

Montreal Gazette (2004), "Sidbec deficit lives on and on", 27 May, B5.

Morgenthau, H. (1945), "Bretton Woods and international cooperation", *Foreign Affairs*, 23, 182–194.

Moskovskie Novosti (1995), "Government of Kazakhstan has cancelled the agreement on management of the Karmet enterprise", 1 November (B9). Translation.

Munck, R. (1999a), "Dependency and imperialism in new times: a Latin American perspective", *European Journal of Development Research*, 11, 56–74.

—— (1999b), "Deconstructing development discourses: of impasses, alternatives, and politics", in *Critical Development Theory: Contributions to a New Paradigm*, London, Zed.

Murphy, Joe (2002a), "Mittal was Vaz's guest ahead of Kazakh deal", *Sunday Telegraph*, 10 March, 2.

Murphy, Jonathan (2003), "Civil society and social capital in the post-socialist Russian north", *Polar Geography*, 26, 2, 132–154.

—— (2003a), "No-one loves you the way we do – poverty and the international financial institutions". Paper presented at the Third International Critical Management Studies conference, Lancaster, UK, 7–9 July.

—— (2006), "Illusory transition? Elite reconstitution in Kazakhstan, 1989–2002", *Europe-Asia Studies*, 58, 523–554.

—— (2007), "Learning from the past: a small quibble with Fred Lee's history of American radical economics", *Review of American Radical Economics*, 39, 108–115.

Murshed, S. (2003), "The decline of the development contract and the development of violent internal conflict". Inaugural lecture by the Prince Claus Chair in Development and Equity, University of Utrecht, 12 May. Accessed at www.uu.nl/content/murshed-inaugral.pdf on 16 January 2004.

NCERT (1994), *Research Based Interventions in Primary Education: The DPEP Strategy*, New Delhi, NCERT.

N'Guiamba, S. (2002), Interview with author, 21 October, Niamey, Niger.

Naidoo, K. (2003), "Civil society, governance, and globalisation", Presidential Fellows Lecture, 10 February, Washington, DC, World Bank.

—— (2003a), "Civil society accountability: 'Who guards the guardians?' " Speech made at the United Nations, 3 April.

Nazarbayev, N. (1985), *Stal'noi Profil' Kazakhstana*, Alma-Ata, Kazakhstan Printing House.

Neu, D., Ocampo Gomez, E., García Ponce de León, O. and Zepeda, M. (2002), "Facilitating globalization processes: financial technologies and the World Bank", *Accounting Forum*, 26, 257–276.

O'Brien, R., Goetz, A., Scholtze, J. and Williams, M. eds (2000), *Contesting Global Governance*, Cambridge, Cambridge University Press.

Olcott, M. (2002), *Kazakhstan: Unfulfilled Promise*. New York, Carnegie Endowment for International Peace.

OECD (1999), *DAC Scoping Study of Donor Poverty Reduction Policies and Practices*, London, ODI.

—— (2001), *DAC Guidelines: Poverty Reduction*, Paris, OECD.

Oliver, R. (1971), *Early Plans for a World Bank*, Princeton Studies in International Finance 29, Princeton, NJ, Princeton University.

Osborne, D. and Gaebler, T. (1992), *Reinventing Government: How the Entrepreneurial Spirit Is Transforming the Public Sector*, Reading, Mass., Addison-Wesley.

OSCE (2000), *OSCE Handbook*, Vienna, OSCE. Accessed at www.osce.org/publications/handbook/files/handbook.pdf on 10 August 2004.

Overseas Development Institute (2003), "Experience of PRSs in the Transition Countries", *Synthesis Note*, 6.

—— (2003a), "Experience of PRSs in Africa", *Synthesis Note*, 7.

—— (2003b), "Experience of PRSs in Asia", *Synthesis Note*, 8.

Pala, C. (2005), "Kazakh banks hit the capital buffers", *Euromoney*, 36, 432.

—— (2005a), "From 'small and risky' to a target for partnership", *The Banker*, 7 March, 62.

Pallister, A. (2002), "Why the Romanians were worried about the Mittal deal", *Guardian*, 14 February.

Pandey, S. (2006), "Para-teacher scheme and quality education for all in India: policy perspectives and challenges for school effectiveness", *Journal of Education for Teaching*, 32, 319–334.

—— (2006a), Interview with author, 14 September, New Delhi.

Pandey, S. and Raj, R. (2003), *Professional Support System and Classroom Performance of Para-teachers*, New Delhi, NCERT.

Parker, M. (2002), *Against Management*, Cambridge, Polity.

Parliament of Trinidad and Tobago (1990), *Senate Hansard*, 27 March.

—— (1992), *Senate Hansard*, 28 November.

Peck, A. (2004), *Economic Development in Kazakhstan*, London, RoutledgeCurzon.

Penrose, E. (1953), *Economic Planning for the Peace*, Princeton, NJ, Princeton University Press.

Pentsov, D., Kolleeny, G. and Horton, S. (1996), "Bankruptcy Kazakh style: the Karmet case", *East/West Executive Guide* 6, 10 (1 October).

People's Daily (2007), "China outbound investment reaches US $16.13 billion last year", 25 January. Accessed at http://english.people.com.cn/200701/25/eng20070125_344770.html on 25 March 2007.

Peters, G. (2000), *Institutional Theory: Problems and Prospects*, Political Science Series 69, Vienna, Institute for Higher Studies.

Peters, T. and Waterman, R. (1982), *In Search of Excellence*, New York, Harper & Row.

Pettifor, A. and Greenhill, R. (2003), *Debt Relief and the Millennium Development Goals*, United Nations Human Development Report Occasional Paper 2003/3, New York, UNDP.

Phillips, H. (1992), *Between the Revolution and the West: A Political Biography of Maxim M. Litvinov*, Boulder, Colo.: Westview Press.

Phillips, M. (2003), "The World Bank as privatization agnostic", *Wall Street Journal*, 21 July, A2.

Pierson P. (2000), "Increasing returns, path dependence, and the study of politics", *American Political Science Review*, 94, 251–267.

Pierson, P. and Skocpol, T. (2002), "Historical institutionalism in contemporary political science", in I. Katznelson and H.V. Milner, eds, *Political Science: State of the Discipline*, New York: W.W. Norton, 693–721.

Pinkham, J. (2005), "A legacy ruined by the world's bankers", *Guardian*, 13 April, 25.

Pirani, S. (2004), "Kazakh stampede continues", *Trade Finance*, October.

Planning Commission (2001), *Approach Paper to the Tenth Five Year Plan, Draft*, New Delhi, Government of India.

Poddar, T. and Yi, E. (2007), *India's Rising Growth Potential*, Global Economics Paper 154, New York, Goldman Sachs.

Polanyi, K. (1944), *The Great Transformation*, Boston, Beacon Press.

Preis, A. (1994), *Labor's Giant Step*, New York, Pathfinder.

Putnam, R. (1995), "Bowling alone: America's declining social capital", *Journal of Democracy*, 6, 1, 65–78.

Quarmby, K. (2005), "Why Oxfam is failing Africa", *New Statesman*, 30 May, 10–12.

Rahnema, M. and Bawtree, V., eds (1997), *The Post-development Reader*, London, Zed Books.

Rawnsley, A. (2001), *Servants of the People: The Inside Story of New Labour*, London, Penguin.

Reagan, R. (1989), "The USSR", speech. Accessed at www.ronaldreagan.com/ussr.html on 18 January 2005.

Rees, D. (1971), *Harry Dexter White: A Study in Paradox*, New York, Coward, McCann & Geoghegan.

Reinicke, W. (1996a), "Can international financial institutions prevent internal violence?

The sources of ethno-national conflict in transitional societies", in A. and A.H. Chayes, eds, *Preventing Conflict in the Post-Communist World* Washington, DC, Brookings Institution, 281–337.

—— (1997), "Global public policy", *Foreign Affairs*, 76, 6, 127–138.

—— (1998), *Global Public Policy: Governing Without Government?*, Washington, DC, Brookings Institution.

—— (1999), "Hands on the bridge", *World Link* (Davos), 40–42.

—— (2004), "Business and civil society in global governance: defining new roles and responsibilities", 21st Sinclair House Debate: Beyond the State? "Foreign Policy" by Companies and NGOs, Bad Homburg, Germany, Herbert-Quandt-Stiftung. Accessed at www.h-quandt-stiftung.de/root/index.php?page_id=846 on 15 June 2006.

Reinicke, W. and Deng, F. (2000), *Critical Choices: The United Nations, Networks, and the Future of Global Governance*, Ottawa, IDRC.

Reinicke, W. and Witte, J. (2005), *Business UNUsual. Facilitating United Nations Reform Through Partnerships*, New York, United Nations Publications.

Reuters (2002), "Kazakh govt says President had $1 bln secret fund", 4 April.

Rischard, J. (2001), "High noon for the global economy", *The Globalist*, 9 March. Accessed at www.theglobalist.com on 25 June 2004.

—— (2002), "A new role for global business", *Optimize*, 11 September. Accessed at www.optimizemag.com on 25 June 2004.

—— (2002a), *High Noon: Twenty Global Problems, Twenty Years to Solve Them*, New York, Basic Books.

—— (2004), Presentation at Board strategy session of the Parliamentary Network on the World Bank. Chantilly, France, 20 June.

Robinson, W. (2004), *A Theory of Global Capitalism*, Baltimore, Md., Johns Hopkins University Press.

—— (2005), "Global capitalism: the new transnationalism and the folly of conventional thinking", *Science & Society*, 69, 316–328.

Romuliowocz, B. (2003), Political Officer, OSCE Kazakhstan, Interview, 30 June, Almaty, Kazakhstan.

Rowden, R. and Icama, J. (2004), *Rethinking Participation: Questions for Civil Society about the Limits of Participation in PRSPs*, Washington, DC, ActionAid USA/ActionAid Uganda. Accessed at www.actionaidusa.org/images/rethinking_participation_april04.pdf on 25 June 2004.

Roy, A. (2007), "It's outright war and both sides are choosing their weapons", *Tehelka*, 4, 10, 31 March, 10–12.

Sanchez, D. and Cash, K. (2003), *Reducing Poverty or Repeating Mistakes?*, Stockholm, Church of Sweden.

Schechter, M. (2002), "Critiques of Coxian theory: backgrounds to a conversation", in R. Cox with Schechter M. *The Political Economy of a Plural World*, London, Routledge, 2–25.

Scott, W. (1987), "The adolescence of institutional theory", *Administrative Science Quarterly*, 32, 493–511.

Selznick, P. (1948), "Foundations of the theory of organization", *American Sociological Review*, 13, 1, 25–35.

—— (1949), *TVA and the Grass Roots*, Berkeley, University of California Press.

—— (1996), "The old and the new institutional theory", *Administrative Science Quarterly*, 41, 270–277.

Shannon, T. (1996), *An Introduction to the World-System Perspective*, Oxford, Westview.

—— (2000), *John Maynard Keynes: a Biography, Volume Three: Fighting for Britain 1937–1946*, London, Macmillan.

Sikka, P. (2003), "The role of offshore financial centres in globalization", *Accounting Forum*, 27, 365–399.

Skidelsky, R. (2001), *John Maynard Keynes: Fighting for Britain*, London: Macmillan.

Sklair, L. (1995), *Sociology of the global system*, London, Prentice Hall.

—— (2001), *Transnational Capitalist Class*, Oxford, Blackwell.

—— (2002), "The transnational capitalist class and global politics: deconstructing the corporate–state connection", *International Political Science Review*, 23, 159–174.

Sklair, L. and Robbins, P. (2002), "Global capitalism and major corporations from the Third World", *Third World Quarterly*, 23, 81–100.

Skocpol, T. (1977), "Wallerstein's world capitalist system: a theoretical and historical critique", *American Journal of Sociology*, 82, 1075–1090.

—— (1995), "Why I am a historical-institutionalist", *Polity*, 28, 103–106.

Smalhout, J. (2001), "Kohler's new IMF team", *Euromoney*, 386, 34–37.

Smith, J. (2002), "Comments to International Conference on Poverty Reduction Strategies", 16 January, Washington, USAID. Accessed at www.worldbank.org/poverty/strategies/review/usaid1.pdf on 26 April 2004.

Speed, N. (2002), "Plaid tables more steel questions", *Western Mail*, 11 February, 2.

Spivak, G. (1999), *A Critique of Postcolonial Reason: Toward a History of the Vanishing Present*, Calcutta, Seagull.

Srinivas, A. (2007), "India's rise as a manufacturing giant", BBC, 13 February. Accessed at http://news.bbc.co.uk/1/hi/world/south_asia/6356767.stm on 25 March 2007.

Stern, N. (2002), "Investment and poverty: the role of the international financial institutions", in N. Stern, *A Strategy for Development*, Washington, World Bank. 173–185.

Stiglitz, J. (2002), *Globalisation and its Discontents*, London, Allen Lane.

Stocking, B. (2005), "Oxfam bites back", *New Statesman*, 6 June, 35.

Stone, D., ed. (2000), *Banking on Knowledge: The Genesis of the Global Development Network*, London, Routledge.

Sull, D. (1999), "Spinning steel into gold: the case of Ispat International N.V.", *European Management Journal*, 17, 368–381.

Taukina, R. (2003), President, Journalists in Trouble of Kazakhstan, Interview, 27 June, Almaty, Kazakhstan.

Temirtau, Istoriia Goroda (2004), Temirtau, Kazakhstan, Temirtau Municipal Administration. Accessed at www.temirtau.kz/history_01.html on 2 August 2004.

Tompkins, P. and Cheney, G. (1985), "Communication and unobtrusive control in contemporary organizations", in P. Tompkins and G. Cheney, eds, *Organizational Communication: Traditional Themes and New Directions*, London, Sage, 179–210.

Travis, A. (2004), "Nuisance neighbours face compulsory life skills lessons", *Guardian*, 1 June, 1.

UNCTAD (2006), *World Investment Report 2006 – FDI from Developing and Transition Economies: Implications for Development*, Geneva, UNCTAD.

UNDP (undated, ca. 2002), "Millennium Development Goals (MDGs)". Accessed at www.undp.org/mdg/Millennium%20Development%20Goals.pdf on 21 April 2004.

—— (2004), *Human Development Report: 2003*, New York, UNDP.

UNESCO (2000), *The Dakar Framework for Action*, Accessed at http://unesdoc. unesco.org/images/0012/001211/121147e.pdf on 3 July 2004.

UNESCO (2002), *EFA Global Monitoring Report 2002*, Paris, UNESCO.

United Nations (2000), "United Nations Millennium Declaration", Resolution A/RES/ 55/2 adopted by the General Assembly, 18 September.

United States Department of State (1948), *Proceedings and Documents of the United Nations Monetary and Financial Conference*, two vols, Bretton Woods, New Hampshire, 1–22 July 1944, Washington, DC: US Government Printing Office.

United States Senate Committee on the Judiciary, Subcommittee to Investigate the Administration of the Internal Security Act and Other Internal Security Laws (1955), *Interlocking Subversion in Government Departments* (The Harry Dexter White Papers), Part 30: hearings, 30 August 1955, 2415–2860.

USAID (2003), "USAID's approach to poverty reduction: synthesis of studies in Honduras, Mali, Romania, and Uganda", *Evaluation Brief*, 9.

van der Pijl, K. (1998), *Transformational Classes and International Relations*, London, Routledge.

Van Dormael, A. (1978), *Bretton Woods: Birth of a Monetary System*, London, Macmillan.

Vasagar, J. (2001), "MP's role in temple deal investigated", *Guardian*, 27 January.

Vazquez, I. (2002), "A retrospective on the Mexican bail-out", *Cato Journal*, 21, 545–551.

Volcker, P. (2000), Transcript of an interview with Paul Volcker on the US PBS network television programme *Commanding Heights*, 26 September 2000. Accessed at www.pbs.org/wgbh/commandingheights/shared/minitext/int_paulvolcker.html on 23 January 2004.

Wacquant, L. (1992), "Toward a social praxeology: the structure and logic of Bourdieu's sociology", in P. Bourdieu and L. Wacquant, *An Invitation to Reflexive Sociology*, Chicago, University of Chicago Press, 1–60.

Walden, G. (2006), *New Elites: A Career in the Masses*, London, Gibson Square.

Walker, L. (2003), *Startup of the Development Gateway*, Washington, World Bank Operations Evaluation Department.

Wallerstein, I. (1976), *The Modern World-System: Capitalist Agriculture and the Origins of the European World-Economy in the Sixteenth Century*, New York, Academic Press.

—— (1979), *The Capitalist World Economy*, Cambridge, Cambridge University Press.

Warren, B. (1980), *Imperialism: Pioneer of Capitalism*, London, Verso.

Weaver, J. (1965), *The International Development Association: A New Approach to Foreign Aid*, New York, Praeger.

Wedel, J. (1998), *Collision and Collusion; The Strange Case of Western Aid to Eastern Europe, 1989–1998*, New York, St Martin's Press.

—— (2004), "Flex power; a capital way to gain clout, inside and out", *Washington Post*, December 12, B04.

Weschler, W. (2001), "Follow the money", *Foreign Affairs*, 80, 40–58.

White, H. (1930–1948), The Harry Dexter White Papers (White Papers), Manuscripts in 13 boxes, Seeley G. Mudd Manuscript Library, Princeton University.

—— (1935), "Outline analysis of the domestic economic situation", 3 May, *White Papers*, Box One, file 2a.

—— (1939), "Proposal for loans to Latin America", 6 June, White Papers, Box Six, file 14b.

—— (1940), "Paper concerning Democratic Party planks", 10 July, White Papers, Box Six, file 15e.

—— (1942), "Preliminary draft proposal for a United Nations stabilization Fund and a Bank for Reconstruction and Development of the United and Associated Nations", White Papers, Box Eight, file 24c.

—— (1942a), "Draft of a letter to the president", 12 August, White Papers, Box Seven, file 22a.

—— (1943), "Postwar currency stabilization", *The American Economic Review*, 33, 1, Supplement, Papers and Proceedings of the Fifty-fifth Annual Meeting of the American Economic Association, March 1943, 382–387.

—— (1945), "The Monetary Fund: some criticisms examined", *Foreign Affairs*, 23, 195–210.

—— (1945a), "Account of a meeting concerning Russia and the 'Morgenthau Plan'", White Papers, Box Seven, file 22f.

—— (1945b), "Continued peace and friendly relations with Russia", White Papers, Box Seven, file 23d.

—— (1948), Unpublished and untitled manuscript on dangers to economic stability, White Papers, Box Seven, file 29.

—— ed. (1945c), "The problem of Germany", unpublished book manuscript, White Papers, Box Seven, document 22h.

White, H. and Black, R. (2004), "Millennium Development Goals: a drop in the ocean", in R. Black and H. White, *Targeting Development*, London, Routledge, 1–35.

Wilks, A. (2001), "Development through the looking glass: the Knowledge Bank in cyber-space". Paper for the 6th Oxford Conference on Education and Development, Knowledge Values and Policy, September.

—— (2003), "The World Bank, the IMF and 'results': increasing dominance in development policy lending", London, Bretton Woods Project. Accessed at http://brettonwoodsproject.org/article.shtml?cmd[126]=x-126–16204 on 5 June 2004.

Williams, G. (1992), "Modernizing Malthus", in J. Crush, ed., *Power of Development*, London, Routledge, 158–175.

Williamson, J. (1990), "What Washington means by policy reform", in J. Willamson, ed., *Latin American Adjustment: How Much Has Happened?*, Washington, Institute for International Economics, 5–20.

—— (2000), "What should the World Bank think about the Washington Consensus?", The World Bank Research Observer, 15, 251–264.

Willmott, H. (1993), "Strength is ignorance; slavery is freedom: managing culture in modern organizations", *Journal of Management Studies*, 30, 515–552.

Winslow, E. (1931), "Marxian, Liberal and Sociological Theories of Imperialism", *Journal of Political Economy*, 39, 713–758.

Wolfensohn, J. (1999), "A proposal for a comprehensive development framework", Memorandum to the Board, Management, and Staff of the World Bank Group. Washington, DC, World Bank, 21 January.

—— (2004), "Mr. Wolfensohn's Address at the Shanghai Conference on Scaling Up Poverty Reduction, May 26 2004", distributed by World Bank Internal Communications to all World Bank staff, 27 May.

Wolfensohn, J. and van Leeuwen, F. (2000), "Schooling for all? We can have it if we mean it", *International Herald Tribune*, 25 April.

Woods, G. (1966), "The development decade in balance", *Foreign Affairs*, 44, 206–215.

Woods, N. (2000), "The challenges of multilateralism and governance", in C. Gilbert and D. Vines, eds, *The World Bank: Structure and Policies*, Cambridge, Cambridge University Press, 132–156.

World Bank (1993), *World Development Report 1993: Investing in Health*, Washington, DC, World Bank.

—— (1993a), *Kazakhstan: The Transition to a Market Economy*, Washington, DC, World Bank.

—— (1994), *The World Bank and Participation*, Washington, DC, World Bank Operations Policy Department.

—— (1996), "Kazakhstan financial sector adjustment project: project information document", Report PIC3530, Washington, DC, World Bank.

—— (1996a), *The World Bank Participation Sourcebook*, Washington, DC, World Bank.

—— (1997), "Algeria structural adjustment loan project information document", Report PIC3006, Washington, DC, World Bank.

—— (2000), "Algeria privatization assistance project project information document", Report P070123, Washington, DC, World Bank.

—— (2000a), "Partners in transforming development: new approaches to developing country-owned poverty reduction strategies". Accessed at www.imf.org/external/np/prsp/pdf/prspbroc.pdf on 19 April 2004.

—— (2000b), "Involving non-governmental organizations in bank-supported activities", Good Practice 14.70, *Operational Manual* (March), Washington, DC, World Bank.

—— (2002), "PRSP questions and answers". Accessed at www.worldbank.org/poverty/strategies/qanda.htm on 14 April 2004.

—— (2002a), *A Sourcebook for Poverty Reduction Strategies*, 2 vols, Washington, World Bank.

—— (2002b), *Republic of Tajikistan: Joint IDA–IMF Staff Assessment of the Poverty Reduction Strategy Paper and Poverty Reduction Strategy Paper*, Report 25059-TJ, Washington, DC, World Bank.

—— (2002c), "Comprehensive development matrix", Washington, DC, World Bank. Accessed at www.siteresources.worldbank.org/CDF/resources/cdfmatrix2002.pdf on 15 August 2007.

—— (2003), "Issues and options for improving engagement between the World Bank and civil society organizations", Discussion Paper, 24 October, Washington, DC, World Bank.

—— (2003a), *Country Assistance Strategy: Niger*, Report 25203-NIR, Washington, DC, World Bank.

—— (2003b), *Project Appraisal Document for a Basic Education Project, Republic of Niger* , 20 June, Washington, DC, World Bank Africa Regional Office.

—— (2003c) "Overview of poverty reduction strategies". Accessed at www.worldbank.org/poverty/strategies/overview.htm on 14 April 2004.

—— (2004), *Global Monitoring Report 2004*, Washington, DC, World Bank.

—— (2004a), "Scaling up poverty reduction conceptual framework", Background Paper for the Shanghai Conference on Scaling Up Poverty Reduction, 25–27 May, World Bank, Washington, DC. Accessed at www.worldbank.org/wbi/reducingpoverty/docs/conceptual.pdf on 2 June 2004.

—— (2004b), *Millennium Development Goals: Global Monitoring Report 2004*, Washington, DC, World Bank.

—— (2005), *Millennium Development Goals: Global Monitoring Report 2005*, Washington, DC, World Bank.

—— (2006), *Millennium Development Goals: Global Monitoring Report 2006*, Washington, DC, World Bank.

World Wildlife Fund (2003), "Alliance for forest conservation and sustainable use". Powerpoint presentation, accessed at www.wwf.no/ppt/wb-wwf-presentasjon.ppt on 5 May 2004.

Wright Mills, C. (1957), *The Power Elite*, New York, Harper.

Žižek, S. (1997), "Repeating Lenin", Article accessed at http://lacan.com/replenin.htm on 8 October 2003.

Zymelman, M. and DeStefano, J. (1989), "Primary school teachers' salaries in sub-Saharan Africa", World Bank Discussion Paper 45, Washington, DC, World Bank.

Index

Figures are indicated by **bold** page numbers.

*For Product Safety Concerns and Information please contact
our EU representative GPSR@taylorandfrancis.com Taylor & Francis
Verlag GmbH, Kaufingerstraße 24, 80331 München, Germany*

T - #0021 - 270225 - C0 - 234/156/11 [13] - CB - 9780415412698 - Gloss Lamination